# Buck Whaley's
# Memoirs

# Buck Whaley's Memoirs

THOMAS 'BUCK JERUSALEM' WHALEY

NONSUCH

First published 1906
Copyright © in this edition 2006
Nonsuch Publishing Limited

Nonsuch Publishing Limited
73 Lower Leeson Street
Dublin 2
Ireland
www.nonsuchireland.com

British Library Cataloguing in Publication Data.
A catalogue record for this book is available from the British Library.

ISBN 1 84588 541 4

Typesetting and origination by Tempus Publishing Limited
Printed and bound in Great Britain

# Contents

# Notice

I am apprehensive that I shall be accused both of presumption and singularity in thus obtruding myself on the notice of my friends and the public; therefore think it expedient to detail the motives that influenced my determination.

Having during my solitary retirement often revolved in my mind the various scenes of life, in which I have been either a principal actor or merely a spectator; and having always had within myself a secret friend and monitor, who persuaded me to make observations, to draw conclusions and to hoard up for riper years the lessons of experience; I thought that a faithful picture of my youthful eccentricities, drawn with justice and impartiality, would not be unacceptable to my countrymen, and particularly to my younger friends, who will find some few examples which they may follow with advantage, but many more which they ought to avoid.

The energetic and sophistical Rousseau, the ingenious and excellent Lavater, the sublime and elegant Gibbon, have given instances and served as models for such publications: why should I not presume in my humble way to follow their steps and lay in my claim to immortality?

It must be confessed that their pursuits in life have been quite different; they have exhibited to the Philosopher, the Legislator, and the Man of Letters many striking traits of originality. Some of them have led astray many a young man, many a good Christian, from the path of religion into the comfortless labyrinth of irreligion and infidelity.

Disclaiming all such pretensions, I shall simply give a sketch of my actions and pursuits: I shall unfold the deepest recesses of my heart and unmask the various arts and stratagems that are used to mislead young men of great expectations, and to ruin their health, morals and fortunes.

The notes I have made and the various Journals I have kept of my voyages, that of Jerusalem in particular, enable me likewise to intersperse my narrative with much instructive matter and entertaining anecdotes; many of which, though more ably communicated by eminent writers, yet have some novelty from the different manner in which I may have viewed and considered them.

The imprisonment and death of the unfortunate Louis XVI, and the boldness with which, from my eagerness to see and observe every thing, I approached some of the most formidable and atrocious characters, distinguished in that incomprehensible and ever to be lamented Revolution, enable me also to throw some light on that land of darkness and to discover some of the secret springs used to lead, under the seducing smiles of liberty, a good and loyal people into all the excesses of savage barbarity. Whatever I have seen and observed I shall faithfully detail, without presuming or attempting to misguide the reader; claiming, as a reward of my sincerity, that indulgence which candour and impartiality are always sure to obtain.

Should but one young man learn from these sheets some useful lesson, and stop in the career of folly and dissipation; or one of my indulgent friends be induced to believe that my extraordinary levities proceeded, not from a corrupted heart, but an eccentric and exalted imagination and ridiculous pretensions to notoriety, I shall think myself amply repaid for having attempted this publication.

# PART 1

# CHAPTER I

Introduction – My Birth – My Mother's Character – My Own – A Journey to France – To Auch – The House Establishment of an Englishman in Foreign Countries – A French Bishop – A Match Proposed – An Intrigue – A Journey to Marseilles – To Lyons – An Acquaintance with Gamblers – Honesty of a Foreign Banker – Paris – A French Courtezan – An Assignation – My Stepfather Introduced.

After having made the tour of Europe and visited several parts of Asia and Africa; having indulged myself in all the pleasures which a young man of a lively imagination, possessed of a large fortune, and entire master of his actions may be supposed capable of enjoying; having vainly sought for happiness in the society of what is called the best company, and distinguished myself as a man of gallantry, a little sober reflection has convinced me how much I was deceived in believing that a life of dissipation could produce enjoyment; or that tumultuous pleasures led to real happiness. I now find that the latter can only be attained in a calm and retired life remote from the vortex of fashionable amusements, in the pursuit of which man may be said to live rather for others than himself; and where the transient pleasures he enjoys are constantly succeeded by pain and languor.

I am at present quietly settled in Ireland, blessed with the society of a wife whose mild manners and amiable disposition form a striking contrast with the frivolousness, the vanity and tinsel which I formerly so much admired in my female acquaintances.

My time is divided between the education of my children, the improvement of my small farm, and the writing of these Memoirs, which I hope may prove of some service to youth in particular and to travellers in general.

The former will discover the different modes of seduction practised by the artful and designing of both sexes; a knowledge by which he may be a considerable saver, both in pocket and constitution.

The traveller will find a description of the manners, customs and prevailing opinions of the different nations I have visited. He will be taught to shun the impositions and artifice practised upon strangers; and at the same time learn to avoid giving offence by that overbearing pride and self-importance too common to our countrymen, and from the display of which, by our ostentatious travellers, the British nation has suffered greatly in the opinion of foreigners.

I would not, however, have it imagined that these reflections are occasioned by a satiety of the world, or an incapacity of enjoying its pleasures; but that they proceed from a full and firm conviction of their truth and utility.

I was born at Dublin in the year 1768. My father was a man of very large property, having amply provided for all his children, not less than seven in number. I had for my own share an estate of 7,000 pounds a year, besides upwards of 60,000 pounds in money.

On my father's death, which happened when I was four years old, the care of my education devolved upon my mother, who sent me to one of the first seminaries of Ireland, where I remained till I was fifteen.

I shall beg leave to introduce my mother to the reader's acquaintance, lest he should imagine that the irregularities of my conduct, which he will have an opportunity of witnessing, by perusing these Memoirs, might have proceeded from her own bad example, or a neglect, on her part, in my education.

My mother at the age of eighteen was married to my father, then in his fifty-ninth year. To a person remarkably handsome were united captivating manners, a well-cultivated mind and the most incorruptible virtue. But what raised her highest in the esteem of all who knew her, was the undeviating rectitude of her conduct towards my father, notwithstanding the disparity of their age, which would have been sufficient to have excited the malevolence of slander against her, had she given the least opening for it, by any levity in her behaviour.

She was the mother of seven children, all of whom she brought up in the paths of religion and virtue: and whatever follies any of us may have committed, the cause could never be imputed to her. All her cares, all her anxieties were on our account; and the most bitter sensation I feel in reflecting on my past conduct proceeds from the pangs I have inflicted on that most excellent woman. Indeed, I may attribute my reform in a great measure to the desire, which I never ceased to feel, of contributing to her ease and satisfaction.

Three years after my father's death she married Mr N---, of whom I shall have occasion to speak more fully hereafter. This choice would in itself have been sufficient to have gained her the esteem of all who knew her, had she not so amply possessed it before.

Ere I proceed in detailing the principal occurrences of my life, I wish to say a few words respecting the opinion I have formed of my own character.

It is a just, though trite observation, that the most difficult knowledge is that of knowing oneself; for which reason I shall not attempt to give a finished picture of my character, but merely sketch a few outlines, by which the reader may be enabled to form some judgment of my behaviour in the different scenes through which I have passed, and in which I have been a principal actor.

The most prominent feature in my character, to which I may in a great measure impute all my misfortunes, is the extreme anxiety and impatience I always felt at the approach of any difficulty. To avoid an impending evil, I have formed plans so wild and extravagant, and for the most part so impracticable, that what I had before dreaded appeared light when compared with the distress I incurred by my own precipitate folly. Added to this, an impatience of all control whatsoever, and a temper always impelled to action in proportion to the resistance which it had to encounter; and it will no longer be a matter of surprise if I were continually entangled in some new and perplexing embarrassment.

When I had attained my sixteenth year, my mother thought proper to send me to France in order to finish my education. For this purpose she assigned me a yearly allowance of 900 pounds, and placed me under the care of a tutor, who had been recommended to her by some persons of distinction in Ireland. He had been in the army, but his pay not corresponding with his expenses he was under the necessity of selling his commission to pay his debts, and had now taken up the profession of governor, or as it is sometimes termed, bear-leader, to young men of family. He had had a good education, and profited considerably by the observations he had made abroad. His heart was good; but his constitution had been impaired by early intemperance; and he wanted that address and firmness of character necessary to superintend the conduct of a young man like me, on whom opposition badly managed, or authority indiscriminately exercised, always acted as a stimulus to excess. Though he proved an indifferent Mentor, as will appear in the sequel; yet I do not by any means wish so far to injure his memory as to lay to his charge the blame of my follies and eccentricities, which I am willing to take on my own account.

I went to meet him at Bath, from whence we travelled to London in order to forward the necessary preparations for our journey to Paris. We had not long arrived at that place before I gave him a specimen of what he had to expect.

One evening he proposed going to the play, which, for certain reasons, I declined.

On his return, he indiscreetly entered my room and found his hopeful pupil with very indifferent company, of which, however, he took no notice, but went immediately to bed. In the morning I appeared before him with all the awkward bashfulness attendant on a first offence, but he soon reassured me by treating the matter as a bagatelle.

Such a morality, so consonant to my own taste, soon reconciled me to the character of my tutor; and for some time we lived together on the best terms imaginable. We remained about three weeks at Paris. I shall not attempt to say anything at present of this famous city, so many descriptions of it having been already given – I mean as it existed ten years ago – for, since the Revolution, it may be described as a place that stood in such or such a degree of latitude, besides, as I often visited it since, I shall take occasion to say something which may give an idea of its present inhabitants.

From Paris we travelled to Auch, where I was to learn French, and perfect myself in the exercise of riding, fencing and dancing. This place was fixed upon by my governor, as he had many acquaintances there whom he was desirous of seeing.

On my arrival I hired an elegant house, set up a pack of hounds, procured a stable of hunters, and established my house quite a l'Angloise. But all this was not sufficient to satisfy my restless disposition. I therefore took a house at Cauterets and a small country residence at Bagneres, both situated in the upper Pyrenees, and much frequented on account of their mineral waters. I had likewise a house at Tarbes which, being the capital of the upper Pyrenees and the bishop's see, with a magnificent episcopal palace, was a most populous and gay city. All these places were but a few leagues from one another, at each of which I took care to have the honours of my table done by some favourites. My tutor, in support of this system, was determined to follow me at least half way; and accordingly took under his protection another fair one, with whom he alternately visited one of my country houses. But though our taste and inclinations, in respect to the sex, were perfectly similar, yet I found that we generally agreed better asunder, and therefore his visit at one of my residences was always a signal for me to remove to the other.

In this manner I spent about a twelvemonth, during which time I made occasional excursions to Bareges, famous for its medicinal waters, where I exhibited all the folly and extravagance peculiar to our countrymen abroad.

I passed the greatest part of my time at my house at Tarbes, as I found there an intimacy with the Prince and Princess de R--- R---, who had been banished to their country seat through the intrigues of the Court. This exile, however, was attended neither with gloom nor melancholy. Their chateau, which was magnificent, was generally filled with people of the first rank, and the most remarkable for wit and talents. Gallantry was the principal pursuit of the inhabitants and visitors of this fairy castle.

I became acquainted here with Monsignor de Tarbes, who spent all the time that could be spared from his pastoral functions, which required his attendance but one hour in the week, at the Prince's chateau. The austerity of the priest he threw aside with his clerical habit, and in our society was all life and spirit. I had the good fortune to be honoured with his particular attention, which from a person in such high estimation could not fail to be very acceptable to a young man of my disposition. I am indebted to him for much useful information respecting France, and I shall ever retain for him the greatest esteem and veneration.

The Prince was one of those characters of whom nothing would be said, if he were not a Prince! The Princess, on the other hand, must have attracted notice in any station: although past forty, she was still a fine woman, and had something peculiarly pleasing in her manners and address. In public she condescended to treat me in the manner she would a favourite son, but in a tête-à-tête she would have been much displeased had I behaved to her with the respect due to a mother; and this, I firmly believe, without any criminal intent, but merely from the vanity of being admired.

The following scene, which passed between the Princess, her daughter, and myself, will shew that however deficient she might have been in female delicacy, she at least harboured no design against me in her own person.

She had a daughter, who was at that time about sixteen, and though not handsome she was lively and agreeable. One day the Princess invited me to breakfast with her on the following morning in her bedchamber. This is so common in France that it created no surprise in me: I accordingly repaired to the place of assignation. When I entered the apartment, the Princess was still in bed and her daughter seated on one side of it. Breakfast was served and we conversed for some time on indifferent subjects. At length the Princess, under pretence of examining a new pair of stays which her daughter wore, took off the young lady's handkerchief and left her neck entirely bare, all the time observing me with a fixed eye, in order to discover how I should be affected at such an extraordinary behaviour. Astonishment, I believe, was strongly depicted in my countenance, and, libertine though I was, I could not avoid being shocked at so great an outrage against female decorum.

When the young lady had quitted the apartment the Princess asked my opinion of her daughter, and without waiting for my answer told me that the young person had conceived a very favourable idea of me, and proceeded without further ceremony to propose a match between us. At first I looked upon this as a feint, as I had conceived the idea that the Princess did not regard me with indifference herself, but on her persisting in the proposal, I expressed my acknowledgment in the warmest terms, and promised to write immediately to my friends on the subject, which I did that very evening. It was not long before I received an answer, which contained a positive disapprobation of the match, on account of the difference of our religions. This, I must own, was a circumstance which never occurred to me. My friends were not content with simply expressing their refusal, but wrote to my tutor, to remove me with all possible speed from Auch, in which perhaps he would have found some difficulty had it not been backed by a motive more powerful than his authority, and which I am going to relate.

In the neighbourhood of Auch I became acquainted with the Count de V---, a young nobleman of a large fortune, which he chiefly devoted to his pleasures. As our dispositions were so congenial, it is not extraordinary that a strict intimacy should soon have commenced between us. At his house I fell passionately in love with a young lady of exquisite beauty. She was a relation of his, and as I had by this time pretty well got rid of that *mauvaise honte* which I carried with me to France, I did not hesitate long before I made her acquainted with my passion, and in a short time succeeded to the utmost extent of my wishes.

Our intrigue was carried on with such circumspection that we concealed it from the knowledge of her mother, notwithstanding all her vigilance. But there was a third witness likely to intrude, of which we were not aware, and which rendered it necessary immediately to concert some measures to prevent its turning evidence against us. The best expedient I could devise was to make the Count a confidant of the whole affair, well knowing the looseness of his morals in everything in which women were concerned, nor was I deceived in my expectations. His advice was to carry off directly his fair cousin from her relations, and remove her to some place where she might remain concealed till such time as it might be thought proper for her to appear again in the world. I accordingly conveyed her secretly to my house at Auch, where I intended she should continue during my residence in that part of the country.

But unfortunately an Abbé of whom I learned French, and who had free access to my house, discovered the secret, and either through envy or resentment at not having been consulted in the affair, he read the poor girl so severe a lecture on the enormity of the sin of being connected with an heretic and the damnation that must ensue, that I found her, on my return, bathed in a flood of tears and given up to despair. I comforted her as well as I could, and exhausted my little stock of morality, in order to convince her of the absurdity of this Abbé's assertions. It became, however, necessary to remove her, for fear of worse consequences, to a place of greater security.

As soon as this was accomplished, I went in quest of Monsieur l'Abbé, whom I found by the luckiest chance on the parade with some officers of my acquaintance. I reproached him and chastised him on the spot, by giving him a very severe caning.

The Abbé made immediate application to a magistrate, who without any process or form of trial committed me to prison. I was, however, soon liberated by the interposition of the Archbishop of Auch, who passed his word that I should appear to answer any charges which might be preferred against me.

In the meantime he wrote an account of the transaction to the Minister, who immediately sent an order that the magistrate should be dismissed for the irregularity of his conduct: for that revengeful Abbé had brought no less a charge against me than of having insulted, violently assaulted and raised my sacrilegious hands against a Priest; a crime which was punished with all the severity of the law, and for which the magistrate thought proper to have me imprisoned and dealt with as a common malefactor. Nor do I know whether I should not have been doomed to experience the same fate which the young and unfortunate Chevalier de la Barre suffered at Abbéville in 1766, had it not turned out, luckily for me, that this fellow only wore the dress of a Priest, and had never been ordained, a fact, the certainty of which it was the duty of the Magister to ascertain, before he had begun any criminal process against me.

I mention this circumstance as one out of many to which I was witness, where the slightest offence was punished with the strictest severity; and which may serve as a lesson to democrats and revolutionists, who have vilified the old government of France as a pretence for their massacres and pillage.

Before I left Auch I consulted one of the most experienced lawyers, upon the best means of conveying away my protégée, without risk to her or myself. His advice was, that she should meet me at a small distance from town, in the presence of some witnesses, who would be ready to prove that it was she who inveigled and carried me off. This was a subterfuge practised in France to evade the severity of the law against seduction.

At length I quitted Auch, where I had expended above £18,000, and repaired with my beauteous Helen to Lyons, and from thence to Montpellier, where she was delivered of a daughter who died shortly after. When the mother was sufficiently recovered to be removed, I placed her in the Convent of the Tiercelets and allowed her a pension which was regularly remitted to her until all communication was stopped between England and France. Since that time all my endeavours to discover what became of her have been fruitless.

After this inconsiderate proceeding, I went to spend some time at Marseilles, on a visit to my sister who was settled in that city; and as she was acquainted with most of the principal inhabitants, I passed my time very agreeably among them. I was enraptured with the vivacity and cheerfulness of these Provençals.

The Marseillese ladies are in general handsome, excessively gay and without the least restraint in their conversation; using the most familiar and unrestrained expressions to gentlemen as well as to each other without the least ceremony. This freedom of speech, however, keeps the bon ton at a distance, and though very pleasing in their own circles, becomes very vulgar and tedious to a nice observer. I was young, had a respectable train of servants and spoke the French language tolerably well: this was more than sufficient to gain me admission into all their parties. But my versatile disposition, or rather my evil genius, prompted me to quit this pleasant and harmless society and return to Lyons, where I met with an adventure, from which I may date all my subsequent misfortunes.

In this city I could find nothing to amuse me, if I except the sumptuous entertainments I gave to all those who chose to partake of them. Magnificent balls and suppers to the ladies, extravagant and expensive dinners to the gentlemen, succeeded each other in quick rotation.

The people of Lyons are very different from those of Marseilles. The latter only think how to make life agreeable, while the former concentrate all their enjoyments in the eagerness of making a rapid fortune. As an instance of their interested character, I shall relate a circumstance not generally known; and which I should not have discovered, had not a Lyonese girl led me into the secret.

At Lyons there is a league formed between the shopkeepers and the other inhabitants against all strangers who come to visit them. It is usual for foreigners to bring letters of recommendation to some of the principal inhabitants for the purpose of procuring lodging and assisting them in the purchase of whatever they may stand in need of. These complaisant conductors have ten per cent from the merchant upon every article which he sells by their recommendation, and for which he of course takes care to reimburse himself in the price of his commodities, so that the purchaser pays ten per cent more than he would have done, if he had gone alone to the shop, and at the same time looks upon himself as much obliged to his friend for his assistance in obtaining what he thinks a good bargain. The rich and the poor are here employed in their shops and warehouses from morning till night. The spirit of gain is the sole active principle which prevails in this vast magazine of luxury, which distributes its various articles to the four quarters of the world.

As to the Lyonese ladies, they possess but few attractive charms. A certain apathy and listlessness of manners destroy the effects of any beauty with which nature may have endowed them. I had no resource therefore, but in the pleasures of the table.

Among my numerous friends and acquaintances were two Irish gentlemen, whose names I shall conceal, because I only wish to impeach myself. I lived with them in so close an intimacy, that in a short time we became inseparable. Some time afterwards I received an anonymous letter, cautioning me to beware of my new friends, who were represented to be a couple of desperate gamblers, come from Spa, for the express purpose of making me the dupe of their execrable trade. They had received information of my residence at Lyons from one of their emissaries, whom they employed in such places as young men of fortune were likely to resort to. I paid but very little attention to this advice, as I never observed in either of them the least inclination for play: Besides, I was so little addicted to it myself, that I did not believe they had sufficient influence over me to induce me to play, even were they so inclined.

However, I shewed the letter to my tutor, who was of opinion that I should entirely avoid their company, and gave me some further exhortation against every species of gaming whatsoever: yet I was so infatuated with my new acquaintance, that I disregarded this good advice and the admonition of my unknown friend.

Some time afterwards we were invited to dinner by the two gentlemen, which invitation my tutor declined, nor could I ever learn what motive induced him not to accompany me to a place which he himself thought dangerous. This gave occasion for many of my relations to think that he was a party concerned in the scheme. But they certainly did him injustice. He was, it is true, a man of free principles, but I could never accuse him of anything unfair or dishonourable, besides, it was no uncommon thing with him to excuse himself from parties to which we were both invited. I therefore went alone to encounter this pair of worthies.

They had taken care to provide a handsome company of female beauties, who by their persuasion and example induced me to sacrifice so liberally to Bacchus at dinner, that before the dessert was introduced the glasses seemed to dance before me. Nothing would then satisfy them but we must drink champagne out of pint rummers, which soon completed the business.

When I was in a proper state for them to begin their operations, they one and all proposed playing at hiding the horse. I was in no condition to refuse anything, and soon acceded to their proposal, and without being scarcely conscious that I was engaged in it I lost £14,800 on my parole, exclusive of my ready money, carriage, jewels, etc.

I know not why they even stopped here, for I was in such a state that they might have stripped me of my whole fortune. I cannot, however, feel myself much indebted for this instance of their forbearance. They contented themselves for the present with a bill for the amount, which I drew on La Touche's Bank, and I then went to bed in a state of torpid insensibility.

The first thing I did in the morning was to communicate the whole transaction to my governor, with which he was visibly affected but as he saw the state of mind I was in, he forbore saying anything that might add to my distress, but rather endeavoured to console me by saying that the evil was not without remedy, and that at least it would have one good effect by rendering me more cautious and prevent me from ever falling into such hands for the future. This, though a negative sort of comfort, joined to the natural strength of my animal spirits, restored me in some measure to a state of tranquillity.

I did not enjoy it long. My banker, on whom I had drawn for so enormous a sum, communicated the affair to my friends before he would honour the bill. They advised him by no means to pay it, and it was returned protested. This was a most mortifying piece of intelligence to the fraternity; yet they were not without their expedients: they advised me to repair immediately to London, where, upon my fortune being made known, I should find no difficulty in getting my bills discounted to any amount I thought proper. As a further inducement for me to undertake the journey, they offered to remit half the debt, provided I should succeed in procuring the remainder.

My tutor was much averse to this scheme, which, he said, would entirely ruin him in the opinion of my relations, whose friendship it was so much his interest and inclination to preserve. But upon my representing to him the advantage of getting rid of half the debt he at length consented, and the following plan was concerted between us, in order to conceal from my friends my departure from France. I was to leave with him a series of letters to my mother, of different dates, according to the periods I usually wrote to her, which he was to dispatch occasionally as if I had been actually on the spot. This, I must own, I did rather to avoid giving my mother pain than to remove any anxiety I felt on his account.

I then drew a bill upon Dublin for two thousand louis d'ors, with part of which I paid some debts I owed at Lyons, and the remainder was to bear my expenses to London. Matters being thus arranged I set out with one of my creditors, leaving the other with my tutor, who I believe would gladly have dispensed with such a companion.

Before I take leave of Lyons and those good-natured friends, I must mention a trick played on me of a different nature; but which, if we consider both the parties concerned, had more knavery in it. In the company of gamblers, we are, or should be, on our guard, knowing that plunder is their trade: but we confide in men of business, from a supposition that they cannot injure us without hurting their own credit. The following fact, however, will be a caution to travellers how they sign bills of exchange abroad without strictly examining their contents.

I had by this time an unlimited credit on P--- at Paris. My friends thought this was one of the many expedients which might be tried to save me from ruin, and reclaim me from my follies, by inspiring me with a sense of honour and gratitude and if it had not the desired effect, it would at all events prevent me from raising money by having recourse to usurers.

This Mr P--- gave me letters of credit on all the principal towns which I visited. I drew on him from forty-one parts of France, and whenever I owed him £2,000 sent me two bills of exchange, as first and second, on my banker at Dublin, of the same amount for me to sign, which I always did without hesitation. But when I came afterwards to settle with my agent at home, I found that many of these bills had been paid twice over. This vile negotiator had drawn them in such a manner as to make them appear of different tenor and dates.

All my attempts to rectify this mistake and recover the money have hitherto been fruitless, for whenever I wished him to confront my checks with his letters of exchange, he always found some pretence or other to prevent the investigation. I have reproached him in his own house with the infamy of his conduct; and this I have done at a time when it was so dangerous to have any difference with a man who was flourishing under the reign of Robespierre. I can assert with truth and upon my honour, that I do not think I have been defrauded of less than £10,000 in this manner. So much for the honesty of a foreign banker.

On my arrival at Paris we took up our lodgings at the Hotel Jacob, Faubourg St Germain. In the evening I went to the opera, where chance placed me near a lady of exquisite beauty, whose occupation it was not difficult to discover, and who, as I soon perceived, set me down as an object worthy of her attention. A conversation therefore commenced between us, in the course of which she proved herself a perfect mistress of that species of dialect which is called jargon in France.

After the opera I offered my hand to conduct her to the lobby, where she took the opportunity of telling me that her horses being all out of order, her brother, who was a captain in the army, had attended her to the opera in his carriage, under a promise of returning after the performance. As she did not perceive him, she hoped it was not trespassing too far to request I would send one of my servants to call a fiacre.

After expressing my astonishment at the want of attention in her brother, I congratulated myself on its effects, as it gave me an opportunity of being in some degree useful to her. I pressed her to accept my carriage, to which, after much well-acted repugnance, she consented. I accompanied her to the house, where I found everything in the most magnificent style, and perfectly consonant with the way of living of a person of the first rank and fashion.

However, there were immediately such preparations made as did not seem intended for her inattentive brother, nor could I help being struck with the analogy of my case to that of poor Gil Blas in a like adventure. However, the good opinion I had of myself, the beauty of the lady, her engaging and fashionable manners made me soon forget the comparison. Nor did I think myself so little versed in scenes of this nature as to suffer myself to be duped by such an artifice. I remained, therefore, perfectly satisfied with my own reflections, and attributed my good fortune to my own merit and address. Supper was soon served up, which consisted of a variety of delicacies and the most exquisite wines.

During our repast she gave me a short account of her history. Her husband had a considerable employment at Court, and was then in attendance upon his Majesty at Versailles. I had dismissed my carriage that I might have some pretence for lengthening my visit, which I procrastinated till three o'clock in the morning, when I left her, highly pleased with my evening's entertainment, and not without having previously obtained her permission to pay my respects the following day.

I became now her constant cicisbeo, and her husband was so much engaged in his attendance at Court, that he had the civility never once to interrupt us. I thought myself the happiest young fellow in Paris or London. One day, however, I found her buried in thought and overwhelmed with the most unfeigned sorrow, nor could I at first prevail on her to disclose to her bosom friend the cause of her uneasiness. After repeated entreaties she confessed to me that the preceding night, having supped at the Duke de ---., she had been induced to play, and had lost, besides her ready money, one thousand louis d'ors on her parole; which, if she did not pay in the course of the day, would not only dishonour her in the great world, but would be the subject of eternal animosity and reproach between herself and her husband.

I was so struck with her grief and the plausibility of her story, that swift as an eagle I flew to my Hotel and laid at her feet every sol I had in my possession, which at that time did not exceed £700. Quite overpowered with my generosity, she thanked me in the most courteous manner, and whatever I could do and say, she would not accept more than £500, saying that with the help of that sum she should be able to make up the whole before evening.

I was never better satisfied with myself in my life, than when I returned to my Hotel, £500 minus in pocket; but with the consciousness of having rescued an amiable young woman of fashion from shame and ruin. I was so intoxicated with her charms and her fondness for me, that if she had asked 2,000 guineas I should not have rested a moment till I had raised that sum.

I do not know how much longer this infatuation would have lasted, if my creditors had not pressed me very much to proceed to England. I therefore left my charmer with all the anguish and throbbings of a young and inexperienced lover, fully determined to return to her as soon as my affairs should be settled in London.

But I suppose she was glad the farce was over; for by what I felt and experienced in the sequel, it could not remain much longer concealed that she was nothing better than an intrigant.

As soon as I arrived in London, I endeavoured to get my bills discounted, but without effect. I had not been many days in the capital, when one evening a stranger entered my room and delivered to me the following letter:

Sir

I am now the miserable inhabitant of a Convent, into which I
have been forced by my friends: were it not for the expectation of
regaining my liberty, I should convince them that I prefer death to a
confinement so repugnant to my temper and disposition. From what
I have heard of your character I have conceived the flattering hope
that you will exert your utmost endeavours to deliver me from this
captivity. As a proof of my gratitude I shall be happy to lay myself and
fortune at your feet.

The person who will deliver you this letter is the husband of my nurse,
who is still with me, they are both in my interest; and you may place an
implicit confidence in him.

Signed, C--- P---

I knew very well that Miss P--- was at Paris, in the same Convent
with Lady B---, her intimate friend, to whom I had been introduced.
I knew likewise that Miss P---'s fortune was £25,000 a year, besides
£200,000 in ready money.

Though I never had the pleasure of seeing this rich heiress, yet considering my personal merits and the lady's acquaintance with Lady B---,
her application to me seemed perfectly natural and consistent with
reason. I read the letter over several times, examined the superscrip-
tion, and at every interval cast a look at the bearer, to trace, if possible,
any marks of deceit in his countenance; but I could perceive none.
He answered all my questions with such simplicity and appearance of
candour that I could no longer doubt of the fact.

He told me that he had received the letter from his wife, who
enjoined him to use all his endeavours in persuading me to return
with him to Paris, as her mistress was very impatient to see me and to
concert measures for her escape. I at length dismissed him, desiring that
he would come in the evening when he should have his answer.

My Irish companion, to whom I communicated the intelligence, was
in raptures at the prospect of such a good fortune, and confirmed me
in the design of repairing immediately to Paris. But, unfortunately, I
had not in my possession more than 10 guineas remaining out of two
thousand I had received two months before at Lyons. In this difficulty
I had recourse to my banker for a supply, which he positively refused,
as he feared, and not without reason, that my return to France would
be but a renewal of my former follies.

Upon this I found myself under the necessity of shewing him the letter, which when he had read I was both pleased and astonished to find him entering as warmly into the project as if he had been a young man of eighteen, without reflection or experience. My banker was a man of strict honour and probity: without guile himself he suspected none in others, and though engaged all his lifetime in business, was as ignorant of the wiles and deceit of mankind as if he had been the inhabitant of another world. He offered me all the money I should want for the occasion, but wished first to see the bearer of the letter, that we might regulate our motions accordingly.

When I mentioned this to the foster-father of the young lady, he was by no means pleased with the communication I had made, and represented the risk he should run of being discovered an accomplice in carrying off a person from a convent, a crime always punished in France with the utmost severity of the law. I quieted his apprehensions by assuring him that he might depend upon the discretion of my banker. He told me he would consider of it, and that he would have no objection to the interview in case he could do it without danger to himself. In the course of two days he returned and agreed to accompany me to the banker's.

We all three met and dined together at a tavern in Covent Garden. After some conversation it was finally determined that he and the banker should set off directly for Paris to prepare matters, and they should inform me whenever my presence became necessary.

While we were giving orders about procuring a carriage, my servant came to inform my new acquaintance that a person wished to speak to him. At this I perceived that he was visibly affected. He went out and soon after returned, saying he was the most unfortunate man in the world: that one of his creditors had found him out and got him arrested, so that it was impossible he could proceed to Paris. The banker demanded how much the debt was, and on being told it was £150, he immediately advanced this sum, upon which the other retired, as we thought, to pay his creditor; but he did not think proper to return, nor have we ever set eyes on him since.

One would imagine that this was sufficient to have unravelled the whole plot, and it is certain that if I had been left to my own determination I would have given up the point without further inquiry. Not so my friend, he was too sanguine in the prospect of my advantage not to persevere while there remained any hope of success. His next step was to consult my creditor, who watched me like a tipstaff lest I should slip through his fingers. His advice was, and for which he had no doubt good reasons, that the banker should procure some person of the law who could speak French to accompany him and advise him in the steps proper to be taken on their arrival at Paris. He was not long in finding one fit for his purpose, whom he engaged under promise of allowing him £500 for his attendance.

They soon arrived at Paris, and lost no time in repairing to the convent, where they were immediately admitted to the presence of Lady B---, to whom they presented their credentials, I mean the letter addressed to me. When she had read it, she desired Miss P--- to be called, who no sooner cast her eyes on the letter than she burst into a violent fit of laughter in which she was joined by her companion, to the manifest confusion of the two adventurers, who, finding the whole to be a gross and manifest forgery, slunk away and made the best of their way back to London.

This was not the worst part of it, for exclusive of paying the attorney the stipulated sum, the banker had the additional mortification of seeing the whole affair detailed in all the papers under the title of 'A Trip to Paris', or 'The Banker Taken In'.

I found afterwards that the whole had been a plot laid by the fraternity for the purpose of inveigling me to the Continent, where they hoped not only to get me arrested for the bill I had drawn on Dublin, and which had been returned protested, but to pursue their further operations and schemes on me with greater security than they could do in London, surrounded as I was by my friends and relations. But though they failed in the main point, their principal agent had profited something by his sham arrest.

My health was now so much impaired that I found it absolutely necessary to apply to medical assistance. Unluckily it happened that I was recommended to a physician of eminence who was well acquainted with my family in Ireland. He immediately conveyed an account of the state in which he found me, and of my conduct in general, with which few indeed were unacquainted. My step-father Mr N--- was affected beyond measure at such an unexpected piece of intelligence, and lost no time in repairing to me himself.

Although the character of Mr N--- be well known, I cannot resist the desire I feel of rendering homage to the eminent qualities of that incomparable man, and to pay him this small tribute of respect and gratitude. He is at once the tender husband, the warm friend and generous benefactor. He is possessed of such extensive knowledge, of manners so conciliating, as would alone have procured him friends, were he not endowed with every other qualification that can command and ensure the love and veneration of his fellow citizens.

I was much afflicted at the sight of this sincere friend; who upon entering my apartment told me that on the first intelligence of my illness, he had come to convey me to his lodging, where I should be better accommodated than at a public Hotel; and at the same time be at some distance from a society to whom I might impute the greatest part of my misfortunes. He reprobated in very severe terms the conduct of my governor, who, he said, might at least have accompanied me to London, since he had not sufficient authority to prevent my coming myself.

He next took my creditor to task for the atrociousness of his conduct in pillaging a young man and enticing him away from his tutor, in hopes of raising money at an exorbitant interest in London, by which he had introduced sorrow and distress into a respectable family. This was so little relished by the person to whom it was addressed, that he thought proper to call Mr N--- to account for the liberty he took with his character. Mr N--- was not a man to be brow-beaten, and the affair might have had serious consequences but for the interposition of some friends who contrived that the matter should be settled in a manner more pleasing to all parties.

# CHAPTER II

My Return to Dublin – An Extraordinary Wager
– A Sea Journal – Description of an Albacore – The
Moorish Fleet – Gibraltar – The Grand Battery – St
George's Hall – Poco Roco, or Eliott's Parlour – Ince's
Gallery – Willis's Battery, or Queen's Gallery – The
King's Bastion – St Michael's Cave – Some remarks
on Gibraltar.

When I had sufficiently recovered my health, I accompanied Mr N--- to Dublin, where I was received and treated like the Prodigal Son. I took a house, hired a number of servants, and upon looking into my affairs, found that I had expended, exclusive of my ready money, about £20,000 of my fortune. Still, however, I might have been happy; I had an ample property remaining and was caressed by my friends, who looked upon my past follies with indulgence and as merely proceeding from the ebullitions of youth.

This quiet life did not suit my volatile disposition: in order, therefore, to vary the scene, I sent over to London for a female companion with whom I had been intimate, and who immediately accepted the invitation. I had no motive whatever in giving her the preference but that she was exotic. My inamorata was neither distinguished for wit or beauty; but I will do her the justice to say that she had none of that rapacity and extravagance so common with the generality of her profession. What I expended on her account was from my own free will and suggestion. I hired her a magnificent house, suitably furnished, and settled an allowance of five hundred a year on her: this was merely pro

forma, for she cost me upwards of five thousand. At her house I kept
my midnight orgies, and saw my friends, according to the fashionable
acceptation of the word.

But soon growing tired of this manner of living, I conceived the
strange idea of performing, like Cook, a voyage round the world; and
no sooner had it got possession of my imagination, than I flew off at a
tangent with my female companion to Plymouth, in order to put my
plan in execution, which was to purchase a vessel of 280 tons burthen,
and to carry twenty-two guns. I entered into treaty  with a builder,
who engaged to furnish me with one of the above description for
£10,000, equipped in every respect, and to be ready in the space of
four months.

This affair settled, I returned to Dublin, where being one day at
dinner with some people of fashion at the Duke of L---'s, the conversation turned upon my intended voyage, when one of the company asked
me to what part of the world I meant to direct my course first, to which
I answered, without hesitation, 'to Jerusalem'. This was considered by
the company as a mere jest, and so, in fact, it was, but the subject still
continuing, some observed that there was no such place at present existing; and others that, if it did exist, I should not be able to find it. This
was touching me in the tender point: the difficulty of an undertaking
always stimulated me to the attempt. I instantly offered to bet any sum
that I would go to Jerusalem and return to Dublin within two years
from my departure. I accepted without hesitation all the wagers that
were offered me, and in a few days the sum I had depending on this
curious expedition exceeded 15,000 pounds.

My whole mind was now engaged on this new project. I was inflamed
with the desire of doing what had not been attempted by any of my
countrymen, at least by those of my own age, and I figured to myself
the pleasure I should feel at my return to my own country after having
accomplished this undertaking: what admiration I should excite by the
detail of my wonderful adventures, my hair's breadth escapes, and the
descriptions I should give of the beautiful Turks, Greeks, and Georgians,
and all the farrago with which my heated imagination was filled.

I was now nearly of age, and Mr N--- peremptorily insisted that
I should again examine the state of my fortune, with which request,
however unwilling, I was under the necessity of complying. I found it
still more diminished by the variety of my dissipation and extravagance.
This worthy man, with the greatest delicacy and gentleness, represented

to me then, that the way of life in which I was engaged must inevitably lead me to ruin, that my extraordinary, not to say scandalous, establishment formed for the English lady did not stand me in less than five thousand a year, that the annual expense of my ship, exclusive of the first cost, would amount to much more, and that at the rate I proceeded, I must in a short time be reduced to indigence, and depend for support upon my friends and relations, that the attachment of the former, as I have since experienced, would cease, when the sunshine of my fortunes, by which they were now attracted, should disappear, and as to the latter, he knew my pride of heart too well to suppose that I could live under the mortification of owing the means of existence to any one, however nearly allied.

He then addressed me in the following affectionate manner. 'My dear M---, do you look upon me as a friend?' I assured him that the proofs he had given me of his friendship were too deeply engraved on my heart ever to be erased; that I looked up to him as a father, and that I should ever esteem it as my greatest happiness to be permitted to call him by that sacred title.

'Well then,' said he, with tears in his eyes, 'I conjure you by your friendship and the regard you allow me to have, that you will part with this woman and abandon the wild scheme of the voyage, that you will bestow your whole attention on the adjustment of your affairs, on fixing an establishment suited to your income, and, finally, that you will think of uniting yourself to some person of prudence and virtue, which will be the means of saving you from that precipice on which you are now tottering: you will then become a good husband, a good father and a good citizen, three essential qualifications for every honest man, and without which there can be no real enjoyment in life.'

Had he required of me any other sacrifice than the two above mentioned, I should have complied without hesitation; but these were my favourite hobby-horses: and though I would not offend Mr N--- by a direct refusal, I requested he would give me till the next day to consider of it, which interval I employed in deliberating how I could best soften my non-compliance with his request, so as to avoid giving him offence. This I could not do in such a manner but that the good man was sensibly touched at my strange infatuation, and any other but himself would have at once abandoned me to my fate. But his zeal to serve me was as steady as my perseverance in my own undoing was obstinate, so that by dint of argument and persuasion, he at length prevailed so far as to exact a promise from me that I would at least comply with half his request, and give up either one or the other, leaving the choice entirely to myself.

As I was now really attached to the lady, I agreed to give up the ship, if he would undertake to get her off my hands, which he did by means of a small compensation to the builder, who, I understand, afterwards sold her to the Empress of Russia.

This matter being settled, my whole attention was directed towards my expedition to Jerusalem, in which I intended my fair one should accompany me. But the inconveniencies of a female companion in traversing so much sea and land were pointed out to me in such a manner as induced me to give up that part of my scheme, and I accordingly left her in London on an allowance of two hundred a year, which was regularly paid her till all my property was sold.

Having now arranged everything which I thought necessary for my pilgrimage, I set out for Deal on 20 September, 1788, where I was joined by Mr W---, who had promised to accompany me. I hired a vessel called the *London*, to carry me to Smyrna and touch at Gibraltar. On 7 October we went on board and set sail immediately.

## 9 October

We commenced our voyage with favourable gales, and this day we found ourselves in the Bay of Biscay. The sea ran prodigiously high, and for several hours the motion of the ship surpassed every thing I had ever seen or felt before. The sea rolled over our heads and washed every thing off the deck. One prodigious wave striking the ship in the counter, set her for some moments on her beam-ends, knocked the man from the helm, and almost killed him, on my endeavouring to assist him I nearly shared the same fate, as I was thrown by another sea with great violence against my companion, and had my hip and thigh bruised in a most shocking manner.

Night coming on, it blew harder and harder, and though the sailors termed it a hard gale, I really thought it deserved the appellation of a heavy storm, nor was I, if countenances are allowed to reveal the emotions of the mind, the only person on board of that opinion. The captain himself acknowledged it to be the hardest gale he had encountered for seven years.

The return of day, however, promised us more moderate weather; and the wind shifting, we had in a few hours even less of it than we wished.

I now began to feel the vanity of human wishes, and the late storm having made me somewhat religious I could not help reflecting how little we are able to judge for ourselves. I had, some hours before, most fervently prayed for less wind, and now I was about to invoke heaven for more! These considerations naturally induced me to be satisfied with the calm rather than have it exchanged for a storm.

My friend and I had been informed, when in London, that it was expedient, considering the hazardous expedition we were going to undertake, that we should let our beards grow, in order that we might be as little noticed as possible in those countries we intended to visit, which could be effected only by dressing ourselves as much as possible in the habit of the country. Accordingly, we had not shaved since we left London, so that by this time we really appeared ridiculous and grotesque figures. We would more than once have undergone the operation of the razor had we not been well assured that a long beard would be of more use to us and protect us more efficaciously than long swords, or all the guards we could procure. This appeared to us a better scheme than either to fight the Arabs or make them large presents.

## 15 October

Early in the morning I was awoken by the noise of the crew on deck, who had a large fish fast at my line; I got up just time enough to see him brought on board. This fish, known to the sailors by the name of Albacore, was the most beautiful I ever beheld. It had in shape and colour much the advantage of the Dolphin, remarkably strong and full made at the shoulder, and tapering towards the tail. He weighed thirty-seven pounds when gutted, and it was out of my power to prevent the cook from cutting him open before he was a moment out of the water. I observed that while he underwent the severe operation of having his inside taken out, he lay as if totally devoid of feeling, but scarcely had his entrails been taken from him, when, as if to make amends for his apparent torpor, he beat the deck with such astonishing violence and rapidity that it was impossible to approach him. At length I was pleased to see an end put to his miserable existence by a blow with an axe, which the cook gave him on the head, which cutting it almost asunder, entirely deprived this beautiful animal of life.

I observed one peculiarity in this fish, which I should not pass over unnoticed: I remarked his heart to be as large as that of a half-grown lamb, and curiosity having led me to take it up in my hand, I was much astonished to find it so convulsed as to force open my fingers when pressed upon it. I laid it down and took out my watch to see how long it would retain its motion, and much to my surprise the heart moved on the deck for nearly two minutes after I had thrown it down. It was a most excellent fish, and for several days was served as the first dish at table. I saw with regret that we could not replace him, and therefore ordered some of it to be pickled, and found it as good as any sturgeon I had ever eaten.

## 20 October

We saw a whale quite near us. This stupendous animal did not in the least appear to mind us: it seemed to keep company with the ship, and followed it for many minutes, spouting up water to a very great height, and once he was so near as to wet our mizzen half way up with the spray. Had we been at all provided with harpoons, we might, I am certain, have made him a very easy prey.

## 26 October

We had now been six days beating to windward, expecting every day to weather Cape St Vincent, and what was most extraordinary was that let us be on which tack we would, whether steering East, West, North, or South, we were sure to have the wind change, as we did, and blow directly in our teeth. This led me to remark that, in order to live pleasantly at sea, two qualifications were absolutely necessary: in the first place, a man must possess an uncommon share of philosophy, and in the next a good stock of patience, particularly if he has the misfortune of being confined to a merchant ship with a long voyage before him, absent from all the endearing objects of his heart, and the wind constantly against him, with no appearance of a change in his favour. In a situation like this, one has much time for reflection. I hope that those I made may be of service to me, and by way of assisting them, I proposed to my friend to drink a bottle of Madeira, and set his philosophy and mine afloat together. This succeeded beyond my expectation: the heavy hours passed away in jocund merriment. We forgot that the wind was against us and, night coming on, we slept as well and contentedly as if we had the most prosperous gales in the world.

The next morning we saw a number of fishing boats off the Spanish land, and through my glass I could discern the village of Saltas in the land of Sinas, or Boddendoes, so called from the redness of its soil. Saltas, as well as I could judge at the distance of two or three leagues, is a neat pretty village situated at the foot of a very high hill. The country on both sides is very beautiful, and mostly covered with underwood.

I should have liked to go on shore, but not having bills of health for the place, and knowing the strictness observed by the Spaniards in preventing all strangers from landing on any part of their coast, especially from on board a Turkey ship, induced me to give up all thoughts of it. Besides, the captain related to me a circumstance which some years before happened to himself. He was then mate of a merchantman bound to the Levant, and finding the ship weather-locked upon the Spanish coast near Malaga, he was desired by the captain to go on shore in search of a few necessaries.

He had scarcely landed when he was seized and carried before a magistrate, who sent him to prison, where he lay for upwards of ten days, till the ship went to Gibraltar and the Governor was informed of the circumstance, who on application had him restored to liberty, though not till after he had paid the gaolers very considerable fees. This was more than sufficient to shake me in my resolutions, and I was obliged to content myself some time longer with the exercise that walking the deck afforded.

At length the wind became favourable, and the captain revived our spirits by informing us, that should the wind keep as it was, we should be in Gibraltar in thirty-six hours. I had now been twenty-one days on board, and when we sailed from the Downs we expected that much less than half that time would have set us on the Rock. I could not help growing a little impatient, and the more so as I had a long voyage before me and little time allotted to perform it.

I had not much leisure to cherish these pleasing expectations, as in a few hours the wind kindly returned to its old quarter. My patience began to be nearly exhausted, for the more I endeavoured to reason with myself the more I was convinced of the fallacy of human happiness: one moment we were elated with appearances, which vanished in another, and reason, which we are told should be our support, only serves to convince us more fully of our wretched insignificance.

In my opinion, a man should either be a Seneca, or quite a fool, to pass through life with any tolerable share of comfort. I am confident that I am no philosopher, and though I have vanity sufficient to prevent me from thinking myself a fool; yet were I called on to give my opinion, which of the two characters I think the most likely to conduce to happiness, I should not find it a hard matter to decide in favour of the latter.

## 27 October

At break of day we saw the coast of Barbary, distant four leagues, and soon after we were abreast of Cape Spartel, when we were very much alarmed at the appearance of several ships within gunshot of us, which we discovered to be the Moorish Fleet. It consisted of six small frigates that seemed to mount from twenty to thirty-six guns each. They appeared to be full of men, above twice the number we have in ships of that size; notwithstanding which they obeyed their signals very clumsily. Yet on the whole I thought the ships sailed well on a wind, and had they been more expert at handling and setting their topsails, they would have kept tolerable pace with us.

We observed them after some time make a signal, which immediately gave us the alarm: the foremost ship ordered the boats to be hoisted out, and on the first being let down into the water we were sufficiently aware of their intentions not to wait for a second. We crowded all the sail we could, and were in about two hours out of their reach.

These boats most undoubtedly were intended to board us: whether their views were hostile or not, I cannot decide, but in either case it would have reduced us to the dire necessity of performing forty days quarantine at Gibraltar, as we afterwards learned, had we been boarded by any ship whatever from the coast of Barbary.

We sailed close along the Barbary shore, and found a strong tide hurrying us into the Gut of Gibraltar, at the rate of seven knots. The coast appeared very wild and the shore very bold all the way from Cape Spartel to a very high land, called Apes' Hill, from the number of animals of that name that is seen on it. The face of the country is rocky, and yet covered with much underwood, which has an uncommonly wild appearance. Here and there you are struck with a romantic prospect, and some spots are very pretty. But as you proceed to the eastward the country carries with it the appearance of an uninhabited sandy desert.

On the following morning we found ourselves in the very centre of the Gut or Mouth of the Straits and on both sides the most beautiful sea-landscape offered itself to our view, on the South the uneven surface of the Barbary shore forming itself into a bay, at the West end of which is the town of Tangiers, on the North, nearly opposite, and on the Spanish shore, is the beautiful village of Tercese. The immense height of the rocks ascending perpendicularly from the surface of the sea strikes the imagination with sublime though awful ideas.

In the middle of the Channel that runs between these two shores, as you open the entrance into the Mediterranean, there runs a tide, which in the summer months always sets in to the westward and to the eastward in the winter months, at the rate of five knots. From the manner in which this tide appears to boil up in different places, I should imagine the ground to be very foul, or that there runs a contrary tide at the bottom, either of which would give it the appearance it now has.

I cannot be supposed to affect feelings that may be fairly called peculiar to the moment, when in the midst of that immense body of water which washes a shore of no less than 3,000 miles, even in a direct course, to the head of the Black Sea, I discovered so many new, interesting and variegated scenes, which were much heightened by the reverberation of the sound of cannon through a chain of mountains, and the setting sun plunging itself into the Atlantic directly central to our situation, and which was sometimes obscured by the interposition of impending clouds.

On Wednesday, 29 October, we discovered the Rock of Gibraltar. I had remained on deck from five in the morning with all the eagerness that curiosity and expectation could inspire. The renown of that memorable siege was too fresh in my memory not to be stimulated by the greatest impatience to hear those facts recorded on the spot which immortalized its brave defenders and their veteran chief

I had from earliest youth formed a wish of visiting Gibraltar, and the eagerness with which I waited for the time of my getting onshore is not to be described. But I was never more disappointed in my life than at the first appearance which this so much celebrated place seemed to present at two miles' distance from the sea: nothing to strike the eye but the height of the rock and a few straggling houses: not the appearance of a battery, or the smallest indication of a fortified place.

Nor was my opinion peculiar to myself in this respect, for I have heard since that a stranger on his first approach to Gibraltar must necessarily be somewhat disappointed from the first view that place offers from the sea. But how soon is he undeceived when he sets his foot on shore, and with what pleasure and admiration does he gaze on everything he sees around him. Nature and art have gone hand in hand for many years, and if nature has been lavish of her favours, art has done much indeed, and is still exerting herself to improve her wonderful productions by rendering this celebrated fortress absolutely impregnable, to advance the grandeur and glory, the interests and honour of the British name.

I was just stepping into the boat to go on shore when the captain requested I would return to the cabin and look at myself in a glass, nor could I help laughing at the ridiculous appearance I made. In dressing my hair the servant had taken care to powder my beard, which was now grown an inch long. I therefore held a council of war whether or not I should appear before the Governor in such a manner, and the majority giving it against me, I was obliged to yield to the considerations of the present, and lose sight of the motives of prudence which had made me take these precautions against the future. Consequently my venerable beard was condemned to undergo the operation of the razor, and it required all the exertions of my persuasive eloquence to get a respite for the poor whiskers.

I inquired my way to the Governor's, and as I proceeded through the streets was much struck with the variety of figures that I met running promiscuously backward and forward, and the odd and confused noise resulting from a dozen different languages spoken at once. Jews of all nations, Moors, Turks, and Christians were indiscriminately mixed together, each having a different dress, countenance, and religion. To me all was masquerade. I could not have been more amused in the centre of the Pantheon, nor hit upon a character to which I could have done more justice than the one I naturally filled at the time, that of a country booby, gaping and staring at all I saw.

I did not find his Excellency (General Geo. Augustus Eliott, Lord Heathfield, KB) at home, but having been informed of my arrival, he had done me the honour of leaving an invitation for my friend and me to dine with him at three. We strolled about the town till that hour, viewing and examining the devastations committed during the late siege. We were received with all that easy politeness and affability of manners which so eminently distinguish his Excellency's character, and denote the gentleman, as well as the social companion. I had the honour of being well acquainted with the General some years before, when he was on the staff in Ireland, during the administration of the late much lamented Duke of Rutland, whose public and private virtues can only be forgotten when time is no more.

He recollected me with pleasure, and I knew sufficiently of my friend the General to be certain of meeting with excellent cheer at the Governor's.

We ate, drank, laughed and talked a good deal for the time, but early in the evening the company broke up and I was going to retire when my friend recommended me to his secretary, Mr B---, who, in order to make me pass the evening as pleasantly as possible, had invited a party of young people to a little dance. Though rather fatigued, and in boots, I could not withstand the temptation, when I was presented to a very beautiful young Spaniard, *agée de seize ans, aussi fraiche que jeune, et aimabie que jolic.* My pretty partner did not dislike a fandango. Her uncle, as he was called by some, though others informed me that he was more nearly related to her, played the *bass viol.* He was a fat friar of the Franciscan order, and so much of the bon-vivant as to have been excommunicated by the Pope.

After I had danced for three hours, I found myself under the necessity of asking quarter from my fair partner, and I found much more pleasure in the conversation of this beautiful girl than I had experienced even in gratifying her in the fandango.

The next day I received visits from several of the officers of the Garrison, among whom I had the pleasure of meeting with many old friends and school-fellows, vying with each other who should shew me the greatest politeness.

Accompanied by some of them, I walked out to see the town. We first examined the storehouses and barracks that had been destroyed in the lower part of the town, and which had not been rebuilt since the siege. Afterwards we visited the different batteries that are constructed at the foot of the Rock: among the most remarkable are Orange Bastion, Montague Bastion, Saluting Battery, King's Bastion, Prince George's Battery, and South Bastion. They are situated on the Line Wall to the west of the town. There are many other batteries on the different heights above, to support these in time of action.

As we were proceeding to make the tour of the different works that defended the bottom of the Rock, we arrived at Waterpoint, where we found the Commodore's, now Admiral Cosby's, boat, just come on shore in order to conduct me on board the Trusty. He received me with the most friendly cordiality; and after inquiring about all our mutual friends in Ireland and England, he offered me every assistance that lay in his power; telling me I might command his boat whenever

I should want her; and as the most curious and interesting part of the Rock must be seen by water, this kind offer, of which I availed myself several times, was of the greatest service, and enabled me amply to satisfy my curiosity.

From thence we visited the Grand Battery, situated on the north, and thirty feet in height. It commands the two entrances from the isthmus into the garrison, and in the last siege this battery, with only half its guns in play, was more than sufficient to prevent any boat from landing at any part of the isthmus, having the entire command of both the northern entrances which run parallel to each other. I spent much time in examining and admiring this great battery; but with the General's hour for dinner approaching, I was forced to make a precipitate retreat, and was lucky enough to find myself in good time.

It is the fashion in Gibraltar, as well as in London and Dublin, to complain in the midst of a most sumptuous repast, of the hardness of the times and the dearness and scarcity of provisions. I was assured, however, that they were then as much so as during the siege, owing to the disagreement which subsisted between the garrison and his Moorish majesty, who had taken it into his head to quarrel with them and refuse them provisions. It was even said that in one of his drunken fits he had sworn by his beard never to be on better terms with Gibraltar.

Our next excursion was to view and examine St George's Hall and Gallery and the different embrasures cut out of the solid rock, that have been made and are still carrying on, at an immense expense. The morning being uncommonly warm, and our intended promenade being on a continual ascent, we thought it proper to hire mules. As we ascended the hill, every object struck me with new and pleasing sensations. The first thing I observed was the apple geranium, growing everywhere spontaneously, and in full bloom, likewise in different places, the variegated geranium; while the general face of the Rock produced at this season a considerable luxuriance and verdure, and was ornamented with neat cottages built by officers, and many gardens formed and cultivated with vast labour and expense, the produce of which every proprietor of grounds sends to the common market, after the wants of his own house are provided for, and which afford a supply tolerably adequate to the great demands of this numerous Garrison.

The uncultivated parts of the Rock produce vast quantities of the Palmetto, with a considerable variety of more humble plants and aromatic herbs. But the quantity of ruins still visible and the number of respectable habitations that were reduced to mere wrecks recalled to the mind of the spectator all the sufferings their inhabitants must have experienced during the siege.

The town below had the most picturesque appearance, the number of different batteries planted in every quarter and seen at one view, make one consider with surprise the temerity of an enemy that would dare to approach within their range. In our ascent we commanded a very distinct view of the Causeway and Inundation from lower Forbiss to Landport, and the whole range of Line Wall from thence past the new Mole as far as to Roscia Bay.

After we had made considerable progress in our ascent to St George's Cave, we stopped for some minutes to see a cavern called Poco Roco, or small cave, in which General Eliott, late Lord Heathfield, resided for some time during the commencement of the late siege. This little rock is situated nearly 400 feet from the surface of the sea, and about one-third of the way up the Rock. The General had the front of it built up, and he lived on this spot for a month when the Spaniards first began the attack. They had the incivility to throw many shells near this humble abode, with a wish to dislodge this brave veteran.

From Poco Roco Cave, now called Eliott's Parlour, we remounted our mules, and rode upwards of one hundred feet higher up the Rock, when we arrived at the entrance of Ince's Gallery, so denominated after the name of the man who planned and executed that great work. We unlocked the door and proceeded forward into this wonderful Gallery, hewn out of the solid rock. It extends in length, from the entrance to the most easterly part, 770 feet. In that whole extent, its gradual descent is about 84 feet: its breadth about 80, and its height from 7 to 9 feet.

It has fifteen different ports or embrasures, each of which is occupied by a long thirty-two pounder. These guns are supplied with ammunition from seven magazines hewn out of the rock of the Gallery, at equal distances; and in time of a siege they can be played with astonishing effect on the Spanish lines, without the possibility of receiving any injury.

When you arrive at the end of this Gallery, you enter St George's Hall. Here, if possible, your astonishment is still increased, and you are really lost in amazement; a vast and magnificent Hall opens to your view, into which you descend from Ince's Gallery by a spacious flight of steps.

St George's Hall has seven large embrasures by which it is lighted: three of them are to the east, three to the west, and one in the centre, to the north. The floor of the Hall from the steps to the north part is 46 feet, its extreme breadth 40, and its height in general 18. The thickness of the rock through which the ports are cut is 15 feet, and each port has a long thirty-two pounder.

I observed to my friend how very highly I thought this vast subterraneous work was finished, and in what a masterly manner the workman must have used his chisel, so as scarcely to leave an edge or the least roughness on any part of the rock, which was polished with the greatest care, but my astonishment much increased when they informed me that it was intended to have the Hall and Gallery wainscoted from one end to the other; this would answer a most salutary purpose in case of a desperate siege, when the barracks of the town should be destroyed. Here would be a capital retreat for the soldiers, and they would be better lodged than troops usually are in the best barracks. Their hammocks might be slung to the ceiling and drawn close by pulleys during the day. Their firearms could be most commodiously hung in gun-racks along the side of the Gallery, and there would be here at once complete barracks large enough to lodge six regiments.

After I had spent full three hours in viewing with much pleasure St George's Hall and Ince's Gallery, we descended the Rock and came to the old batteries at Willis's, so called from the name of the person who first constructed them.

Under Willis's we went to see another curious work, now carrying on and nearly finished, called Queen's Gallery: It is similar to St George's and extends north and north-west When finished it will add exceedingly to the strength and security of Gibraltar; as there will be an excavated communication between all the lines, by which ammunition of every kind can be conveyed at all times wherever it is wanted.

From Queen's Gallery we descended the hill and went to the King's Bastion, begun fourteen years ago. The first stone, which weighed seven tons, was laid by General Boyd (Lt.-Gen. Sir R. Boyd, KB, Colonel of 39th Foot, in 1788 Lt.-Governor of Gibraltar, pictured on following page) on 28 March, 1774. His speech upon this occasion seems to have been dictated by the spirit of prophecy.

'May this work, which I nominate the King's Bastion, repel the united efforts of France and Spain, and may it be as ably defended, as I make no doubt it will be skilfully constructed.' The brave veteran lived to see his prayer fulfilled in all its parts, and his remains are now deposited in a tomb constructed by his own order in the centre of the Bastions.

This great battery is of a semicircular form: its estimate was laid at £21,000, but, like all other estimates, by the time it was completed it did not cost less than £50,000. It was from this Bastion that the flat-bottomed boats, or floating batteries, were destroyed by red-hot shot during the late siege. General Eliott had dining tables made from the wrecks of these boats, on which I had several times the pleasure of dining with the Governor.

After our morning's excursion we returned to town a good deal fatigued, I in particular, by the excessive heat, to which I was not inured like my companions. I dined this day at the mess of the 18th Foot, with my friend, and as it turned out, my future fellow-traveller, Captain M---.

I partook here, as indeed at all the other tables in the Garrison, of most excellent cheer, a well-regulated mess, good cookery, excellent wines and a most gentlemanlike society. With these inducements I trust I may be pardoned for having been tempted to excess; particularly as I had an object in view, which I thought of much importance, and was determined to carry my point this evening, if possible.

My friend with whom I dined was at this time just going to become his own master, having obtained leave of absence and being about to return to England with the Commodore, who was then quitting this station. It was my anxious wish to prevail on him to defer his visit to England and join me in my intended expedition, in which I was so fortunate as to succeed, and from this moment we considered ourselves as embarked in one common cause, in which we felt equally interested.

We terminated, at a late hour, a jovial, pleasant evening, and parted to meet the next morning for another excursion. I was determined to explore St Michael's Cave, as I did not wish to leave Gibraltar without seeing this wonderful work of nature. The Governor had promised me every assistance I should want, and accordingly he had the goodness to send me twelve chosen men with torches, and a guide, with 200 fathoms of rope to facilitate my subterraneous descent, as I was determined to go to the bottom of this cave, or at least, as far as any other person had ever been.

At nine in the morning I set out, accompanied by Captain S--- of the Royal Engineers and my friend Captain W---. We were mounted on mules and clambered up a very steep ascent. We arrived after an hour's ride at the mouth of the cave, where having refreshed ourselves with some Madeira, and summoned up our courage, we followed, with torches in our hands, our Genoese guide, and after encountering many difficulties, arrived at the first great chamber of this wonderful Cavern.

It would be ridiculous in the extreme for me to attempt the description of those awful beauties which surrounded us on all sides. The different crystallizations and the many fantastic structures which appear to support the ceiling of this great ante-chamber require, to be truly delineated, that descriptive talent which so peculiarly distinguishes the writings of some of our poets, where the beauties of nature are heightened by the glowing traits of taste and imagination. From what I had seen I felt myself inspired with the most eager desire to proceed.

We descended from this first great apartment, by the assistance of ropes, about sixty fathoms lower, where we landed ourselves in nearly the same kind of chamber we had left above. Having provided ourselves with straw, we had it lighted, and in a few moments the whole place was illuminated. Reversed pyramids of petrified water, thirty and forty feet in length, hanging from the ceiling everywhere, and reflecting the light in different colours, had the most beautiful appearance, and struck the imagination with the most sublime ideas. The air still retained its salubrity, and the only unpleasant circumstance that occurred to us was the number of bats, which everywhere flew against us and interrupted our solitary meditations.

We remained in this second chamber till all our straw was consumed, and then proceeded on our journey by the help of ropes which were fastened at the entrance. We descended almost perpendicularly fifty fathoms. I now began to find my body rather heavy for my arms to support much longer; and with some impatience asked my guide below me whether we should soon get to the bottom. He answered me that we had already reached it. I made haste to follow him, and soon found myself on my legs. I remained some time panting for breath and much exhausted.

As soon as my friend W--- had joined me, the rest of the party having already deserted us, we proceeded to the spot which our guide informed us was the bottom. This last apartment was not half the size of the other two, and the crystallizations had totally altered their form. Instead of the long petrified icicles, the whole ceiling and sides of this chamber appeared covered with large bunches of grapes, of different colours, red, white and blue, as exact as if the fruit itself had been hung up everywhere. I broke off several, and have kept them since as a great curiosity.

Our guide now told us that we had seen all that was worth visiting, and advised us, on account of the foulness of the air, to go no lower. I asked him if he had ever known anyone to have gone farther. He said he had himself gone about twenty feet lower, and afterwards found it impossible to proceed, as the passage became too small for a man's body.

I was however determined to go on, and lighting a new torch, I ordered him to lead the way. We descended with much difficulty, as the air began to be quite mephitic. Our torches went out, but happily we had left a large flambeau burning at the entrance of the second cave, which my guide was obliged to fetch, leaving me all the time in the dark. I began to be much incommoded with the damp, as we were in the most violent heat, occasioned by the hard exercise of lowering ourselves by ropes.

I saw nothing here so curious as what we left some hundred feet above our heads: the crystallizations were smaller, and the water in greater abundance, dropping from all quarters. Our guide was pressing us to return, when I perceived a small aperture, which he wished to prevent my seeing. I asked him why he had not shewn it. He said that no one had ever been lower, except the two soldiers, who two years ago, had attempted to force themselves into this hole; that, indeed, they had succeeded in getting in, but never found their way back.

On examining the size of the hole, I thought it sufficiently large for the dimensions of my body. I thrust my head and shoulders into it and perceived that at the distance of five or six feet it took a different direction, and appeared to go perpendicularly downwards. I ascertained this fact by throwing my torch into it, which disappeared suddenly: we heard it for some seconds falling with a hollow noise, which at last subsided, and on looking into the hole, I perceived a very clear light at a great distance. I was therefore determined to endeavour to proceed a little farther, and if possible to go to the bottom.

When we examined our rope we found that we had only about the sixth part of the two hundred fathoms remaining. I fixed it round my shoulders and between my legs, and began to let myself down. The hole grew so small that it required much strength and resolution to proceed. I did not lose courage, but forcing myself forward I found I was, after a struggle of a few minutes, as low as the torch, and to my great surprise at the bottom, where no human being had ever yet been. I called to my friend, whose voice I could distinctly hear, informing him that I was really at the bottom, and that the air was by no means bad but very cold.

He was determined to follow me; I endeavoured to dissuade him, as I knew the size of his body to be too large for the narrow parts of the passage, but he was positive, and got as far as the spot I dreaded, when, forcing himself on, he remained fixed for some time without being able to proceed up or down, nor could he, as he afterwards informed me, utter a syllable. What first apprised me of our danger was the quantity of smoke, which not finding vent above, from the obstruction of his body, almost suffocated me below. I made all possible haste to get back, as the smoke increased in such a manner as almost prevented my respiration. I now found myself in the last extremity, but was determined my courage and presence of mind should not forsake me, and finding that my life depended on my exertions, I struggled like a person in the last agonies of death, and in a little time found myself returned to the spot where I had left the guide. My friend was quite exhausted and breathless, nor could we speak for several minutes, and had he remained a little time longer in the narrow passage, he and I must inevitably have perished.

We found ourselves so weak that our return to the land of the living was by no means an easy task. It was both difficult and fatiguing to raise and pull ourselves up by our hands, placing our feet against the rock and holding fast by the rope, which was now become so wet that it required much strength to prevent its slipping through our hands, and our falling to the bottom.

After some hours' severe labour we had the pleasure of once more seeing daylight, and found ourselves at the mouth of St Michael's Cave where I answered the inquiries of my friends by fainting away, and it was some minutes before I recovered my senses. We had been five hours in the cave, and were it not for the ridiculous vanity of saying that we had gone lower than any other person, and quite to the bottom, half an hour would have shewn us whatever was most curious and best worth our notice. I had the rope measured, and found that I had been as low as the level of the sea. The only benefit I reaped from this expedition was the ample materials for mirth and raillery it afforded my friends, who pretended that it had been my intention to perform my journey to Jerusalem through the bowels of the earth.

After having spent a few days more in examining every natural and artificial curiosity of this place I thought it prudent to proceed on my voyage. I therefore took leave of all my friends and acquaintance, thanking them for the friendly and encouraging reception they had given me.

I cannot dismiss this subject without making a few general remarks on this spot. For, in my opinion, there can be nothing in Europe, or in the world, that can offer to the curious traveller so many objects to admire and investigate as Gibraltar. He might spend a whole month very pleasantly in examining its natural beauties alone. And the artificial works, surpassing everything of the kind in the world, would afford him ample materials for study and improvement.

To appearance, indeed, Gibraltar must strike the eye as a barren rock, yet wherever it is cultivated, which is done in some spots by collecting earth together, it yields vegetables in great abundance. Sometimes it does not rain here for four months, and of course everything would be burned up were it not for the heavy dews which fall every night. But after a few hours' rain every cultivated spot assumes the most lively verdure. A garden here, of about half an acre, could not, I was assured, be cultivated at a less expense than £300 a year, and yet the tenant, notwithstanding that enormous sum, was a considerable gainer by its produce.

Though the Rock of Gibraltar is surrounded by the sea, well water is to be found all over it, pretty good, and fit to drink, though heavy and often brackish; but the rain water from the mountain, which is filtered through the sands without the south port, is exceedingly good and wholesome, and remains uncorrupt a long time. It is collected into a reservoir, and from thence conducted to the town. This aqueduct was first begun by the Moors and carried by earthen pipes, in their time it reached the city, supplying the Atarasana and the Castle: that now existing was planned by a Spanish Jesuit, and only reaches to the grand parade. The hill universally abounds with cavities and receptacles for rain, which mostly centre in the Reservoir, affording an inexhaustible stock of excellent water, greatly contributing to the health of the inhabitants.

I was much surprised, in one of my excursions, to spring a covey of partridges of about twelve brace. I saw nothing for them to feed on, but was informed that they eat the seed of the Palmetto, which grows in great abundance on every part of the Rock. I met with numbers of them afterwards nor was I astonished at it, when I knew that there was a strict rule observed forbidding any person of whatever rank or condition to fire a shot on any account, unless at an enemy, and they have had sufficient sport in this way to satisfy any reasonable people for some time.

At the southern end of the Rock, some way up, above St Michael's Cave, there are many wild boars, which are sometimes seen a dozen in number. I should willingly have paid those gentlemen a visit, had shooting been permitted. On the Sugar Loaf there are monkeys in hundreds, and though the soldiers often complain, when on guard, of being pelted by them with stones, they are not permitted to defend themselves by shooting at them.

There is very little society at Gibraltar, but a perfect harmony subsists between the Garrison and the few inhabitants, and with apparent wishes to promote conviviality, they spend their time in a very pleasant manner. I felt so much comfort and satisfaction among them that it was with much regret I left this celebrated Rock, not less endeared to me by the hospitality I experienced there than it is known to the rest of the world for its memorable defence.

# CHAPTER III

The Sea Voyage resumed – The Island of St Peter
– Sicily – Mount Olympus – A Storm – Smyrna – A
*Tendour* – *L'Avant Souper* – The Custom-House – A
Caravan – A Mosque – A Turkish Bath – A Lead-
foundry – Character of Pauolo, my Servant – A
Turkish Burying-Ground – Journey to Constantinople
– Magnesia – Its Governor – Preparations for a Battle.

## 6 November

We re-embarked on board the *London*. Nothing remarkable occurred to us on the first days of our navigation; nor shall I attempt to describe the various scenes and trifling occurrences which do not fail to attract the attention of the inexperienced navigator. It was not till the thirteenth that we discovered land, which proved to be the island of Sardinia.

On the same morning I was very much entertained with the appearance of a vast number of pilot fish. This fish is known to live in perfect amity with the shark, whose caterer he is said to be, in the same manner as the jackal is the lion's. We endeavoured to catch some of them with lines, but did not succeed. We tried to strike them with the harpoon, but being rather too small to be killed in this manner we only got two of them after labouring for three hours. We had them dressed for dinner and found eating them tolerably well.

Having unfortunately stood too much to the northward, we perceived that most likely we should not be able to weather the island, which would be one hundred miles out of our course, and to my great mortification, our apprehensions were but too well founded.

## 14 November

We stood in for the south end of the island, close off St Peter's, the shore of which is safe and bold, and the rocks very lofty, resembling much the northern parts of Ireland, off the point of Bengore and along the Giant's Causeway.

In different places of the island of St Peter's I observed the inhabitants employed along the shore in burning charcoal. The weather was extremely sultry, but the serenity of the sky and smoothness of the waters, which are experienced here as much as in any other seas, more than atone for the other inconveniences. We sat down to dinner in good spirits, and though the fare was none of the best, we contrived to make amends for it by vying with each other who should most enliven the conversation. We did not sit long at dinner, though the conversation turned a good deal on a favourite subject, sporting, in all its branches. And though this subject naturally led us to mention most of our Irish friends, yet two bottles of port saw the end of our discourse, and we went on deck to admire the beauties of the setting sun, and there renewed our conversation till the rising moon brought forward other pleasing and interesting sensations

## 17 November

We saw the little island of Maretimo, exhibiting nothing to the view but a rock uncommonly high above the water; it is of a circular form, and rather flat at top. Having passed Maretimo, we saw two more small islands, Fangnana and Farognana; the former resembles Gibraltar very much in respect to the shape of the rock. They are very steep and have a most uncommon appearance from the sea.

## 18 November

We discovered this morning, close on the shore of Sicily, the city of Marsala, which is built on the southwest promontory of the island. It appears from the sea a large and beautiful town, has several good houses, a great many steeples, and is surrounded by a wall.

As you proceed southward, the island of Sicily is very flat for many leagues along the shore, but as you carry your eyes into the country it rises by degrees and terminates in lofty mountains.

A very beautiful plain extends from Marsala a great way along the coast: at the distance of ten miles is Mazaria, beautifully situated close on the sea coast. It is fortified and the base of its walls is washed by the waves. The intermediate country between these two towns is most beautiful, and carries with it the richest appearance. At small distances from each other you discover here and there several villas most delightfully situated. The circumjacent country has the appearance of being very populous. The greater part of it is thickly wooded, and the whole is interspersed with villas whose situations are chosen with judgment and exhibit an uncommon degree of neatness, wealth and cheerfulness.

As we sailed further along this beautiful island we were at every moment amazed and delighted with the different cities, towns, and villages, many miles up the country; all of them exhibiting handsome churches with lofty spires. I stayed all day upon deck, admiring the beauties of this garden of the world, when on a sudden at four in the evening the weather changed, and threatened us with an impending storm. As the night advanced the gale increased in heavy squalls accompanied with thunder and lightning, and, indeed, our night was in every respect very uncomfortable.

Before daybreak we could see Mount Etna emitting a little fire and vast clouds of thick smoke, but in the morning we discerned it more perfectly, and all went on deck to view this celebrated mountain, where the ancient poets had placed the forge of Vulcan, whose assistants, the Cyclops, fabricated the thunderbolts of Jove. We could discern it at the distance of twenty-five miles, having then the appearance of a small bonfire. On a nearer view I could perceive its top, covered with snow and volumes of smoke, whilst the sides, on account of the fertility of the soil, were carefully cultivated and planted with vineyards. The changes in the atmosphere were more frequent during this day than we had yet known them: foul and fair weather, light breezes, and then a storm, thunder and lightning, and then a serene sky, excessive heat at one time and soon after extreme cold alternately succeed each other during the last twenty-four hours.

## Saturday, 22 November

After a very tedious navigation we discovered the Morea and passed Cape Matapan in the evening. The coast of this peninsula, all along as far as the island of Cerigo, has the appearance of being very barren and quite uncultivated. The surface of the coast is very high and uneven, the shore bold and steep. We saw no houses or animals of any kind till we had nearly passed the island of Cerigo, formerly Cythera and known for its temple dedicated to Venus, when we discovered the small village of that name. It has a very mean appearance, and the country a worse. No verdure or cultivation of any kind, and the land looks as if it produced nothing but stones.

While we were passing the once celebrated land of Peloponnesus, we were naturally led to consider and converse on its ancient grandeur, and could not, without inexpressible regret, reflect on the melancholy revolution which time and despotism have here effected; that a country once the seat of the fine arts, the nurse of literature, and famed for her progress in science not less than she was for the celebrated system of jurisprudence of the renowned Spartan law-giver, should now exhibit the most rude, barren prospect that can be conceived, where poverty and ignorance have succeeded to opulence and improvement, where the noble, generous, arduous, and exalted spirit for which the Spartan youth were famed, and which led them to vie with each other in emulating every act of heroism, magnanimity, and virtue, is now totally extinct, and we behold their posterity sunk to the lowest pitch of human degradation, mean, cruel, cowardly, ignorant, dishonest, and embracing contentedly the fetters of slavery, to which their ancestors would so much rather have preferred death.

## 23 November

In the evening we discovered Mount Olympus to the northward. I had seen it in the morning but took it then for clouds, which it very much resembled at a distance. Its being always covered with snow accounted for the extreme cold we had lately felt, and the northerly wind blowing strongly over its top was a sufficient cause for the sudden change of climate. I cannot see why the ancient poets have placed on it the residence of the gods, and made it the seat of Jupiter, as they certainly allotted to him a residence which they would have found very uncomfortable.

As the evening advanced, the weather began to wear a very threatening aspect. We spied at a distance a French merchant ship of the size of the *London* furling her sails, as about to lie to for the night. I was much pleased to find that the captain thought it advisable to hail her. He allowed the French to be better acquainted with these seas, as they frequent them more than we do. He always made it a rule to profit by the experience of the natives of those countries that he visited, particularly in what regarded the weather, as it stands to reason that people who have been long accustomed to its continual vicissitudes, will earlier foresee and judge more correctly of any change that is about to take place. I perfectly coincided with him, and his modesty increased the good opinion I had of his skill and prudence. We soon came up with the Frenchmen's ship – she was from Marseilles, and bound, as ourselves, to Smyrna. Her captain told us that the face of the sky portended a storm, and advised us on no account to venture among the islands, but to follow his example and lay to for the night.

Scarcely had we time to follow his advice before it began to thunder and lighten. I observed that the lightning took a horizontal direction, about a fathom above the surface of the sea, and that two flashes of the silver forked lightning always went together, which we were informed to be the sure forerunner of a storm in these seas. The remainder of the night fully justified the Frenchman's fears and convinced us how right our captain was in following his advice.

The wind was moderate till nine, when it began to blow a true hurricane, accompanied with the most dreadful thunder and lightning. The darkness of the night increased the terror of the storm. The rain poured down in such torrents as rendered it impossible for the men to keep their feet on deck. The storm had continued raging for several hours, and threatened to grow worse before any change for the better could be hoped for.

At two in the morning we carried away our mizzen sail, the sea was running over our decks, the boats were in danger of being staved, the binnacle was dashed to pieces, every movable on deck was washed away, and with difficulty the compasses were saved.

It is impossible for anyone to figure to himself the distress of our situation. We were obliged to let the ship drift at the mercy of the waves. She made much water, and her seams, by her labouring, were opening everywhere. The water poured even into the bed-places: all was confusion and a dismal scene of distress.

My Jerusalem friends often occupied my thoughts, and had I gone to the bottom, I am certain that I would in my last moments have regretted not having been permitted by providence to perform my journey, and to win the bets which these gentlemen were confident they had laid with so great odds in their favour.

The rain stopped at a little after five, and the wind by degrees became more moderate, we began then to cheer ourselves with the hopes of fine weather. We had not drifted so much in the night as we imagined, but found, to our very great sorrow, that our good friend the

Frenchman had disappeared. Where she went, God only knows! I really felt very much distressed on her account; and as we were certain that she could not have made sail during the night, we could only dread the worst. *Haud ignarus mali, miscris succurrere disco.*

I have often heard that 'after a storm comes a calm'; and I was glad then to find even a probability of it. Insensibly the wind died away and the weather promised fair. The captain assured us at breakfast that during the whole course of twenty years' experience, he never had witnessed a more dangerous night than the last and contrary to the usual custom of sailors, who only pray as long as the danger lasts, he returned thanks to providence for our escape, and for not having ventured among the islands where we must have inevitably perished.

The next day we were nearly abreast of the island of Candia, ancient Crete, the largest island of the Archipelago, subject to the Grand Signior, formerly so renowned for the government and laws of Minos, now only remarkable for its poverty and the wretchedness, ignorance, and barbarity of its inhabitants.

The calm continued almost uninterruptedly for several days, and though we were sorry not to move more expeditiously towards the end of our voyage, yet we could but enjoy the fineness of the weather for two days when we were very near Candia, the mountains of which are very high. At length we passed it, and entering the Aegean Sea we found ourselves in the midst of the Cyclades.

The sailing was here truly delightful, and every object interesting. We passed most of our time on deck. The water was smooth as a continued sheet of glass, so that we were scarcely sensible of its undulation, while the moderate heat of the sun and the happy temperature of the air rendered the climate grateful in the highest degree.

This day we passed the islands of Melos, Paros, Narcos, and Delos, and Andros, and thought we could discover on Delos the remains of the temples of Apollo and Diana which are still to be seen there.

In the narrow passage which separates Andros from the peninsula of the Negropont, on which Athens stood, we were a whole day becalmed, and regretted indeed not having it in our power to visit the ruins of that renowned city but we knew too well the danger of our landing without permission or janissaries to protect us.

## 28 November

We this day ran along the island of Chios, or Scio, celebrated for its fertility, and at the present day far excelling every other island of the Archipelago, as well in the beauty of the country as the industry of its inhabitants. The neighbouring islands draw from it the corn necessary for their support; and large quantities are also annually exported for the Constantinople and Smyrna markets: they likewise carry on a considerable trade in silks and wines.

Our spirits were considerably elevated by the information we here received from our captain, that we were now distant from Smyrna not more than twenty leagues, which he expected to run by the next day. The night was very still and on the morning of 29 November we were abreast of Cape Colaburno, which forms one point of the Gulf of Smyrna; and here we had the mortification to lie the whole day becalmed, and on 30 November, made the Isles des Anglois in the Gulf of Smyrna.

We this morning passed the Orlac Islands, and assisted by a light breeze we soon were off the castle of Smyrna, where we saluted the Turkish flag, which has not here any means of enforcing respect, as the castle is literally a ruin and mounts only two or three pieces of old ordnance. Proceeding to make sail for the town, we discovered an English frigate, the Ambuscade, which we also saluted with five guns, and received the compliment in return.

It fell calm at twelve in sight of the town. We received a visit from one of the officers of the Ambuscade, Mr S---, who came on board to inquire the news from England. He informed us that they spoke of the plague at Smyrna, and that some people had already died of it. I must confess that my courage failed me at the very sound of the word plague, and I found myself rather alarmed; but I learned afterwards that the death of two or three persons in one day was thought of as being of no consequence at Smyrna.

In the evening we saluted the town and received the *bienvenue* from above fifty ships of different nations, by each of them firing a salute on our arrival. We were also favoured with visits from different gentlemen of the town; among them were the Messrs. L---, from whom we received the most cordial reception; we accompanied them on shore, and had the pleasure of being most agreeably surprised by finding at their house a most amiable mother, with four still more amiable daughters, to whom they introduced us with all the ease and unreserved familiarity of old and sincere friends. I was, without further ceremonies, to seat myself at the *tendour*, next to Mademoiselle Margotten, who with all the naiveté in the world began to explain to me the use and advantages of this piece of household furniture, of which she well perceived I had never seen the like before.

In Turkey none of the rooms have fire-places. The *tendour* is used in their stead. It is a square table with several quilted coverings spread over it which reach down to the ground. Underneath the table is a large copper in which charcoal or embers are placed, the knees of each person round the table are covered with the quilted counterpane, and the head confined under the *tendour*, renders this place the most comfortable and of course the most frequented spot in the apartment. Round this, little parties are always assembled, either to read, work or for other amusements. In cold weather the hands are warmed under the coverlids, and sympathy sometimes brings them into contact with those of your fair neighbour.

Of the society in this family I cannot say too much, and we afterwards experienced much pleasure with many advantages from this acquaintance. Mrs M--- aunt to our hosts, the two Mr L---, was a most amiable, cheerful woman, and passionately fond of her four most amiable daughters. Never did exist a family more united, and I may say, more deservedly happy. The girls, beautiful and accomplished, were all that the prudent mother could wish them; they repaid with every grace the pains taken by their parent in their education. These fair sisters were the first Smyrneottes we had seen, and from their beauty we formed a most favourable opinion of the charms of their countrywomen. Affable and unaffected in their manners as in their conversation, they heard with a wish to learn, and always answered with much sense and politeness, divested of all constraint, with a certain vivacity which was really fascinating.

At six o'clock tea was served á l'Angloise, and after it was over the ladies requested us to accompany them to what is called at Smyrna the *Avant Souper*, where we went on foot, attended by servants with lanterns. This society is supported among the Christian families of the city, and is held at the house of each person every night alternately. It was held this evening at the house of a member of the British factory, where we met Mr --- our Consul, and all the principal persons of the town. The scene was novel and interesting, and the various habits made the rooms appear as if they were open for a masquerade, and having hunted me successfully at a Pharao bank held by two Greeks, at eleven o'clock I accompanied our party home and immediately returned to our ship for this night, having left our trunks and other necessaries still on board.

## 2 December

We employed this morning in preparing our dispatches for Europe, as we were informed that a mail for Marseilles was to be dispatched this day. After we had written our letters we returned from on board, and on our landing we were told that it was absolutely necessary for us to go to the custom-house in order to get our trunks. The Customs of this great city were managed by a proud Turk, who did not understand our not appearing ourselves before.

Informed of this gentleman's way of thinking, and of his great attachment to a small fee, I put a spyglass in my pocket and, accompanied by Mr L--- and his dragoman, we proceeded to the custom-house, where we found this long-bearded *fermier-général* already waiting for us, and were informed that he meant to receive us in state.

Having been shewn into his presence-chamber, we found him seated on the ground: he did not favour us with a look, but ordered us to be seated and pipes to be given. I had not been long enough in Turkey to have adopted the custom of smoking, yet I was informed by Mr L--- that it would be deemed highly uncivil if I did not at least affect to smoke. I was therefore compelled to put a pipe to my lips, and having sat a quarter of an hour without one syllable being uttered, though there were more than twenty people in the room, sweetmeats were served and afterwards a little coffee without sugar.

The refreshments over, this Head of the Customs at length broke silence, and inquired if we had anything in our trunks besides wearing apparel. Being informed that we had not, he immediately gave orders that our luggage should be carried off unopened. I presented him afterwards with my spy-glass, which he did me the honour of accepting without looking at it, or even thanking me for it.

I was struck, for the moment, with such uncivil manners, but on becoming more acquainted with the genius of the Turks, I found this to proceed not from ill breeding but pride. They do not wish you to suppose that anything so trifling could raise a smile on their countenance, or afford them the least satisfaction. Besides, a Turk, when he receives a present from a Christian, imagines that he confers the obligation, and would not have you suppose it possible you could oblige him, were you to present him with half your fortune. However, having no wish to induce my custom-house friend, by so high a compliment, to change his opinion, I gave him leave to pocket my spy-glass, with whatever ideas he pleased. I wished to be gone, and desiring the dragoman to pay him, on my part, as many compliments as he thought proper, I took my leave and returned to Mrs L---'s.

In the evening we had the honour of receiving visits from the most respectable gentlemen in the town, among whom was Mr Hays, the British Consul. After tea, we again had the pleasure of accompanying the family to the *Avant Souper*, which was held at the house of a Dutch gentleman.

We met nearly the same company as the preceding evening, and had the good fortune of being introduced to a gentleman who had travelled much in Syria. I am indebted to him for no little information, respecting the different modes of travelling; as also the necessary measures to be taken to prevent frequent impositions and to escape the attacks of the Arabs. He informed me that I ought not by any means to wear the European dress, that wherever I passed I should be very circumspect in my behaviour; appear to possess as few valuables as possible, that I should travel with a small guard in preference to a great escort, join no caravans, as they were frequently in league with those wandering tribes of Arabs whose only pursuit is plunder and robbery, that I should proceed with few attendants, as little baggage as possible, but by all means that I should be well armed.

This gentleman advised us likewise, that in case we were stopped by the Arabs, we should not appear in the least dismayed, but peremptorily refuse giving up any part of our property, however, that we should at all events be prepared with a purse containing some money, which we should give them with the worst grace possible, in case they threatened to ill treat us, as it is much more prudent to pacify than fight them, informing them at the same time that sooner than be stopped a second time, by any of their fellow freebooters, we were determined to risk our lives in our defence.

I treasured up the advice of this well-informed and good-natured gentleman, fully determined to profit by it when circumstances should render its application useful.

## 3 December

We went to see a caravan that had arrived the preceding evening. It was composed of 250 camels, with one hundred leaders and fifty soldiers to defend them. When on their march, two of the soldiers are at half a mile's distance, forming an avant-garde, in order to reconnoitre. The others are in the centre, assembled under one banner, always ready to repel the attacks of the wandering Arabs, whose chief object is to disperse the caravan, that they may plunder it with the greater facility for they are very averse to come to desperate measures, unless some of their Arabs are previously wounded. The caravans that proceed to Mecca and have a general rendezvous are not so numerous as the others.

Nothing can be more interesting and curious than the manner of loading the camels, who regularly obey the whistle of their masters. At the first whistle they bend the first joint of their fore-feet and rest on the second, if this posture be too elevated, the leader whistles a second time and the animal squats as low as possible. On the third call it rises and proceeds on its journey. Nothing can exceed the docility and patience of these animals. Though they take very large strides they proceed but slowly, and do not perform a greater journey in one day than a man at an ordinary pace can accomplish. They travel about thirty miles in thirteen hours, sleep but very little, tremble at the shaking of a leaf and are stopped by the smallest impediment.

Their moderation in eating and drinking is greater than that of any other known animal. They are sometimes four days without drinking and their food consists of some dry or burnt leaves, sometimes they give them a ball of paste, which they swallow and afterwards chew for the whole day. They proceed without a bridle or collar, and obey the voice of their leader. If you add to all their qualities the advantage that is derived from camels-hair, of which those stuffs known by the name of camlets are manufactured, it may be easily supposed that these animals are in the greatest request

On our return we rambled about for more than two hours, till we completely lost our way, and it was not possible for us to get any information from those we met by any signs we could make, as we were not attended by a guide, Smyrna being one of the few towns in Turkey where foreigners are allowed to go out without janissaries. In this dilemma we walked from one street to another, till at length we found ourselves before a very magnificent building, which appeared to us to be the banqueting-room of some rich jolly Turk.

Perceiving the door of the portico open, we attempted to enter it. We had not proceeded far when on a sudden we were stopped by a Turk who appeared very angry: he made many gestures to shew us his displeasure; and had his long harangue been intelligible to us, we should, no doubt have found it replete with abuse.

We were submissively taking our departure when another Turk of apparently superior consequence to him who had roughly addressed us, approached, and after speaking to him, made signs to us to follow him into the building. As soon as we entered the first door our conductor took off his slippers and made a sign to us to imitate his example; this we immediately complied with, and on opening the second door we found ourselves, to our great surprise, in a Mosque.

The Turks on entering departed from us, and left us to make our own remarks, and we soon perceived that they had withdrawn for the purpose of devotion; as we saw them on their knees, as well as many other Turks in different parts of the building bowing frequently to the ground and apparently worshipping with the most fixed attention and ardent devotion. All was silence, and everything to us solemn as it was novel.

We stood for a considerable time here looking at the building and examining the walls, which were divided in compartments, and adorned with texts from the Koran and different articles of their faith in gold characters, which seemed clumsily executed. During this period not one Turk out of twenty that were there even lifted up his eyes to regard us, so intent were they on their devotion, which they perform with a degree of propriety and respectful solemnity that we rarely see observed by the more enlightened congregations of European churches.

Having now satisfied our curiosity we thought it prudent to withdraw, and having resumed our shoes at the door, we soon gained the street, where we fortunately met a Greek who understood Italian and directed us in our way home, where, after having related our adventures, we were felicitated on our narrow escape, as they termed it, in not having been most grossly insulted or in not having met with even worse than insults, as has happened more than once to Christians. If we had proceeded by ourselves as far as into the Mosque with our shoes on, which, had we not been met, we should certainly have done, there is no doubt but that our indiscretion would have been attended with the most serious consequences.

The next place where curiosity led us was a Turkish Bath, and we examined very minutely the process in using this principal article of luxury among the oriental nations.

You first enter a large vaulted apartment, very lofty and of an octagonal form. In the centre is an immense bath of four feet in depth. On our entrance there were about twenty Turks in it, sitting and squatting in the bottom of this basin; nor did they appear to take the smallest notice of us, tho' we were paying particular attention to them, and were asking numberless questions.

The sides of this bath were of marble, and round it is a kind of gallery which serves as a place of exercise to those who have done bathing and who walk several times round it. In the walls of this apartment are several niches, each large enough to contain two persons. These are always occupied by those who are just come out of the water for the purpose of being rubbed with a kind of coarse, hard cloth, which has a much greater effect than a flesh brush.

The steam that arises from the basin in the centre, which is kept moderately heated, makes the room warm enough to permit those in the niches to remain there as long as they think proper without running any risk of catching cold.

There were not less than fifty naked people in the different parts of this chamber, who appeared not at all discomposed at our presence, but preserved all their characteristic gravity. Some had been rubbed with the hand, others with the cloth, and some remained still sitting in the bath.

After they have amused themselves here as long as they like, they repair to an inner apartment of about half the size of the former, where the heat is considerably increased.

There are large flat stones on which they seat themselves, and seconded by the intense heat of the vapour which issues from every part of the room, the perspiration soon begins; which, after it has continued for some time, the patient (for though the Turk undergoes this ceremony for pleasure, I cannot help giving him this appellation) is shown into another chamber where the heat is still more violent. Here he can go no further, nor could anything but custom and habit from his infancy enable him to go thus far; for the heat of this place was so intense that I found much difficulty in respiration, though I did not remain in it many seconds.

Notwithstanding the excessive heat of the apartment, a Turk will amuse himself by sitting here for an hour at a time, till every pore is open. He then calls in his slaves, who alternately rub him with their hands and pull his joints till he thinks them sufficiently supple; when, after perfuming his beard with the most costly essences, he retires into his *haram* to finish the day.

Having paid three piastres, the price of my curiosity, I quitted the Bath and proceeded with my friends to visit the manufactories.

We first visited the Lead-foundry, where they make shot and cast bullets: of the latter there were several tons ready to be sent to the Vizier's Camp. There are about two hundred persons employed in this foundry: but the clumsiness of their implements, their ignorance of the mechanic powers, a knowledge of which would so much facilitate their operations, and, above all, their bigoted attachment to their primitive usages, which precludes every possibility of improvement, declare them in this, as in other arts, centuries behind European nations.

I observed to my conductors how much I was surprised at seeing the tail of the bullets left just as they came from the mould. I was informed that the Turks preferred this mode, from a supposition that the wound made by a ball in this state would be the more difficult to cure, and consequently more destructive, never considering that it would impede the velocity of the ball and render its range so uncertain as to prevent the best marksman from hitting his object.

Having seen enough of this despicable manufactory, and finding the hour of dinner at hand, we proceeded homewards and on our way stopped for a few minutes at a great carpet manufactory, for which this city is famous. We were shewn a great variety of carpets, some of which were very beautiful. The colours were lively and the designs executed with a great deal of taste.

My time now becoming precious, I found it necessary to proceed on my journey; and therefore determined to set out immediately by land for Constantinople. I sent for Captain M--- of the *London*, who agreed to wait three weeks or a month for my return, when he was to land me at St Jean de Acre, or the Port of Jaffa, on the coast of Syria, and likewise to touch at the island of Cyprus on his way. This business being arranged, I applied to my friend Mr L--- to assist us in procuring a guard of janissaries, as well as a guide and mules. This worthy gentleman, on my first mentioning our intention of going to Constantinople by land, remonstrated with me against it, on account of the season, and more particularly on account of the war: dreading that we should meet with parties of the victorious Turks, returning from the camp, who are always insolent, and frequently rob and murder travellers. He used many other arguments to dissuade me from this arduous undertaking, but finding me determined, he acquiesced with reluctance, and promised to afford us every assistance in his power.

## 4 December

I completed, to my very great satisfaction, one principal piece of business respecting my journey. I hired a servant, a guide and interpreter, a companion and a guard and all these essential qualities I found centred in one man. He was an Armenian, and well versed in the modes of travelling in Turkey: he spoke all languages, had travelled over most of the globe and had a very good character from many respectable gentlemen of Smyrna. This fellow proved afterwards of the greatest service to me, and I really think that without him we should never have arrived at Constantinople. He had already been there twice by land, and assured me that there was no other danger to be apprehended than that resulting from extreme fatigue. He recommended plenty of ammunition and to provide ourselves with guns, pistols and carabines. I already liked my Armenian, and he on his side swore by the Holy Sepulchre that he would with much pleasure lose his life to serve me. He began to relate his wars with the Arabs on his way to Jerusalem, where he had likewise been, and assured me that he had shot many of those wandering plunderers. Whether the fellow was lying or telling the truth, I considered not; he succeeded in amusing me a good deal, which I found was his intention.

Captain W-- who had accompanied me from London, and who had been confined for some days by a rheumatic complaint, not thinking it prudent to encounter the difficulties and fatigues to which we were likely to be exposed, decided on staying here until he should be re-established. This, of course, lessened our party; but Captain M--- and I persisted in our intention, and now all our arrangements being made, we took our leave of the amiable and friendly family from whom we had received so much kindness, and at four o'clock in the evening we set out on our journey.

Mr L--- the younger, and Mr M---, brother to the young ladies I have before mentioned as members of Mr L---'s family, insisted on accompanying us part of the way to Bournat-Bat, five and a half miles from Smyrna, where we intended to pass the night. Captain M--- and I were mounted on very good horses, which our friends had procured for us for our whole journey. Our party consisted of seven persons, one of them a janissary, who served us as guide, the rest servants and a black slave, to drive our mules that carried our beds, baggage, etc.

Never in my life was I more charmed with an evening ride! The country had the appearance of richness. We saw some cotton plantations and a variety of shrubs, the spontaneous productions of the soil, and the month of the year, though December, bore all the appearance of the finest evening in June. The air was warm, the sky serene, the birds were singing on every bush, the Spring had already commenced, and vegetables of various kinds were growing spontaneously on each side of the road. What most particularly engrossed my attention were the hedges of myrtle which form the most common fence to the gardens about Smyrna, and are here and there interspersed with the wild geranium, in full bloom. These hedges diffused the most fragrant as well as the most refreshing odours. The most common trees, in the neighbourhood of Smyrna, I observed to be the orange and lemon and a variety of evergreens.

We arrived at the little village just as silent night was about to draw her sable mantle over the earth. I had almost forgotten the Fountain of Diana, which is on the road to Bournat-Bat. Indeed were it not for the fineness of the spring, which is in this country a great acquisition, and the name of the chaste goddess with which tradition has honoured it, it would little merit attention. The remains of an arch, apparently a very ancient structure, by which it was covered, are still visible; and some slabs of marble are placed beside the spring in form of an oblong square, on which the story says that the goddess and her nymphs were wont to perform their ablutions.

This part of the fable, I believe, induced us to examine the well with more attention than we should have otherwise done, and however impious it might be, we could not suppress a wish that the goddess and her nymphs had been there, hoping that we should be thought at least as worthy of their divine favour as Messrs. Pan, Orion, and Endymion, with all of whom the chastity of the goddess has been impeached, notwithstanding her most singular petition to Jove to grant her that, which to deprive others of, he had assumed so many forms, under all of which he was equally successful. Oh happy ye, when a Cuckoo, a Bull or a Swan (how different from our times!) had equal influence over the female mind with a shower of gold!

Bournat-Bat, situated at the opposite side of the Bay of Smyrna, is a very neat village, and can boast of having the best house in all Asia for the reception of travellers. It is kept by an Italian woman, who keeps a billiard table. This house is properly speaking the Vauxhall of Smyrna, and a place of meeting for amusement and recreation for all the captains of the trading vessels in the Bay. The lady did us the honour of presiding at table, and as she had no doubt premeditated a long bill, she also entertained us with long stories, by way of passing the time more pleasantly.

Her claret however was excellent, nor did she wish that we should spare it. We had tolerably good beds, which is a very great rarity in Turkey; and this is perhaps the only place where anything better than the bare boards could be procured.

During all my travels in Asia I thought myself happy when I could get some clean uncut straw on which I might spread my blankets. I mention uncut straw because the Turks, feeding their horses and cattle principally on it, cut the straw very small, immediately after the corn is threshed, and put it into large hair bags in which they send it to the market. They never litter their horses, but make them lie on the boards, and we were frequently compelled to do the same. We rose early on the following day and took our leave of our good landlady, who made us pay thirty-six dollars, being equal to 5 pounds 8 shillings sterling, for her friendly and comfortable accommodations.

Our escort consisted of nine mules, three of which carried our provisions for the journey, as we had nothing to expect on the road, and having to travel nearly 300 miles on the same animals, it was necessary to spare them as much as possible, which would of course render our progress slow. The sun was just rising as we ascended the mountain called Yachaku, which commands the town and Bay of Smyrna. I do not remember ever having seen so beautiful a landscape, nor can I suppose that there is in the universe a richer or grander prospect than presented itself to our view from this mountain. The variety of flowering shrubs, particularly the arbutus, now quite covered with berries, growing in vast quantities on the sides of the mountain; the flocks and herds grazing in the valleys; the noble appearance of the town, the extensive Bay and shipping of every nation, formed altogether the most beautiful *coup d'œil* in the world, and with the splendour of the morning inspired us with sensations most pleasing.

I could not help observing to my friend how surprised I was that more of our countrymen did not direct their travels to this delightful country; for I will venture to assert that no part of the globe is better worth their attention, or would more amply repay their trouble and expense than the country from Smyrna to the old and magnificent town of Magnesia, once the capital of the Ottoman Empire which, as well as its environs, still retains so much grandeur.

Having spent half an hour on this mountain, almost lost in admiration, we set off by the advice of my faithful Pauolo, full gallop to come up with our baggage and janissaries, who had gone on before us. We soon overtook them at the entrance of a wood, which consisted chiefly of forest trees such as oak, elm, and pine, all, however, of inferior growth, and intermixed with the fig, olive, and almond. There was also a vast quantity of dwarf holly, which formed a very thick underwood. The arbutus and the oleander were likewise frequent.

We now heard, for the first time, the drowsy noise of a caravan, which we soon overtook. It consisted of about thirty camels, all heavily laden. They formed a long string, and were fastened to one another by a ring which passed through the nostrils of each, and was tied to the tail of the foremost. Their pace was about the same as that of one of our heaviest wagons in England, but they have the advantage of performing much longer journeys, as they seldom stop to feed. This novel sight for some time engrossed our attention; but in the course of a few days we were habituated to it, and it soon lost its power of pleasing from the frequent repetition and the tedious sameness of the object.

The country around seemed in a state of nature, yet displayed a uniform appearance of richness and fertility. We perceived but few cottages, and these were only the temporary abodes of shepherds, where the ragged ensigns of poverty were displayed, and the appearance of the inhabitants bespoke their wretchedness, as much as the neglected state of so fine a country indicated the badness of the government to which it was subject. From the hills we perceived many villages in a plain to our right, and saw the ruins of one that had been destroyed not long before by a minister of the Porte, the inhabitants having refused, most likely from inability, to furnish a large sum of money which this avaricious and cruel tyrant had demanded. The name of this dismantled village is Palamont, it had been inhabited by about five hundred families, who were all put to the sword without distinction of age or sex. Thus do these devoted people frequently fall victims to the rapacity and relentless cruelty of barbarous and despotic tyrants, who under the mask of duty to their sovereign veil the most atrocious acts of cruelty and oppression.

After three hours' ride at the rate of about four miles an hour we arrived at a coffee-house, where our guide, Pauolo, advised us to stop in order to refresh ourselves and our mules. You meet very frequently with these houses in Turkey; and here the traveller may stop if he chooses, and be accommodated with coffee without sugar and a pipe. We entered a little cottage not unlike an Irish barn. It was built of mud and straw, and not more remarkable for its furniture within than its architecture without. The only movables in the house were a couple of mats on which we spread our repast, and though we were surrounded by Turks, who were enjoying their pipes, we made an excellent meal of cold partridge which our good friend at Smyrna had packed up for us, with a liberal allowance of Madeira wine to last for our journey.

The first object that engaged my attention, after leaving our hotel, was a Burying-ground. It was surrounded, as all these places are, with lofty cypresses. I was much surprised at the sight of such an immense number of graves, most of them recently dug: but I soon recollected that I was travelling through a country where the plague seldom intermits for any length of time; and upon inquiring I found that above one thousand of these graves had been made about four months back when the plague raged at Smyrna and in its vicinity. These considerations for some time damped our spirits, and inspired us with gloomy and dismal ideas. Over each of these graves is a stone of about four feet in height, set upright and a turban carved on the top. They are painted in different colours, such as red, white and green. Those who are honoured with the latter have their origin from Mahomet and call themselves his descendants. They are looked upon as of the same family and no others are permitted to have the green turban on their tombs after their decease.

We travelled for the remainder of the day over a fine country, the soil of which shewed everywhere marks of richness and fertility. The road, if we may give it that name, was very bad, and indeed not passable for carriages, but we saw no obstacles to impede the equestrian traveller, as the grounds were without enclosures. The greatest part of the country was planted with cotton trees, and those plantations were remarkably well cultivated and cleared of weeds, the cotton plants being set at equal distances of about three feet.

Towards evening we arrived at the summit of a very lofty mountain, from whence we discovered the extensive plain of Magnesia and could trace with the eye the winding course of the celebrated Meander.

The town itself is at the distance of about six miles. We intended stopping at Magnesia for the night, and therefore made as much haste as we possibly could in order to have sufficient time to see the town.

On our arrival we found much difficulty in getting lodging for the night. My faithful Pauolo at length obtained permission for us to lie under the gateway of a large court where the caravans put up. There was a little room without windows, which did not hold out to us the most pleasing prospect of the rest of our entertainment for the night. We had our beds spread on the ground, and sending Pauolo to buy us some provisions we went, accompanied by a janissary, to stroll about the town.

We did not perceive any vestige or monument of Magnesia having been once the seat of the Ottoman Court. The houses are all built and mostly of wood, the streets narrow and dirty. This had been the seat of the Eastern Empire, till, on 19 May 1453 Mahomet the Second took Constantinople from Constantine Paleologus, and removed his Court to that celebrated city. Magnesia contains above 100,000 inhabitants, and next to Smyrna is the town of most trade in Turkey; being situated in one of the richest and most extensive plains in the universe. It has been distinguished for the fertility of its soil, and it is now one of the chief sources of supply to the cotton market of Smyrna.

This district, even in the time of Themistocles, 450 years before the Christian era, was bestowed on him, on account of its fertility, by Artaxerxes Longimanus, King of Asia. And that noble Athenian chose this spot for his residence, when dismissed by Artaxerxes from his Court at Susa, whither he had fled to seek an asylum from the persecutions of the Greeks and Lacedemonians. Cornelius Nepos informs us that the revenues of this district then amounted to fifty talents ($£11,250$), and at the same time makes mention of the other districts which Themistocles held through the liberality of the Persian monarch. That illustrious general resided here many years, and on being solicited by his benefactor Artaxerxes to march an army against the Athenians he here swallowed poison, to avoid at once the imputation of ingratitude and the odium he must have incurred by fighting against his country. The Magnesians erected a magnificent monument to his memory in the great square in this city, which existed in the time of Plutarch; but neither square or monument is now visible.

The Governor of this great and profitable district is a most extraordinary man. Though a Turk, he is possessed of talents much superior to those of his countrymen in general, and has extended his knowledge beyond the limits of the very small circle to which theirs is generally confined. He has raised himself by his abilities into some degree of credit with the Porte, and obtained the confidence of the Grand Signior. The information he had acquired respecting the commerce of this country induced him to fix on this spot as an eligible situation in which to establish himself. He first made a calculation of its produce, considering at the same time the failure of the crops, to which all countries, but some parts of Turkey in particular, are more or less subject. He afterwards made his agreement with the Porte on the subject of the tribute he was to pay. He succeeded in it with such surprising accuracy and managed this important matter with so much address that he has constantly been able to gratify the most unreasonable demands of the Ottoman Ministry.

He judiciously foresaw that his success and elevation would soon be followed by the loss of the favour of the suspicious Sultan, and wisely anticipated the exorbitant increase of tribute which his enemies would require when they saw him deprived of the countenance of his Sovereign. This in reality happened a few years afterwards: his imposts were at once more than doubled and successive augmentations having taken place, he now pays 100,000 pounds sterling per year, which is more than double the sum that the whole produce of his district was ever supposed to be worth. This he has been enabled to do by gradually improving the cultivation of his lands and introducing an economy in farming hitherto unknown, and by which he is said to have realised an immense fortune.

This wonderful man is the friend of the peasant and adored by his dependants. The regular remittances of a sum which so far exceeds the expectation of the Porte, is said to be the thread on which the head of this enlightened Turk now depends, and should a peace take place with the Russians, which must lessen the demands on the Grand Signior's coffers, it is supposed that he would fall one of the first victims to the jealous rage of the party now in power. Such is the ingratitude and unjust conduct of this abominable Government, under which a subject must ever be wretched and unhappy.

## 7 December

We proceeded on our journey, and the first part of this day's ride was very unpleasant, as we had for three miles a bad causeway to travel over till we approached the Meander, over which there was a wooden bridge of considerable height and length, without battlements and very narrow; and the construction of it appeared so feeble that we did not cross it without apprehensions. Here we paused to view this celebrated stream, and bring to our recollection the great events which took place on its banks and will perpetuate its name. Here we fancied we trod the ground where the great Antiochus sustained a total overthrow from Lucius Scipio 150 years before Christ in which he lost 50,000 men and 4,000 horses as well as fifteen elephants.

At twelve we reached a poor village called Zachonona about fifteen miles from Magnesia. We had sent our mules with the baggage forward. As we reached this place before them, and had not passed them on the road, we were seriously alarmed, and apprehended that the black slave who was with the baggage had either run off with our effects or was plundered. We remained for two hours in this painful suspense, and were at length relieved by the arrival of the negro, who had taken a different road, by which he had gone several miles out of his way. After having blamed each other for having separated from him, as he had in his possession every valuable and all our money, we resolved to be more prudent for the future.

We retired to a kind of barn, where we made a violent attack on our cold provisions. We removed part of our valuables from the trunks and secured them in our own pockets. Here we were honoured with a visit from the Governor of the village, accompanied by fifty other Turks, who all appeared in uniform misery. They seated themselves on the ground around us and entertained themselves with admiring our fire-arms, which, we were pleased to find, they were sensible of being well loaded.

After our dinner we went eighteen miles farther to the town of Auctozaar, and alighted at a caravansary inhabited by Greeks who carried on a manufactory of cotton, for sail-making and other common purposes of the country. The accommodation was most wretched. We were all obliged to lie down in the same room, nor could we get provisions of any kind. It had rained all day, we were wet through, and to complete our misfortune, we had neither fire nor fire-place, nor could we procure even a dish of charcoal to dry our clothes. A traveller, however, must expect to encounter difficulties and disappointments, particularly in these countries. Habit teaches us to despise them, and the pleasure we experience from having surmounted obstacles seems to be in proportion to their magnitude.

The next morning bore a more favourable appearance. We travelled over a country uncommonly beautiful, diversified with eminences, covered with woods and vast herds of cattle and the most beautiful flocks of sheep with flat tails and long pendent ears, the former of an immense size. We observed no habitation, nor passed any village, for the first five hours of our ride through a most romantic country. We halted to breakfast by the side of a fountain built by the bounty of some penitent and charitable Turk. This is considered by them an act most meritorious and benevolent; and so it really is, when situated so as to furnish to the weary traveller the refreshing draught which he could not otherwise procure.

We soon bid adieu to the fountain which had refreshed us, and continued our route over a mountainous and very wild country, and in five hours arrived at a small village called Gelembe, where a small mud-walled room afforded us shelter. We had some very tough fowls killed for our supper, and comforting ourselves with the hopes of a good night's rest, we went to bed at eight, having had some clean straw spread under our mattresses.

In the night, the dogs made so much noise that our sleep was hourly interrupted. It was not the first time that we had been annoyed by these animals, which abound in most of the Turkish towns. Not appertaining to any individual, they infest the streets in large packs, and in the night (particularly when it is moonlight) they keep up a most dismal howling. We have frequently counted a hundred of them together. They are of the wolf and mastiff kind, and very large. It is extraordinary that in this country where the heat is excessive in summer these dogs are never known to go mad.

In the morning our landlord had prepared for us a couple of boiled turkeys, some eggs, and milk, which made ample amends for our bad supper.

We had proceeded but a few miles when it began to rain violently and continued the whole day without intermission. Our Greek capotes, which we were assured at Smyrna would resist twelve hours' rain, were wet through in less than three. The additional weight of our clothes when wet soon knocked up our wretched mules, so that after a most disagreeable ride of eight hours we were obliged to take up our residence for the night in such a habitation as few Europeans have ever visited. It was a wretched hovel of twenty feet long, at one end of which were some cows and sheep, which we turned out to make room for horses, while we were obliged to content ourselves with the other corner.

To complete our misery, we had no provisions left, and could procure nothing but some stinking camel's flesh, highly seasoned with garlic, here esteemed a most delicate viand by the conductors of caravans who frequent these roads.

In the morning I was astonished to find that my faithful Pauolo had, during the night, baked some bread, made of some coarse flour which he was fortunate enough to find in the village, and procured some sheep's milk, so that we were able to make a most delicious breakfast. It cannot be imagined how much such little attentions are valued in a servant: when removed from all friends and relations, in a savage and remote country, your personal influence and property lose their weight and consequence and you are left to shift for yourself, with those advantages which nature and not any fortuitous circumstances may have bestowed on you. In such a situation the servant has, very often, the advantage over his master, either by his personal strength, his unimpaired constitution, or his knowledge of useful arts.

If to these qualifications he adds, as my dear Pauolo did, a good and feeling heart, a sensible mind, a cheerful disposition and a fidelity that cannot be shaken, he then becomes a most valuable friend: he is your companion, and you cheerfully and implicitly look up to him for that assistance which you cannot derive from your own powers, and which he bestows with the beneficence of a friend and the respectful submission of an inferior.

On the two following days we had a most disagreeable and fatiguing journey to perform, as the country was wretched and scarcely exhibited any appearance of population or improvement of any kind. The hills were covered with brushwood, and the rains had made such deep ruts in the roads that in many places we had much difficulty in getting over them.

We met with nothing curious or interesting, except on the second day we overtook a Turkish guard consisting of an Agha and about twenty janissaries. They had with them an unfortunate Greek as a prisoner: he was tied by his legs under the horse's belly, and his hands were tied behind his back. On inquiry we were informed that this man was one of the relations of the late Governor of Scio who had been beheaded some time before at Constantinople. This poor prisoner was going then to suffer a similar fate. He appeared much dejected and seldom spoke to those about him. While I most sincerely sympathized with this unhappy victim, I felt a glow of exultation which I could not suppress, when I reflected on the pre-eminence of that most excellent constitution which we enjoy as British subjects, by which our lives and properties are so well secured. We continued with this escort for upwards of three hours, when we found that our mules were not equal to the fine horses of the Pasha, and that we could not accompany them at the rate they travelled, though it did not exceed four miles an hour.

We stopped under the shade of a beautiful hanging rock, covered with arbutus, where we refreshed ourselves, at the same [time] allowing our horses to pasture around us. We were met here by some foot-travellers who informed us that in all likelihood we should be attacked before we reached the place of our destination, which was at about twelve miles' distance. They said that there were a number of deserters from the Grand Vizier's army, who had encamped in this part of the country; that they robbed and massacred every traveller they met and had already assassinated many people.

I concealed my apprehensions as well as I could, for fear of alarming our janissaries. Captain M--- and I consulted what was to be done. We determined to load our fire-arms anew and to make a most desperate resistance, being well convinced that nothing but the most determined courage could extricate us from the hands of such desperadoes. I informed my Armenian servant of our intentions, who seemed pleased to meet with an opportunity of manifesting his fidelity and courage. He swore that he would die by me; and threatened to shoot the first of our band who should attempt to run away, or refuse to assist us when attacked.

His animated and enthusiastic manner of talking inspired the whole troop with an ardent desire of signalizing their valour. I knew that I could trust to the courage of my Irish servant, and if I entertained a doubt of any one it was of those who should be the foremost in protecting us – I mean our guard and guides, whom we had hired at Smyrna for that very purpose.

At four in the afternoon we perceived, at the distance of a mile, a number of people to the amount of thirty, who were assembling together and coming towards us. Through my glass I could discover that they were but indifferently armed. Only ten or twelve of them had guns; the rest were armed with bludgeons and daggers. I informed my little caravan of this circumstance, which appeared to diffuse universal joy.

However, as we drew nearer, it was deemed necessary to form some plan of defence. M--- being the soldier, I submitted to him the direction of our manoeuvre; and it was accordingly resolved that we should proceed two by two. He and I went first, each of us having a double-barrelled gun and a case of double-barrelled pistols. My servant Pauolo and a janissary came next, my Irish servant and another janissary afterwards, and close behind followed our baggage. My servants, to do them justice, did not appear in the least intimidated, but all the rest seemed irresolute and much agitated, and had not M--- and I gone foremost, I am convinced we should have been deserted by the janissaries.

The gang was now within pistol shot of us, when it was proposed that we should halt and wait their coming up; this was agreed on by all, except the impatient Pauolo, who was for giving them the first fire, and then impetuously rushing on them to disperse and put them into confusion. However, he obeyed my injunctions, which were not to attack until the party's intentions should appear hostile.

When they saw us stop, they did the same, and it was easily perceived that they were more frightened than we were. Whereupon, I ordered Pauolo to ask them what their intentions were. They assured him that they were poor sailors, on their way home, and that their intentions were perfectly peaceable and friendly. I was convinced of the truth of this, and gave them some money, by way of compensation for having so wrongfully suspected them. Breathing again a little more freely, we congratulated each other that we had not been forced to fight. The alarm, however, proved of some use to us, as it served to make the janissaries uncommonly alert in driving on the tired mules, wishing to get to the place of our destination before dark.

We pushed forward with all possible expedition and arrived by seven. We alighted at a coffee-house where by much pecuniary eloquence, which is as persuasive in this country as in any other, we prevailed on the landlord to dislodge some Turks who were in possession of the room, smoking and drinking coffee. Here we were tolerably comfortable for the night.

## 11 December

It had rained all the morning, and we travelled through a most comfortless country, till we arrived on the bank of a very large river, now called Maccatitch, but formerly Maceston. Here a most violent dispute arose between Captain M--- and a janissary; the former insisting on his driving the baggage-horses before us, and not allowing them to stop behind, sometimes for half an hour. The janissary grew so very angry, that he drew his sabre and vented his rage on a poor mule that carried our bedding, by cutting him in a most shocking and savage manner. The poor animal, who was then standing on the brink of the river, at least twenty feet from the surface of the water, was forced into it, and swam upwards of a mile down a most rapid stream, and would undoubtedly have perished had not Pauolo immediately undressed himself and mounted another mule, on which he swam to its relief.

The quarrel began again, which I feared would have ended very unpleasantly. The janissary drew his sabre, and had not Mr M--- levelled his gun at him he would most likely have been dreadfully wounded. I now interfered, in hopes of making peace, as the janissary insisted on leaving us and returning to Smyrna. I was much alarmed at this, apprehending that his desire of revenge might induce him to get assistance from the peasants, or join any party in order to plunder, and perhaps murder us. I therefore used every means I could devise to pacify the scoundrel, but to no purpose, till at last Pauolo putting his arms round his neck kissed him several times in the most affectionate manner, which appeased him a little. He kneeled down, put his fingers in his mouth and made the most ridiculous grimaces, using at the same time the most impertinent language, such as 'Christian Dog,' 'Void of faith,' 'Unbeliever', etc. Thus his rage exhausted itself, and Pauolo renewing his embraces, he at last consented to accompany us.

These altercations took up much of our time, so that we did not reach Maccatitch till ten in the evening, where we met our usual difficulties in procuring a lodging and supper. These are weighty concerns to a traveller, though they may appear uninteresting to my readers, to whom I wish to apologise for my tedious repetitions. But as Homer made his heroes eat and drink, and even Voltaire, in his poems, took care not to starve them, so I trust I may be forgiven, if in my narrative, which is truth itself, I record, perhaps too frequently, occurrences so unimportant as my breakfast, dinner and supper.

## 12 December

We had now only six hours' ride from this place of misery to the village of Scala, where we were to take a boat for Constantinople. Throughout all Turkey the places where goods are embarked or disembarked are called Scala, which literally signifies a ladder; and in many places we find not only the quay or spot of disembarkation, but the entire village to which it appertains, to go by this common appellation. This prospect of so speedy a termination to our troubles raised our spirits, and we set off very early and travelled along the banks of the Maccatitch for some miles. The country was on both sides very beautiful and watered with many rivulets.

At half-past four we arrived at this little seaport which contains only a few houses, but its situation is extremely pleasant. On our arrival we did all in our power to prevail on some of the owners of the boats to set sail with us, but as the wind was not directly fair, all our entreaties and every inducement we held out were in vain. They have no idea of going to sea but with a very fair wind. This disappointment, as it occasioned a delay of no less than forty-eight hours, almost exhausted our patience. We amused ourselves with killing some ducks with which the river was covered. We crossed a rivulet to a little island formed by this stream, and two small lakes to the south of the river Maccatitch where we had most excellent sport, having killed many wild ducks, teal, snipes and three hares of an uncommonly large size.

At last the weather setting fair, our *nokidah*, or pilot, ventured to get under weigh, and after a very short navigation we landed at Top-Hanna Scala, on 14 December at four in the evening.

# CHAPTER IV

Constantinople – Pera – Dancing Boys – The
Grand Signior's Procession to St Sophia – View of
Constantinople – The Grand Signior's Barges – Mosque
of St Sophia – The Character of Capitan Pasha – Our
Reception – The Turkish Fleet – Dervishes – The
Seraglio.

At Constantinople, as well as in other European capitals, you are obliged
on your arrival first to proceed to the Custom-house, not so much for
the purpose of paying the duties imposed by Government as to satisfy
the rapacity of its Officers, and we found that money had as much effect
on this bearded gentry, as on our Christian tide-waiters. We were immediately dismissed, and repaired to a house, which is called the French
Tavern, where, having dressed ourselves as expeditiously as possible, we
went to pay our respects to our Ambassador, Sir R--- A---, for whom
we had letters from England. He received us with all that affability and
good nature so congenial to the character of that worthy gentleman.

Here we met several of our intimate friends, and the hospitality and
convivial manners of his Excellency, to whose table we were invited
during our stay at Constantinople, made us soon forget all our sufferings from fatigue and hunger during our journey from Smyrna to
this place.

## 15 December
This was the day I had fixed upon to be at Jerusalem, it being my
birthday, yet as I had sufficient time before me, I did not feel myself

disappointed. It was proposed that we should make a party to the 'Sweet waters.' This is a remarkable place for snipe-shooting, and runs through the Grand Signior's plantations. We accompanied Capt. F--- of the *Pearl* frigate on board his ship, and were joined there by many of the British officers.

The Grand Signior has on this little river, which empties itself into the harbour of Constantinople, a very fine Kiosk, a *tuakish*, or summer-house, with many temples erected on its banks. There is great abundance of grass here in the summer, and it is on these meadows that the Arabs encamp who attend the Grand Signior's horses, which are turned out in April for the remainder of the summer. We had but little diversion, but the beauties of the place made us ample recompense for this disappointment. In the spring and autumn, this river is the fashionable resort of the grandees of the metropolis, where they come in the most splendid barges of fifty and sixty feet in length, rowed by their eunuchs and accompanied by their women.

We walked afterwards about the town of Pera, and paid visits to some English ladies. Pera is a Greek word, signifying 'beyond,' this suburb being situated beyond the gate of Galata. This is a most delightful situation, from which you have a view of the coast of Asia, and the Seraglio of the Grand Signior. The English, French, Venetian and Dutch ambassadors have their palaces here. Those of the Emperor and the King of Poland reside at Constantinople. The foreign merchants have their dwellings and warehouses at Pera as well as at Galata, amongst Jews, Greeks, Turks and Armenians. The French Palace is a most beautiful building, and contains a chapel which was kept by Capuchin friars.

We visited the Gun Wharf and saw some brass guns singularly constructed. They were of uncommon length, particularly a sixty-two pounder above twenty-five feet long, and many others as extraordinary in various respects, which did not induce us to entertain a favourable opinion of the Turkish ordnance, or the progress this nation has made in the artillery branch of military science, notwithstanding the assurances Monsieur de Tott has given us of his having brought it to the highest pitch of perfection at Constantinople.

## 16 December
We dined at Monsieur de B---'s, the Spanish Envoy, where we had a most splendid entertainment. This gentleman was well acquainted with Irish hospitality, and gave us a great variety of most excellent wines.

He promised us letters for the Terra Sancta at Jerusalem. This was a most desirable offer; as that convent is principally maintained by the bounty of the Spanish Court; and these letters afterwards proved of the greatest service to us, both at Jerusalem and in many other places in the Holy Land.

We were likewise so fortunate as to be introduced to Madame la Baronne de H---, who engaged us to accompany her the following day to Buyukdereh, a beautiful village on the Canal at the entrance of the Black Sea, where she had a country house, and intended soon to give a *fête champêtre*. This was too agreeable a party to be refused. His Excellency was likewise engaged, who mounted us on his horses, and rode himself a most beautiful Arabian, which had been presented to him by the Capitan Pasha.

We had a most charming ride of twelve miles, and on our arrival were introduced by the lady to her beloved consort, whom I soon discovered to be a great botanist, and famous for the cultivation of rare and curious plants. This gentleman, between whom and his youthful wife there was a great disparity of years, spent most of his time in his garden, while her ladyship contented herself with now and then paying a visit to a most beautiful geranium flower, which was occasionally placed in one room or another of the castle.

He had been married before and had a daughter a few months elder than her beautiful step-mother; so that there existed a kind of jealousy between these ladies: who should please or be noticed most, a circumstance which generally turned to the advantage of the visitors, and it was not difficult to discover that Mademoiselle Curregonde, rather than remain in her present state, would do anything to be placed under the protection of a husband, even were he as old as her father. However, we must not be too severe on those ladies, who made us spend two very agreeable days. Their hospitality, their engaging manners, I shall remember with the most lively sense of respect and gratitude.

## 20 December

We got up by sunrise fully determined to make the best use of the day, in visiting and examining the different curiosities of Constantinople. We stopped at a sort of Turkish Tavern or Coffee-house, to see the Dancing Boys who are kept at those places.

There were two Turks at breakfast in the gallery who were entertaining themselves in a manner horrid to the ideas of a rational being. Those boys have a method of cracking their fingers and fixing little bells to their wrists, with which they produce sounds and play tunes that are much admired. Being disgusted with this species of entertainment, I hastened from the horrid scene.

We went next to see the Grand Signior go to the Mosque of St Sophia, which was by far the finest masquerade that was ever exhibited. As my talent at the descriptive would not enable me to do justice to the grandeur of this curious procession, I endeavoured to supply the deficiency by a sketch which I made on the spot; but which I unfortunately lost on my return from the Continent, with a collection of many other valuable drawings. I regret this loss the more, at present, as it deprives me of the satisfaction of presenting a print of it to my subscribers.

The Grand Signior sets off from the Seraglio at nine o'clock in the morning, to go to the Mosque of St Sophia, or of Osmenie, the latter being the burial place of all the Ottoman Princes. There is on those occasions a degree of magnificence displayed in the dresses of the various guards and officers of the household, in their turbans and plumes, of which a European who never visited the Eastern countries can have no idea.

Their fine horses with the uncommon riches of their trappings have an appearance of pomp and splendour that far surpasses that of any European Court, while the abject homage which the Sultan receives from his subjects, and the unrivalled grandeur of the exhibition inspires a stranger with a momentary idea, that the pompous title of 'King of Kings,' which the Grand Signior arrogates to himself, is realised, and that he absolutely beholds the greatest of earthly sovereigns.

On our return we met with a very uncommon kind of vehicle, much resembling a covered cart, which is used by the Turkish ladies of fashion, who are seated in it cross-legged on a mat. I perceived ten in the one I met, stowed together in such a manner that they must have suffered extremely from the heat, as there was but one small window to admit the air. I was informed that this fine equipage, drawn by two buffaloes, was the property of a *renegado* who was formerly a rich French merchant, and having failed, thought proper to change his religion in order to meliorate his circumstances, in which he has so well succeeded that he is now able to keep seven wives and concubines without number. I could not help wondering or doubting whether his temperament had increased proportionately with his wealth and years.

At one I set off accompanied by Capt. F--- to see the Grand Signior's Barges. The Canal of Constantinople, from the entrance of the Harbour to the Towers at the head of the Black Sea, affords one of the finest *coup d'œils* in the world.

On entering the Harbour, there is on the left the Seraglio of the Grand Signior with its extensive gardens and lofty walls, afterwards you see the superb Mosques, raising their heads above the other buildings, which in Constantinople are generally but one or two stories high. On the right the view is terminated towards the 'Sweet waters,' by a magnificent Kiosk belonging to the Grand Signior, where he has likewise very extensive gardens. On the front, along the rising ground, is the Arsenal, Pera, Galata and the other suburbs of Constantinople. The beautifully situated town of Scutari also attracts the attention of the traveller, besides numberless other neat villages that extend the whole length of the Bosporus, both on the European and Asiatic side, as far as the mouth of the Black Sea.

The number of ships of all nations, besides Tartans, Schebecks, and the most magnificent Barges, with which the river is always covered, and the hundreds of *Kiakas* filled with ladies, with their proprietors going on parties of pleasure, give the most lively appearance to the scene, and one cannot help regretting that so heavenly a spot should be in the possession of such barbarians. From the peculiar advantages of its situation, it is admirably well calculated to be the seat of the arts, as well as the emporium of the most extensive commerce. What a pity that with all these advantages this capital should be doomed to remain subject to a barbarous despot, whose character seems merely a compound of ignorance and tyranny. The Grand Signior's Barges surpass anything of the kind in pomp and grandeur. The largest of these wonderful pleasure boats is 96 feet in length, ornamented in the most costly manner. They have from 48 to 60 oars, and have canopies, each of a different construction, supported on ivory or silver and gilded columns, exquisitely wrought. Under the canopy the Grand Signior seats himself on a carpet of the most costly embroidery, which commonly costs upwards of 25,000 pias-tres, or 2,500 pounds sterling, and which is always the last brought from Mecca.

The gun-holes are of solid silver, beautifully carved in Turkish char-acters, and the magnificence as well as taste displayed throughout the whole is really astonishing. Notwithstanding the ornaments with which these boats are loaded, they are well constructed for swiftness, being built sharp, somewhat resembling those on the Thames.

Every year an immense caravan sets out from Constantinople to Mecca, to visit the Tomb of the Holy Prophet. It consists of persons of the first rank in Turkey, and of no less than three, four and sometimes five thousand pilgrims. The Grand Signior always sends costly presents for the Sepulchre of Mahomet, among which is a carpet to cover the Tomb, and the one sent the year preceding is brought back to Constantinople and placed in the Seraglio. On that carpet the Sultan is usually seated when he appears in state; and it is considered by all good Mahometans as the safest and most sacred guard the Grand Signior could have in his Palace, in case of an insurrection taking place at Constantinople, where his person might be in danger.

On the following day we visited the Mosque of St Sophia, which is worthy of notice, both on account of its antiquity and structure. On our arrival the Imam made some difficulty about admitting us, which however our janissary soon removed. We gave three Venetian sequins for allowing us to ascend the gallery, from which the whole inside may be seen, as Christians are never permitted to enter the lower part of the Mosque without a firman to that effect, which is an order from the Grand Signior written by his own hand.

This building is of an oblong square, 250 feet in length and 180 in breadth. It stands east and west, according to the Grecian custom, and forms the figure of a cross. It is said to have been begun by the architect Artemius and finished by Isodorus. Four immense columns, united by arches, support a cupola of a vast magnitude. It was formerly ornamented with mosaic work, which the Turks have almost entirely demolished. At the head of the cross stood formerly the Sanctum Sanctorum. The ancient altar has been destroyed to make way for the *mehrabé* or Turkish altar, towards which the Turks turn themselves when at prayer. It is only a niche in which is placed a very large book of the Koran, with a green veil, and a pair of immense chandeliers are suspended on each side.

Near it is a kind of corridor in which the Grand Signior adores his Prophet, it is but little ornamented, and has gilt blinds. Here the Sultan is obliged to come almost every Friday to offer his devotions, and I have been informed that if he were often to neglect this duty, it would occasion a rebellion The floor of the Mosque is mostly covered with carpets, and is of a very fine marble of the island of Marmora.

The columns of the galleries are likewise of the most beautiful marbles of various kinds.

The building is in many places in the most ruinous condition. Many of the columns are held together by iron hoops, and it is probable that the slightest shock of an earthquake would bring this boasted monument of ancient architecture to the ground.

This Mosque has four minarets, one of which is built on the ancient steeple, and of a different architecture from the others. The *souchtar*, or Turkish priest, ascends five times a day to the highest gallery and calls the faithful to prayer.

On leaving the Mosque we intended to go on a sailing party, but the day being too windy we were obliged to give up the idea, and returned to visit the different line-of-battle ships that were laid up at Tersakhaneh. We only ventured to examine their outside, as the plague was then raging on board, and our curiosity was not quite so violent as to overcome our apprehensions of danger. These vessels have much useless finery about them, being encumbered with carved images, painted, or rather daubed over, in green and gold. They mount cannon of different calibres on their main deck, and carry nothing but swivels on the others, trusting more to their pistols and sabres than to the guns, which are very badly worked by their sailors.

We received at this time a message from the Capitan Pasha, brought to us by the Ambassador's dragoman, informing us that we might wait on him the following day. He likewise gave us to understand, that we should be obliged to take off our shoes at the door, in conformity to the custom of the Turks. We did not relish the idea of walking barefooted, but must have submitted to it had not the Capitan Pasha sent an order that he would dispense with that ceremony.

Before I give an account of our reception, I must introduce this extraordinary character to my readers, such as he was represented to me by several persons of the highest respectability, and particularly by Sir R--- A---.

Hassan Pasha is now in his seventy-sixth year he was born at Teflis in Georgia, from whence, as a boy, he was brought to Constantinople and sold as a slave. His first master soon dying, he passed through various bands, and went at last to Algiers in the service of a Turk who fell victim to the plague. Hassan was immediately seized and sold to pay off some of his deceased master's debts. Being of a very fine figure and lively disposition, he was purchased for the Dey, and entered into his service where he remained for some years, till an opportunity presented itself of making his escape. This he effected in a Spanish corn vessel, trading from Algiers to the port of Carthagena.

Having taken a little money with him, he procured his passage in a vessel bound to the coast of Italy, from whence he crossed into Dalmatia, and proceeded to Constantinople, where he entered in the capacity of *cagliongi*, a post one step higher than a common sailor, on board the Turkish Fleet. By his good behaviour in this station he soon obtained advancement, and was gradually promoted to the rank of Capitan or Commander of a ship. He filled this post at the time the Turkish Fleet was burnt and destroyed by the Russians, in the bay of Cismi, commanded by Count Alexander Orlow, in the year 1771.

He shewed so much gallantry and good conduct in that unfortunate affair, that on the death of the High Admiral, who fell a victim to the poignancy of his grief two years afterwards, he was appointed his successor. He has for fifteen years past filled this important station with much credit and honour to himself He has always held the highest place in the confidence of his capricious sovereign and enjoys the happiness of seeing himself both loved and feared by all the officers and sailors of the fleet, and is looked up to by his country as its principal ornament and support.

Though he is now in an advanced age, he appears both healthy and robust and he has a fine open manly countenance that is strongly expressive of that ungovernable ferocity which manifests itself on certain occasions, and which may rather be attributed to the want of a liberal education and to that general system of despotism which exists in that country, and in a certain degree pervades every class, than to any propensity to cruelty with which his disposition might be naturally tinctured. He is brave almost to a degree of temerity, active, strong and vigorous.

In his youth he excelled all his companions in their exercises. He managed his horses with more address, threw his arrow to a greater distance and with more judgment than any man. Impelled by his vigorous arm, the *gerite* (a kind of dart about eleven or twelve feet long) flew with unerring precision and double velocity. He uses his pistols and sabre with superior skill but his pre-eminence was most conspicuous at the public spectacles of the Grand Signior in the circus, where the young men opposed themselves in fierce combat to the lion, or other ferocious animals and where the meed of victory constantly adorned Hassan's brow.

Courageous, generous, benevolent and, except when under the immediate influence of passion, most humane, impartial in his official distribution of rewards and punishments, warm and sincere in his attachments; affable and courteous to his inferiors; ever ready to alleviate distress; but implacable in his enmity to oppressor, it is only to be lamented that a character rendered brilliant by so many excellent qualities was not destined to shine under the more happy influence of a Christian Government, where the prejudices inseparable from a Turkish education, which have been productive of the only blemish that tarnishes so bright a character, could never have existed.

In the high post he enjoys as Lord High Admiral, his privileges are very nearly as great as those of the most despotic prince, and the lives of all his inferiors are at his disposal.

At all the conflagrations in the city or suburbs of Constantinople, which are pretty frequent, the Grand Signior, Grand Vizier, and Capitan Pasha are obliged to assist, in order to animate by their presence and persuasion those who are employed in putting out the flames. The last of these great personages who arrives forfeits a certain sum of money, 1,000 Venetian sequins, in favour of the first. The Capitan Pasha is constantly the first, though he is by many years the eldest of the three.

On the night of 21 December, when a fire broke out in the palace of the Grand Vizier, who was with the army, the Capitan Pasha was at his beautiful villa, situated about four miles from Constantinople. He was immediately informed of it, and in a moment set off on horseback, with forty attendants, and reached town in less than twenty minutes, though the road was scarcely passable, being covered with snow some feet deep, and the night unusually dark, so that out of his forty attendants, one only was able to keep up with him, all the rest having been thrown from their horses, and unable or unwilling to follow him.

Now for an account of our audience. At ten in the morning I set out, accompanied by the Hon. Captain F---, and the officers of the *Pearl* frigate, for Top-Hanna, where we found the boats of the Captain and his first lieutenant waiting for us. The men were dressed in their Barge jackets, and the officers in their full uniforms. We proceeded by water to Capitan Pasha's palace and arrived at the Gate of the Seraglio in less than a quarter of an hour. On entering the first Court we were met by the dragoman of the Palace, who with a suite of attendants conducted us through a range of apartments to the Levee room, where we found the Pasha ready to receive us.

He was seated in state, on superb cushions. Behind, according to custom, was a display of all his most costly arms, beautifully mounted on gold, silver and precious stones. We were all struck with the noble air and countenance of this venerable and truly respectable old man. He rose half way from his seat to receive us and this was considered as the greatest condescension possible on his part, as a Turk is scarcely ever known to rise to salute a Christian, and it was a matter of astonishment to his officers and attendants.

He was most superbly dressed and wore his turban of state, a white band round his forehead, and a high cap with a large diamond feather. The Levee room was very large, furnished *à la Turque* with beautiful cushions spread upon the ground. He ordered us to be seated. I had the honour of sitting at one side of him and Captain F--- at the other; the other gentlemen were seated in a semicircle at the end of the apartment. He began the conversation by telling us that he had always loved the English nation, he inquired much after our ambassador, who he said was a man of courage and probity, who could be depended upon. He took notice of my clothes, which in comparison to his were short indeed.

I informed him of my intention of visiting the Holy Land, and that consequently I was preparing myself for the long dress. This idea seemed to afford him great amusement, and he was so polite as to offer me letters of protection to all the different Governors and Capitans commanding in the Mediterranean, and even promised to procure me a firman from the Grand Signior. I said everything I could to testify my gratitude, and presented him at the same time with a remarkable telescope, with which he was very much delighted; the more so, as he had lately broken the only one in his possession, and had not had an opportunity of replacing it. I likewise presented him with a pistol which from its peculiar construction could fire seven balls one after another with one loading; it cost me 100 guineas. But Capitan Pasha, not wishing to be behind hand with me in point of generosity, sent me the following day a most beautiful pelisse, and a whole bottle of attar of rose, which in England as well as in Turkey is worth 400 pounds, as it required no less than twelve acres of roses to produce that quantity.

We were then served by a vast number of attendants with fifty different kinds of refreshments, such as cakes, sweetmeats, etc. Each article was served by a different servant, all dressed in the richest robes of embroidered satin: another slave carried an embroidered muslin napkin

richly ornamented with gold and silver fringe and spangles: nor was
a napkin carried by the same person twice, and this was changed as
often as a different kind of sweetmeats was offered; this sort of luxury
being carried so far that we were not permitted even to wipe ourselves
a second time with the same napkin. There could not be less than two
hundred attendants, all armed with a fine case of pistols, and a sabre
large and sharp enough to cut off the head of an ox.

After this procession of sweetmeats, coffee was served and then attar
of roses, to perfume the beard. Pipes came afterwards, and I having by
this time learned to smoke, shewed myself quite an adept in the art.
Having stayed about an hour and a quarter, we took our leave and
asked permission to see the Pasha's stables, which he readily granted,
and which was considered as the greatest honour he could pay us, as
the Turks, among other superstitious notions, firmly believe that if a
Christian cast his eyes on their children and horses, the two principal
objects of their affection and attention, they are thereby exposed to the
danger of losing their eyes.

We were conducted to the stables by the Master of Horse. We went
through several vast apartments and descended by a flight of steps
into a private passage, through which we passed into the stables. They
contained upwards of one hundred horses, most of which were exquisitely beautiful; they were chiefly Arabian, and many well worth 1,000
guineas in England. Each horse had his proper attendant, and though
the stables were very spacious, there was scarcely room to move, as the
grooms had all assembled in expectation of receiving some presents
from me. I gave them but a trifle, with which they appeared much
satisfied. All the horses were in the highest condition, and their coats as
fine as satin, which considering that it was December, and the coldest
weather remembered at Constantinople for some years, was a remarkable and astonishing circumstance.

We stayed an hour in this place, and were returning to take leave,
when, as we had advanced some way into a large apartment, I perceived
the Capitan Pasha and several of his attendants on their knees. Our
Dragoman came up too late to prevent me from being noticed, and
we were going to retire when the Capitan made a sign and said that
we should not mind him but walk on through the *megite* or private
chapel. This was another remarkable instance of his politeness, as it is
considered by the generality of Turks highly degrading to be distracted
by any object when at their devotion, especially in the presence of a

Christian. His prayers did not continue above five minutes when he arose and gave orders that we should be shewn into a Kiosk belonging to the Grand Signior, where he seldom comes but in the summer, and then incognito to see the Pasha, who had made a present of it to the Grand Signior. It is of an octagonal form, most beautifully fitted up, with a fountain in the centre. The floor is of the finest variegated marble, and the whole surpassed in elegance everything of the kind I had ever seen. I was credibly informed it cost the Capitan Pasha upwards of 15,000 pounds.

Our boats had been ordered round to one of the doors of this beautiful building, close to the water, so that from the Kiosk we took our leave and stepped into them. We saw him peep through the window blinds and laugh excessively when the Barge-men dropt their oars together in the water. I heard afterwards from Sir R--- A--- that he liked the practice exceedingly, and intended to introduce it into the Turkish Navy.

The Turks send every year a Naval armament to the different islands and provinces bordering on the sea coast. This fleet is regulated as to the strength and number of the ships by the magnitude of the services which it is meant or expected to perform. If the Porte is not engaged in war with any foreign power, it is commonly composed of five or six ships. They collect the enormous taxes to which all those islands are subject; particularly those inhabited by Greeks and other Franks. Before they set sail an annual ceremony is observed and performed with as much pomp and ostentation as if preparations were making against a most powerful enemy. And, as it may give a further idea of eastern magnificence, I shall give the same description of it that was given me by a well-informed gentleman who was witness to it last year.

On 4 May, at eight in the morning, the Sultan repairs in his Barge of State to one of his kiosks, built close to the water. He is attended by his chamberlains and officers of State, his janissaries, pages, Body and inferior Guards parading around their Sovereign in different Barges according to their respective ranks. The Sultan is seated under a superb canopy till he arrives at his kiosk. He is soon followed by the Grand Vizier, who takes his station close to the Wharf in his Barge. On this occasion the harbour is covered with boats belonging to the different noblemen, with their women, come in the greatest pomp to be spectators of this beautiful sight.

The Capitan Pasha on his side embarks with great solemnity at Casum Pasha, the place where the ships are stationed and where he has a Palace, in a galley of fifty oars rowed by slaves. He is attended by three whole and three half galleys, and by a vast number of boats, in which people of the first consequence come to pay their respects to him.

This procession is conducted with so much solemnity and deliberation, that they are two hours rowing to the Grand Signior's kiosk, though but a mile's distance. The Pasha's galley being arrived abreast of the Wharf, he goes on shore attended by the Captains of the different ships under his command, and there he is received by one of the Officers of State, who invests him with a garment, the insignia of his office. He is then conducted by two *cauci* into the presence of the Grand Signior, who wishes him success in his enterprize, and a happy and safe return. He then takes leave and returns to his Barge, where he is received with a general salute from all the galleys, all the ships in the harbour, and afterwards by the batteries of Top-Hanna. He next proceeds along the Canal to the village of Besci Jacci, near the Black Sea, on the European side of the Canal, where he receives a grand entertainment from the Prime Vizier. This last ceremony over, he departs for his station.

## 23 December

Having heard much said respecting the ceremonies of the Dervishes, I proposed to my companion to pay them a visit this morning. As they wish to make the bystanders believe that they are actuated by inspiration and religious zeal to the horrid deeds they commit on themselves, they are always pleased to see strangers, particularly *giaours*, Christian dogs, witness their ceremonies, in hopes of obtaining the reward which is reserved for them if they convert any one by so great a display of faith to the Mahometan religion.

And so much are weak minds enslaved by the blind bigotry of the Greek Church, that I have been informed from good authority that it is forbidden by their priests, under pain of non-absolution, to visit these assemblies of Dervishes, from an apprehension that the sufferings which they voluntarily undergo and inflict on themselves for the honour of their religion might have so forcible an effect upon the understanding of the greatest part as to shake their Catholic faith and convert them to Mahometanism.

At nine o'clock we were conducted by our janissaries to the hall where these Dervishes were assembled, to the number of a dozen, and attended by upwards of one hundred spectators. The scene was opened by a dance of a most ridiculous nature three of the Dervishes stood up at a time in a most curious dress, one part of which was a sort of petticoat fastened very high upon them waist, with a short jacket open before and their arms bare.

They began by turning themselves round for upwards of half an hour, till quite overcome with a vertigo they all three fell senseless on the ground, amidst the acclamations of the spectators. The next object that presented itself to our view was a man pinching the flesh on his arm with a broad pair of pincers made for the purpose, till there was not a spot on his left arm and shoulder that was not bursting forth with extravasated blood. This fellow wished to impress the bystanders with the belief that his religious zeal prevented his suffering any pain from this dreadful operation.

And though, to do him justice, his countenance did not betray the whole extent of his sufferings, yet could he not succeed in persuading any rational being that God would deaden a man's feelings, and prevent him from suffering the pain that he voluntarily inflicted on himself through his folly or fanaticism.

I afterwards witnessed many similar sights, all equally disgusting; but what shocked me the most was a Dervish, who first held a red-hot bar of iron in his teeth till they were nearly burnt out of his head; and afterwards held it in his hands, till the flesh was almost entirely burnt off his fingers. This rendered the place so offensive with the smell of his broiling flesh that I was obliged to take my departure.

There is another ceremony among these poor deluded wretches which I did not want to see – it is their devouring serpents alive. They accomplish this by first laying hold of the animal by the neck and beginning their repast on the head, while the tortured animal writhes itself round their arm, to the very great entertainment of the ignorant spectators, who shout applause and ever after consider these miserable fanatics as saints.

Leaving this disgusting spectacle, we went to Top-Hanna and embarked in a boat to cross the Canal, with an intention of taking a stroll about the town of Constantinople, and particularly to examine as much of the Seraglio as may be viewed without much danger or inconvenience.

This Palace occupies the place where anciently stood Byzantium, on the point of the Peninsula of Thracia, near the Bosphorus. It was erected by Mahomet II., and is three miles in circuit. Its form is triangular: the buildings are on the top and declivity of the hill, and the gardens extend as far as the sea. The exterior has nothing striking or remarkable, and if we are to judge of the beauty of the gardens by the quantity of cypress-trees they contain, we may fairly conclude that they are not better cultivated or more curiously laid out than those of other individuals in Constantinople.

The only particular care that appeared to have been taken was to overload the grounds with shrubs and evergreens in order to conceal from the inhabitants of Galata and the other neighbouring places the sight of the Sultanas while they are walking in them. On going into the first court of the Seraglio, we were shewn a kind of wall with niches for exposing the heads of great state criminals. The first court of the Seraglio is immense, and is guarded by fifty *capigis*, who are only armed with a small stick. It contains the infirmary, the bake-houses and other offices, as well as barracks for the *Baliondgis*.

On the left hand of this square is the ancient church of St Irene, which was built by Constantine the Great, and is now converted into a storehouse for arms. In this court is also a fountain to which the Greeks come on certain festivals to drink of its waters, for which they pay very handsomely to the Grand Signior. Everybody is allowed to enter this court, where a most profound silence reigns; for if anyone was to make the least noise, it would be construed into a want of respect to the Master, and the delinquent would be bastinadoed on the spot.

The second court is more regular and much more agreeable than the first. It is likewise guarded by fifty *capigis*, and has two towers, near which is the Hall of Execution, where the viziers are tried and beheaded. This explains a Turkish Common expression, which is applied to those who are checked in their career: 'to be stopped between the two doors,' as there is one at each side of this place of execution. Here is still to be seen the mortar and pestle that were kept for pounding the *Muflis* and *Mamas* when guilty of treason or other offences. The property of these people being subject to confiscation, they were certain of carrying nothing out of this world with them; not even whole bones.

There are three passages leading out of this great court. The first to the right leads to the Divan, which is the highest tower of the Seraglio. It is a large square building, in which the councils of state are held. The second passage is in the centre of the court, and leads to the Gate of Felicity; it also conducts you to the presence chamber where the Grand Signior receives the foreign ambassadors. Between this gate and the square is a small kiosk where the Kislar Agha holds his Divan, and woe unto those who come under the cognizance of this court of inquiry. The third passage leads to the kitchens, nine in number, and other offices. The remaining buildings on the same line are the Treasury, the Treasurer's House, a Mosque, two kiosks and a beautiful bath.

The buildings at the back of the Divan are the apartments of the Grand Signior, and near them the great *Haram*. The interior of these apartments displays the highest degree of richness and sumptuous magnificence. I have not been enabled to ascertain the number of beauties they contain. I understood that those only were called Sultanas who had been honoured with a peculiar preference by the Grand Signior, and could add to that distinction the far more envious title of 'mother.'

The Seraglio contains two distinct orders of favourites. Those who have been honoured but once with the gracious embraces of the Sultan are called *odalisks*, and the *asakis* are those who can boast of having been noticed several times. Unhappy victims who are obliged to solicit and pine after the embraces of a surly, debauched, and enervated tyrant. With all his riches and power, he can command only sensual enjoyments; and has perhaps never felt or communicated that heavenly enchantment, which is the result of the close union of two congenial souls.

The strictest policy is observed in the Haram: the women can enjoy, and are promoted to places of rank and emolument. Crimes are punished with death: the guilty are tied up and thrown into the sea. But whatever riches or dignities they enjoy, they are nevertheless subservient to the control and caprice of eunuchs. They are allowed a physician when sick, who must, however, feel their pulse thro' a gauze. The eunuchs mount guard in the interior of the apartments; their chief is called *Capiaga*. The black eunuchs, and of them the most hideous, alone approach the *odalisks*. The *ichoglans* are the pages of the Grand Signior; they are very handsome young boys, and were formerly selected from among the captives: but now many families among the Turks solicit that honour for their children, and often pay a sum of money to obtain it. The Mutes are a particular class of servants, always at hand and ready to execute the secret orders of the Prince. They express their meaning by signs with an astonishing perspicacity. When the Emperor walks in the gardens with his women a bell is rung, and the gardeners and labourers are obliged to retreat precipitately under pain of death.

# CHAPTER V

Constantinople, continued – Pera – Its Antiquities –
Obelisks – Cistern of Basilica – The Slave Market – The
Coffee Manufactory – The Watch-Tower – The Seven
Towers – *Ramaden* – A Bath for the Ladies – Character
of the Turks – Dress – The Ladies – Their Food – Their
Diversions – Arts and Sciences – A Turkish *Billet-Doux* –
The Plague – The Police – The Grand Signior – Public
Buildings – Marriages – Janissaries.

On going from the Seraglio a foreigner is much pleased with the
beautiful front of St Sophia, close to which stands one of the finest
fountains in Constantinople, built by the Grand Signior and richly
ornamented with gold and Turkish characters. We afterwards went to
see a Mosque built by Sultan Achmet; it is a very beautiful building and
in its interior far exceeds that of St Sophia, having six lofty minarets
and three galleries. The immense square, in the middle of which it
stands, was begun by the Emperor Severus and finished by Constantine.
Proceeding on the right, you enter the largest street of Constantinople,
called Divan Yole Dgiami. All the *amabadgis*, guards of the highest order
of the Grand Signior, have their houses here. At the bottom of this street
are still seen some ruins of superb arcades, which formerly belonged
to the Palaces of the Emperors, and the famous staircase by which the
princes ascended to the celebrated place At-meidan, which under the
Greek Emperors was called Hippodrome. It was a Circus in which the
public spectacles of horse-racing, bull-fighting etc. were represented. It
is more than 1,200 feet long and 300 broad. The few antiquities to be

seen at Constantinople are chiefly in this square, and reduced to two obelisks and a few columns.

The first obelisk is about thirty-five feet high: it consists of two pieces of red oriental granite, which are in high preservation, as well as the Egyptian hieroglyphics, which cover it almost from top to bottom. It stands on a pedestal of white marble, and on the side fronting the Mosque are seen Latin hexameters, still legible, by which it appears that it was erected by the Emperor Theodosius. On the base are several figures in basso-relievo, but mostly effaced by the ravages of time. Theodosius is represented on one side, with a palm and a crown in his hand, and on the other is the representation of a battle. There is another obelisk at the extremity of this great place, of fifty feet height. It has four sides, and is built of large square stones which are crowded with figures in basso-relievo. It is erected on a pedestal, on which is a Greek inscription almost obliterated. A little farther on, an immense pillar of bronze, resembling three large serpents entwined together, presents itself to view. These serpents have lost their heads, and their bodies are nearly defaced by the stones which children are incessantly throwing at them. It is supposed that this pillar served as one of the tripods in the temple of Delphi, which was consecrated to Apollo, and that it was removed to this city by Constantine the Great.

From this place we went to examine a very great Cistern, anciently called the Cistern of Basilica, which, though the Turks have curtailed more than two thirds, is still immense. It is now quite dry, and contains several hundred persons preparing and winding silk for the manufactories, who fasten their skeins or hanks to the different pillars that support this vast reservoir. Some Greek inscriptions are still to be seen, but I could not find any of them legible. No traveller or antiquarian has yet been able to ascertain the use of this reservoir.

As it was now near our dinner hour, and we were at some distance from the ambassador's Palace, we hastened our return home, but by another road, and had the pleasure of viewing en passant a place called Catergha Limanis, or the Port of the Galleys. This is a very pretty part of the city, where formerly stood the Baths of Julian. We likewise saw a very fine Palace belonging to the Sultana Esma, situated towards the South and commanding a most beautiful prospect.

I observed on our way a vast number of granites scattered here and there, half buried in the ground, and some of them serving as corner stones to the streets. We finished our course by taking a slight view of the Slave-market, where both men and women are exposed to public sale, and thanks to the Jews and pirates, this commodity is most abundant at Constantinople. The Turks come here to purchase men, women and children, as they happen to be in want of them. I saw a beautiful young Georgian bargained for, and examined by several connoisseurs, and owing to the very extravagant demand of her owner, she was some time before she could get a purchaser, though the poor girl did everything in her power to engage notice and command attention, thinking, no doubt, any kind of slavery preferable to the horrid idea of being thus daily exposed to public view, and belonging to a cruel and avaricious dealer in human flesh.

The buying and selling of slaves form a considerable branch of commerce, nor do the ladies of the first distinction among the Turks think it beneath their notice. They often purchase pretty little girls, whom they educate with the greatest care and fondness, and engage masters to instruct them in music, dancing and singing. They bestow so much care in perfecting them in all external accomplishments, and particularly in the art of attracting men, and inspiring violent passions, that it is not uncommon to see young women thus educated rise from the humble sphere in which fortune had placed them to a more elevated station, and become the favourites, and often the wives, of men of the first rank and consequence.

## 24 December

We began our excursion this morning by taking a view of a kiosk called Kirdeb Kioski, which is a kind of state prison, in which the viziers are confined till the time of their exile. Near it we saw another fine building, which was a House of Justice, and passed an immense iron gate commanding a subterranean passage extending under the city as far as the Mosque of St Sophia. I was also shewn here some remains of brick-work in the wall of the Seraglio, said to have formed a part of the ancient Church of our Saviour.

As we were in the neighbourhood, we paid a visit to the coffee manufactory called Belick Jaamizi, where all the coffee consumed in Constantinople is burnt and ground. More than 300 persons are employed in it, and near 4,000 pounds of coffee are daily sold. This may appear immense to persons who do not know, or consider, that the Turks are accustomed to drink coffee perhaps a dozen times in the day, as it is, the quantity appears rather small in proportion to the daily consumption, for the common people here, of the lowest order, live on coffee as the poor in Ireland do on potatoes. No person ever thinks of stirring out till he has first drank his coffee. In the poorest habitation you enter, a cup of coffee is offered you; nor are you suffered to drink it alone, as the owner of the house is sure to pledge you, though he may have already done the same with a dozen prior visitors. This, together with the offer of a pipe, is the most common way of shewing their hospitality: If you refuse either, you are sure of offending, or at least, of giving them a very unfavourable opinion of your taste and manners.

We had been previously provided with an order, or permission to enter all mosques, otherwise we should have been prevented from examining many beautiful buildings of this kind, nor should we have been allowed to see the place where Constantine the Great was buried. He is interred in the mosque called Osmanie Dgiamissi. It is a very fine building, both for its architecture and internal workmanship. The tomb of the Emperor is in the dome of the Church, it is made of one solid block of porphyry, excavated with the chisel, and close to it lies the lid. This beautiful piece of marble is nine feet in length, by three and a half in breadth. Its excavation, which has been the effect of skill and labour, is three feet deep. The thickness of its sides is four inches.

From this we passed through the street called the Street of the Burnt Column, so named from the column that stands at the north end of it, which had suffered materially by a dreadful fire. It is of porphyry and surrounded with bars of iron, its ornament consists of a beautiful foliage, and it is crowned with a capital of white marble. On its top stood the statue of the founder of this city. The column itself is formed of several pieces of porphyry, the parts of which are so admirably well fitted, and the joints so effectually concealed by wreaths of laurel, that till lately they could not be discerned, and it was supposed to be an entire piece of porphyry; but time, that great developer of things, having defaced its ornaments, the joints are now visible in many places.

The Emperor Manuel Comnenus imagined that by diminishing the height of this celebrated column, he would save it from the ravages of time and weather, but instead of replacing the statue of Constantine, he crowned the column with a capital of white marble of the Doric order, and had an inscription engraved on it which at this time is scarcely legible, importing that this admirable work had been restored by the very pious Emperor Comnenus.

We passed afterwards thro' a very long covered street, in which live all the librarians, book-binders and Turkish clerks. The latter amount to many thousands, as there are no printing offices in Constantinople. On expressing my astonishment at this to Sir R--- A--- he assured me that the very attempt to introduce printing would occasion a rebellion;, as the clerks would consider it as a deprivation of their only means of Support or livelihood, and they would be seconded by the mob of Constantinople, which is a very formidable body when assembled.

The Watch-tower of Constantinople next attracted our notice. From its top you can almost see the whole city; and guards are here continually on the watch, that they may give the alarm on the first appearance of fire, which is done in the following manner. Three of them are always on the look-out, who are provided with drums and trumpets of different forms and sizes. When all these are sounded at once, the fire is supposed to be general over Constantinople, and every one, let whatever be his rank or situation, is by these signals ordered to give assistance. When any of the smaller drums are beaten, the fire is in some particular quarter, and when the trumpets are sounded, it is known to be in Pera. By this means, every one knows to what quarter, and even to what street he is to direct his assistance on such an occasion. This is a most excellent institution, and without it the whole city would be consumed a dozen times in the year, supposing it could be rebuilt as often. During my short stay, there were about twenty fires in the city and suburbs.

From this place we directed our steps to Mahomet's Bath, the most famous in Constantinople. It is built on the spot where once stood the Cistern of Arcadius and Modestus, and the traveller still meets with some fragments of masonry belonging to this once celebrated basin. There are in many places pieces of broken pillars, and at the door of the bath two very beautiful marble capitals. This bath is by far the finest I ever saw, and the interior of it is finished in the highest style of eastern elegance.

We afterwards went through a gate built by the Emperor Theodosius, surrounded on one side with walls in arcades and flanked by towers. In ascending to the Mosque of Hassakei, or the Mosque of the Women, we were struck with the noble appearance of the pedestal on which formerly stood the Pillar of Arcadius: there remain only three feet and a half of the column, which is of verde antico, and the pedestal on which it stands ten feet in height is of red granite. We arrived afterwards at a fountain called Balukli, which is highly venerated by the superstitious Turks, who often come here to cast their nativity and consult future events, according to the form and appearance of a number of little fishes with which this fountain is well stocked.

The next day at ten o'clock I set out once more for Constantinople, to see some inscriptions to which I was induced to direct my attention by the advice of the Abbé S---, a very sensible, facetious man, and a great antiquary, who resides in the Ambassador's Palace. In viewing the walls of Constantinople, traces of antiquity may everywhere be discovered well worth the notice of a traveller.

The ancient walls of Byzantium have in some places braved the destructive hand of the Turks as well as of time. Superb columns are still to be seen, and some gateways are still existing. Inscriptions, the laboured monuments of Grecian art, are to be met with in many places on the walls and gateways, both in the Greek and Latin languages, but the greatest part have suffered so much by time that they are scarcely legible. They in general announce the different repairs that have been made by different Emperors.

At the end of the wall, which extends to the west along the sea-shore, are two towers, on one of which the inscription engraved on two long slabs of white marble is still legible, and informs us that these towers had been repaired under Constantine and Bassilei. You then pass the Gate Top-Capoussi, or Gate of Cannon, so called from Mahomet II having pointed his artillery against it. It was in that attack that the unfortunate Constantine Paleologus lost both the empire and his life. The ruins of the Palace of Constantine the Great are still to be seen.

The remains of the Tower of Belisarius, who lived to experience Justinian's ingratitude, are almost entirely demolished.

We were not permitted to enter the Castle of the Seven Towers; nor did we venture to approach very near, as our janissary apprehended that, being Christians, we might be fired upon from some of the windows. The castle is flanked by seven towers, from which it takes its name, and is surrounded by a very high wall. Two of the towers are of white marble. The treasures of the empire were formerly deposited here, but it is now used as a place of confinement for state prisoners, and particularly for the foreign ministers whose Court is at war with the Porte.

While I was at Constantinople, the Russian Ambassador was confined here, but the Turks allowed him £1,000 per month during the time he was deprived of his liberty. I beg leave, for the information of my younger class of readers, to mention here that the Mahometan era takes its date from the time Mahomet fled from Mecca to Medina, on account of the persecution he experienced from the Government of that city. This is called *hegira*, which signifies 'flight,' and commenced on Friday 16 July Anno Domini 622, the day on which he effected his escape and began to preach his doctrines and propagate his religion. On that day commences the first of their year, which consists of 354 days, and *Muharrem*, which answers to our July, is their first month.

The ceremonies of the *Ramaden*, month of March, when the Turkish Lent begins, are performed in the following manner.

As soon as the first moon of that month is perceived, information of it is immediately given to the *cadi* or whatever judge resides in each place. He immediately passes an act in his court for the commencement of the Fast. In garrison towns the people are acquainted of it by the firing of guns. Their mode of observing this fast is neither to eat, drink or smoke from sunrise till after sunset, so that during that month they usually turn day into night and night into day. Pregnant women, invalids and travellers, or the military when encamped in time of war, are not compelled to a rigid observance of this fast; but they are expected to perform it as soon as these legal impediments are removed. Having accomplished half of it, should these impediments again occur, so as to cause a second interruption of the fast, whatever number of days were wanting of the appointed term, they are afterwards obliged to complete. But these obligations are not incumbent on children till they have entered into their eleventh year.

Previous to this fast, it is a principle invariably observed that all private enmities should subside. When two persons meet, between whom some animosity has subsisted, they both immediately manifest their inclination to forgive and forget what is past, by a mutual embrace.

The ancient monastery of St John next attracted our attention. There only remain of this ancient building one range of columns, of the aisle of the church a Cistern supported by twenty-four columns, and a beautiful bath, which, as I have been informed, is solely consecrated to the use of the fair sex. It is forbidden, under pain of death, to pry into this sanctuary. But I prevailed on a Grecian beauty of fashion, with whom I had formed an acquaintance during my stay here, to give me the following particulars.

The baths for the ladies are constructed in the same manner as those for men. When a lady intends to go to the bath, an indulgence which a husband of a certain rank and fortune who has these conveniences in his own house seldom will grant, she covers herself with a double veil and is always accompanied by a female slave. As soon as they arrive they throw off their whole apparel, and in the simple and, it is to be hoped, the innocent attire of nature they pass three or four hours in various amusements. They are sometimes two hundred in number, some in the bath, others negligently lying on couches, while their young and beautiful slaves, disencumbered like their mistresses of all artificial covering, perfume and plait their hair.

The news of the town and the daily petty occurrences, as may easily be imagined, furnish ample materials for mirth and conjectures of various kinds. This is a real relaxation for these poor women, who are deprived of all rational amusements, and are continually kept in a state of dependence and slavery. They laugh, sing and dance, and sometimes form plans of future pleasures and happiness, in the execution of which the Turkish ladies, in spite of their walls, slaves, matrons, eunuchs and mutes, are much more expert than our European women of fashion – as if it were the happy provision of human nature, that our spirit of intrigue should increase in proportion to the danger and difficulties we meet with in obtaining the enjoyment of a dear and beloved object.

I was very a propos diverted from these philosophical reflections, which otherwise might have carried me to an elaborate treatise on the subject, by Pauolo rushing into my apartment, to inform me that a spectacle of a most striking nature was to be seen – the Grand Signior's going to the chase – nor was I disappointed in my expectation, for the scene was very grand. The march began with 4,000 janissaries on foot, in two lines, and armed with sticks only. They were followed by 300 *chiaour* or carriers of the sublime commands, covered with gold and silver stuffs, and mounted on beautiful horses richly caparisoned. Next came fifteen horses for the use of the Grand Signior, led in hand and preceded by two hundred officers of the court in their respective gala dresses. The Grand Signior immediately followed, mounted on a beautiful Arabian, covered with gold brocade spangled with pearls and diamonds. He was surrounded by 500 *soulaces*, body-guards. The viziers, grandees of the court, and first officers of the Seraglio marched in the rear.

We followed him into the fields, where he was only attended by his principal officers and two hundred falconers, each carrying a falcon in his hand. In a moment the plain was covered with these birds. I was sorry that I could not follow the party, for the sport seemed really delightful, and this is the chase which the Turks prefer to all others. Being engaged to dine at the French Ambassador's, the Count De C---, where there was to be a ball in the evening, I took my leave of the Grand Signior with reluctance.

I had this day, also, for the first time, to try on my Turkish dress, which I had got made preparatory to my voyage to Syria, and I found myself so much at my ease in it that I could not be prevailed on to leave it off. I therefore went, dressed like an Arab, to Monsieur De C---, and prevailed on my friends to do the same. The whole company was in a high flow of spirits, and my Jerusalem expedition was the general topic of conversation, as it was my intention to set off on the Monday following. His Excellency asked me if it was a fact that I had a considerable wager depending on it. I answered in the affirmative. The ladies were curious to know the amount of the sum, some pretending it to be £15 or £20, others £30,000. As I had good reasons for not making it known that I had such a large sum depending on it, I evaded answering their questions.

In the evening the company assembled to the number of one hundred persons, and as there were more ladies than gentlemen I was induced to dance, in spite of my Arabian dress, and during the dance, which was English, I am convinced that my figure and movements were truly awkward and ridiculous.

My departure from Constantinople was delayed by a very dangerous illness, which I caught by going on a hunting party, when the intense cold of the morning and the heat of the meridian sun, together with the fatigue of walking for several days in the snow, brought on a fever of the most malignant kind, which left no hopes of my recovery to my friends or physicians. My strong constitution resisted the violence of the disorder, and notwithstanding a severe relapse, occasioned by my own imprudence, I was sufficiently recovered in the course of a month to be able to proceed on my journey.

But before I leave this city, may I be permitted to give a short sketch of some of the prevailing customs, manners, dress and religion of the Turks, such as they appeared to me from my own observations?

The Turks of Europe and those of Asia are not alike. The former are valiant, industrious and laborious, the latter idle, cowardly, and effeminate, totally ignorant of the arts and sciences. Hypocrisy is their distinguishing characteristic; they are avaricious in the extreme but ostentatious, and so incontinent that their Seraglio cannot satisfy their libidinous passions. Practices the most abominable, as well as the most unnatural, are added to the long catalogue of Turkish sensual gratifications.

Their avarice does not stop at the most criminal means of acquiring riches, and yet they are equally prodigal of that ill-gotten wealth in purchasing dress and procuring sensual enjoyments. They are in general about the middle stature, their features are regular and expressive, their eyes and hair black. But owing to their manner of living they scarcely retain any traces of beauty after they have passed the prime of youth.

The inhabitants of Turkey are a mixture of different nations. No less than seventy-two different denominations of people, nations, religions, and sects are to be found among them, such as natural Turks, Arabs, Tartars, Moors of Africa, Wandering Tribes, Jews and Christians of all denominations.

The dress of the men consists of trousers, a long shirt cut in the same manner as those of the European ladies, a *doliman*, or sort of robe which reaches to their ankles, has short and narrow sleeves, and is fastened by a girdle, which is of the greatest use to the Turks, as they carry their handkerchief dagger and pistols in it, and place in its folds their money, tobacco and papers. Over the *doliman* they wear a larger robe, with long and wide sleeves this is called *feredge*. It is made of fine stuffs for summer, and in winter is lined with furs. They put on cloth stockings over their leather socks, in the form of buskins. Their shoes, called *babouches*, resemble slippers. Their head-dress is very ample, no less stuff being used in making their turbans than their robes, which renders them extremely heavy.

It is by the size and shape of the turban that every man's rank and occupation is known. The variety of them is great, as the distinctions are so numerous. The emirs are supposed to be descended from the Prophet, and are always permitted to wear the green turban. I have been told that thirty yards of muslin are frequently used in this part of their dress.

The Rayacks wear the *kalpac* instead of the turban; it is made of lambskin of a white, black or grey colour, and is not near so becoming as the turban. The Turks are very particular in these distinctions of dress, and should a Christian or Jew venture to appear in a green turban, he would be torn to pieces.

In Turkey, as well as throughout all parts of Greece, smoking is a prevailing habit in both sexes. By the length and beauty of the pipe you may judge the rank of the smoker. The mouthpiece is usually made of polished amber, the stem of jessamine, covered with scarlet or green cloth, richly embroidered; the bowl is made of red clay, beautifully gilt. They mix with their tobacco musk, aloes-wood, frankincense, etc. This they manufacture with a white gum into small lozenges, one of which is put with the tobacco into the pipe. This composition improves the tobacco and diffuses a fragrance thro' the room. These lozenges are said to possess other virtues, but I never experienced any. There is another sort made in the Seraglio at Constantinople, which the grandees eat as well as smoke. These are very costly and used only in their *harams*, where it has other effects besides that of improving their tobacco.

The women are, in general, fat and lusty. Their dress resembles that of the man, except in its tightness, by which they endeavour to improve their shape. A gold or silver buckle, set in precious stones, fastens their girdle. Their drawers are of an extraordinary fullness. They wear Morocco slippers and a little iron plate, like a crescent, forms the heel of their little boots, which they put on to walk. They have a kind of corset under their robe, which leaves their neck uncovered, or merely veiled with a gauze. Diamonds form their principal riches; they have bracelets of them; aigrettes, ear-rings, necklaces, watches, snuff-boxes, and pin-cases of different sizes, to a very great value, nor is the propriety of wearing or possessing these jewels ever disputed with the women, in whatever circumstances their husbands may find themselves. When they walk out, they wrap themselves up in another long robe.

The dress of a woman of quality, tho' never seen in public, is far more costly than those worn in Europe. They wear a profusion of pearls, diamonds and other precious stones, with the richest stuffs and furs the most costly. That part of their dress next their skin is of the most extravagant price.

To sing in their houses is considered a mark of ill-breeding, but to fall asleep in company incurs no such imputation.

Their bath is the most fashionable place or amusement, and it is considered as high a compliment to take your friend there as it would be in London to accompany her to the Opera. Their carriages scarcely deserve the name, being little better than carts. They are not on springs, and are closely shut up.

All the ladies in Turkey, of whatever religion they may be, keep themselves constantly veiled which led an ill-natured cynic to make this observation, 'that in Turkey alone vice is not barefaced'. A large triangular handkerchief constitutes their veil, it covers the whole face, and the ends are tied behind so that nothing of their face is to be seen but the eyes and the tip of the nose. They usually paint their nails and eyebrows with a plant called *kene*, which gives them a yellowish-red colour. They sometimes paint the hands and feet, describing thereon flowers, etc. They are great coquettes, and possess in a superior degree the art of deceiving their husbands and lovers. For this reason they are not allowed to walk out often, and are obliged to remain confined at home, passing the tedious hours in embroidering or conversing with their female attendants. The ladies of some Bashaws who are absent may be excepted from this restriction as they are generally very fond of strangers, but such intrigues are not always carried on without danger. They are generally commenced at the Bezistan, where the jewellers, silversmiths and merchants keep their shops. When a lady meets a gentleman to whom she wishes to disclose her partiality, she gives him a gentle push with her elbow. If a lover wishes to insinuate himself into the good graces of a mistress, he approaches her window and indicates his passion by striking his breast.

Jewish women are very expert in the art of favouring the Turkish ladies in their amours. They introduce into their apartments beautiful young men, under the disguise of female slaves, carrying various kinds of merchandize. Grecian and Armenian ladies enjoy more liberty; yet they do not often go out. I was told that a young man, a violet-soap merchant, had so turned the heads of all the ladies at Constantinople that the Grand Signior was entreated by several Bashaws to send him into exile. Every man of wit, talents, or an agreeable figure, is sure to incur the displeasure and hatred of all the married part of the male community. In the country I have seen women bathing in a stream, who took no care to conceal themselves on perceiving that we were Christians. Our janissaries, however, advised us to act the part of Joseph, else in case of a surprise we might be accused of a capital crime and, to my shame, I must confess that it was with much reluctance I followed so perfect an example.

The manner of salutation among the Turks is to lay the right hand on the heart and make a small inclination. If you approach a man of consequence, that is to say, a very rich man, or a man holding a place under the government – for in Turkey, as is the case in many other places, a man meets with outward respect in proportion to his reputed riches, or the importance of his office – you take the end of his robe and kiss it with apparent respect. It would be an insult to take off your turban to anyone.

Their common nourishment consists of mutton, rice, peas and cucumbers. After their repast, they drink either water or whey. The sherbet, composed of lemon juice, cherries and other fruits is reserved for the table of the affluent. They are not so abstemious at their feasts, and seldom leave the festive board before they are intoxicated with narcotic draughts. They do not often eat at each others' houses, and pay but few ceremonial visits. The ladies are never admitted into company. The men, when together, devote the greatest part of their time to smoking. The master of the house himself presents to each of his guests a lighted pipe: perfumes are afterwards introduced, with coffee and sherbet. The company wash their hands in rose-water and dry them in the smoke of perfumes. The Turks are seen smoking everywhere, even in the streets and public walks.

Their only amusements are to draw the bow, to go to the chase with falcons, and to play at chess, but 'tis considered a great sin to play for money. I once saw a young Turk launching a falcon against a wild duck, which immediately plunged into the water: the falcon followed it on the surface of the water, beating its wings whenever it lost sight of its prey. Another Turk, thinking that one falcon was not sufficient, sent his own to its assistance. This excited such a jealousy between the two birds that instead of offering mutual assistance they rushed furiously against each other, and had they not been separated the scuffle would have ended in the death of one or the other.

They likewise amuse themselves with equestrian exercises, for which purpose they often assemble at the Hippodrome, the large square which I have already noticed. There they separate in two bands and range themselves at the extremities. At each signal two riders armed with long lances start, and, rushing forward with the utmost violence, meet in their mid-career and parry with much skill the blows they aim at each other. I have seen several of them leap on and off their horses with as much adroitness as those at Astley's. Quoits also, and wrestling, constitute part of their diversions.

They are fond of cultivating flowers, particularly tulips. The highest compliment a Turk can pay you is to send you one of his tulips as a present. They have even instituted a festival in honour of this flower.

They have made some proficiency in the mechanical arts in general, and have manufactories of silk and cotton. Their watchmakers are all

Armenians, Jews or Franks. They begin to think the Koran is not the only good book in the world, for they now apply themselves a little to history, and are very fond of absurd tales related of their own people. I had the curiosity to have the history of an inn-keeper of Constantinople translated. Love filled up two-thirds of this whimsical composition. He had been a pirate in his youth, and enriched himself by the capture of several Maltese vessels. His battles and victories over both sexes had rendered him famous. He then turned physician, and his skill in that profession procured him the honour and advantage of being employed in the Seraglio at Ispahan.

He was afterwards sold as a slave, and in that state filled the office of steward and innkeeper. He mentions the various love-letters he wrote. A Turkish billet-doux is both simple and ingenious, of which the Turkish ladies often avail themselves, as they can without much danger of discovery communicate their wishes, and carry on their intrigues, by means of this species of hieroglyphics, in which they use neither pen, ink or paper; but put into a purse bits of straw, a few grains of wheat, some salt, a bit of wood, a bit of cord, a grape-stone, or the like trifles, each of which has its separate signification, and this composition answers all the purposes of our best-written love-letters.

I took a copy of one of these curious letters, which I shall transcribe.

He sent, in a purse, a grape-stone, a straw, a jonquil, a match, some paper, and gold thread, which have the following signification:

| The grape-stone | *uzum* | My eyes |
| The straw | *hazir* | Suffer that I be your slave |
| The jonquil | *pull* | Be sensible to my love. |
| The match | *gizo* | I burn, I burn, my flame consumes me. |
| The paper | *kileal* | My senses are bewildered. |
| The gold thread | *til* | I am dying, come to my relief. |

Most of these words are taken from the Arabic, which is the richest language in the world.

The Turkish ladies affect the most favourable opinion of their husbands in every respect, so that when they are not blessed with those fruits of love so much wished for in the married state, they always ascribe it to a defect in themselves, and to atone for their supposed sterility they introduce into their *haram* the most beautiful young girls they can procure. A child is generally the issue of this truly conde-scending kindness, which is considered legitimate and inherits as if so in reality.

It is not more strange than true that the opulent eunuchs frequently have women in their seraglios, and these the most beautiful. These poor creatures become free on the decease of their patrons, when they make up for their lost time during their slavery.

The plague is not more dangerous in Turkey than a fever is in London or Paris. But physicians are not to be had there as in France or England. The most malignant kind is said to be generated in Egypt. It is supposed to be wafted to Constantinople by the winds that prevail for months together at the summer solstice, and never fails to take its leave upon the arrival of the autumnal equinox, when the winds blow strongly from the north.

It seems to be the general opinion that those who have been once afflicted with this dreadful disorder are never known to take it a second time. But this I must, from good authority, take the liberty of contra-dicting. My servant Pauolo assured me that he had been three times afflicted with the plague; and shewed me the marks of its venom, by the cicatrices on all parts of his body. Persons of a strong constitution are more liable to take the infection than those of a delicate frame.

The first symptom of this disorder is a violent headache accompanied with a burning thirst, which is followed by a weakness and almost total loss of the use of the limbs, and people in the last stage of it are seen staggering about the streets as if violently intoxicated; and tho' it is so universally known that the disorder can be taken by the touch only, yet so inconsiderate are the Turks, that they take no precaution to keep out of the way of persons infected; nor indeed would a good Mahometan think himself justifiable in leaving his house, tho' every individual in it were infected, such is the force of predestination. No wonder, then, this disorder should make such ravages among this bar-barous and ignorant race.

But how much must the reader's indignation be kindled, and every sentiment of pity for such insensate barbarians be suppressed, when he is told that the very clothes and cushions on which the afflicted had died are sold the day after in a public place appointed for that purpose, and immediately worn by the purchaser, without even the precaution of fumigation or airing. From all the information I have been able to collect on this subject, I have no doubt that the plague is neither more or less than a violent fever, of the malignant putrid kind, which, if treated at Constantinople as such disorders are treated in London, would in all probability be as easily cured. But I have already observed that they have no physicians among them, nor can they, consistently with their absurd tenets and doctrine, admit of medical assistance even in extreme cases.

In the Plague of 1785, the most destructive that has happened this century, no less than 5,000 died every day. Prayers are never offered to the deity to stop its ravages till the mortality arrives to such a height that only one less than a thousand are carried out at the same gate to the Burying-ground. It is then deemed advisable to invoke the Prophet, and the Turks assemble for this purpose in their Mosques.

Sir Robert A--- assured me that during his residence at Constantinople, for twenty-one years, he knew but few instances of Europeans dying of the plague, to their manner of living in respect to diet, but more especially to a strict attention to cleanliness, may be ascribed their escaping this dreadful disorder.

During the time the plague is thought to rage, which is only when two or three hundred persons die daily, the Franks shut up their houses, and all intercourse outward is at an end till such time as the disorder ceases.

There are persons who for a fixed salary attend the palaces of the ministers and respectable merchants' houses, and furnish them with provisions of all kinds in the following manner. A large tub or cistern of water is placed under the most convenient window in the house, into which is plunged all the butcher's-meat that is intended for the consumption of those within, where, after it has lain a sufficient time to wash away any infection it may have caught, a bell is rung by the caterer, when a basket is suspended from the window and the provisions are drawn up, by which means all danger is avoided.

The police of Constantinople are very vigilant. The shops must be shut with the setting sun, and the patrols, during the night, stop every person they meet in the street.

When a Vizier, Bashaw, or great officer of the empire is doomed to die, the Emperor sends him a cord by one of his mutes, and the criminal has the privilege of being his own executioner. Private individuals do not enjoy such an enviable prerogative: they are either hanged or impaled alive: the latter is one of the most cruel tortures. The criminal is stripped naked, and laid on the ground. The executioner then opens the lower part of his body with a razor and by repeated strokes drives a sharp pointed stake, eight feet long and very thick, into the lacerated passage till it comes out at the extremity of the shoulder. The sufferer is then set upright, his hands are tied to the stake, and the mob are suffered to load him with abuse and execrations.

When the Grand Signior appears in public, if any subject has a complaint to make, he places a lighted flambeau or some burning coals in an earthen pot, on his head, and thus presents himself to the Emperor, who is obliged to hear his petition.

This prince in summer and winter dines at ten in the morning, and sups at six in the afternoon. He sits cross-legged on cushions; a napkin is placed on his knees, and another on his left arm, for the purpose of wiping his hands. A piece of morocco serves him for a table, on which are placed three or four different sorts of excellent new bread, quite warm, suitable to the general taste of the Turks. He uses neither knives or forks, and such is the plainness and simplicity of the sideboard that two wooden spoons compose the whole apparatus of the table, one for the soup and the other for the syrups, for by the laws of his Prophet he is not allowed to use any other at his meals. He seldom drinks more than once at each repast, and he has always before him a number of mutes and dwarfs, who endeavour to amuse him by their buffooneries.

The Turks shew their taste for magnificence in their public buildings only. Their houses are very simple, and are but two stories high. It is customary to have some passages selected from the Koran written on the doors and windows. In the yard of every house stands a little fountain, surrounded with verdure. The staircase is a kind of ladder, with a roof over it. The furniture of their rooms consists of mats and carpets along the walls, with large sofas instead of chairs. They always sit cross-legged leaning on cushions.

No beds are to be seen, being put up into presses constructed for the purpose. When the Turks lie down they put on a small turban instead of a night-cap. They always keep a lamp burning in their bed-room, and sometimes two heated stoves, one on each side. If they awake during the night, they order coffee to be brought, smoke a pipe, and eat some pastry. The house of a nobleman generally occupies a large space of ground, and is surrounded by very high walls. The apartments of the women are secured by double doors and guarded by eunuchs or matrons. The ceilings are either gilt or painted, and the floor is of marble or china.

When a Turk wishes to marry he sends to the parents of the intended bride, to demand their conditions. If they agree, they join hands and the bargain is concluded. This ceremony is finished by a prayer from the Koran. Afterwards the bride, covered with a red veil, is led to her spouse, who for that evening is obliged to discharge the office of chambermaid and put her to bed. It is usual on these occasions for the lady to have the strings of her dress tied with double knots, which the impatient lover is eager to loose, and by that means time is given to the young woman to say her prayers; sometimes to laugh at the awkwardness and precipitate impatience of her lover, and to make serious reflections or entertain fantastic notions of the new state of life into which she is just going to enter.

A Turk is allowed to marry four wives, and keep as many concubines as his circumstances will allow. A wife has a right to institute an action in several cases, particularly if he is not observant of his conjugal duties, a tribute which is commonly fixed on Thursday evening or Friday morning, the time of the week usually consecrated to this purpose.

Their interments do not materially differ from ours. The loud lamentations of the women is the principal ceremony at the death of a Turk, which they continue till the corpse is laid under ground. The men carry the bier on their shoulders, and the women scatter flowers on the tomb every Monday and Friday, and with much importunity inquire of the dead why he chose to die! They wear black for mourning, and leave off their jewels.

The janissaries amount to 100,000. They sometimes render themselves formidable to the nation, and even to the Emperor himself. Five thousand of them mount guard every day at the Palace. The Emperor orders provisions to be distributed among them. If they are dissatisfied, they shew it on that occasion by overturning the dishes with their feet, in which case every attempt is made to pacify them. Their first institution was under Morad II, and they were composed of young Bulgarians and Macedonians, sent in tribute to Constantinople. They were originally called *hadgini*, which in the Turkish language signifies 'strangers', afterwards janissaries or 'new soldiers'. Most of them have some trade, are allowed many privileges and exempt from duties to which the rest of the army are subject. Corporal punishment is not inflicted on them where death is not merited. In such cases they are allowed the privilege of being strangled, whilst others for similar offences are impaled or decapitated.

The janissaries are looked upon as the finest troops of the empire, and are styled infantry; yet those who are sufficiently wealthy to purchase horses are allowed to do so, and are therefore a confused body of horse and foot without order or discipline. Their cavalry is divided into twenty legions, and are totally ignorant of tactics. They are commanded by the chief of the artillery. Their cannon are enormously heavy, and are generally drawn by buffaloes.

There are many corps of volunteers, who choose their own officers. Their sole motive for embodying themselves arises from the hope of plunder. They receive no pay till they arrive at their quarters; and to defray the expenses of their journey they generally plunder the traveller. On their arrival at the camp, they receive the same pay as the janissaries.

They get no clothing from government, and therefore have no kind of uniform, so that every individual dresses as he pleases.

The arms of the wealthy are highly ornamented with silver. They consist of a gun slung over the shoulder; a long case of pistols which they carry under a belt; likewise a dagger and sabre, the 'cutter,' as sharp as a razor and very crooked. They charge with great impetuosity, the sabre in the form of tierce over the head, and aim at the throat of their enemy, but they are soon broke by the German Horse, owing to their steady coolness and discipline.

The army is divided into three encampments, none of which they ever take the precaution or advantage of entrenching. They pitch their tents, without any order, near the most convenient watering place. In the centre is the Grand Vizier's camp. On the right the Agha's, who is second in command; and on the left is the artillery. Their tents, are very magnificent. I was told that in the late war the Grand Vizier's cost no less a sum than 100,000 piastres. A retreat is always followed by a total defeat, as they never take any steps to secure themselves from surprise. On these occasions they grow quite outrageous, and frequently rob and murder each other. In one of their campaigns they attacked the Grand Vizier's tent, which contained the military chest, in which much treasure was deposited. They carried it off; and at the same time destroyed his beautiful pavilion. So much for their order and discipline in 1789. Since that period, I have heard that some considerable improvement has taken place, and that the present Sultan Selim has introduced French tactics, and employs many engineers, all of whom are French.

# CHAPTER VI

Departure from Constantinople – The Dardanelles –
Ancient Troy – Return to Smyrna – Homer's Cavern
– Population of Smyrna – Ephesus – The River
Meander – Fogia Nova – Scio – Patmos – A Greek
Seminary – St John the Evangelist – St John of Acre
– Nazareth – The Church of the Annunciation – The
Governor of Nazareth.

Everything being ready for my voyage, having engaged the sloop
*Constantinople* to convey me to Smyrna, and taken leave of my friends,
we went on board on 21 January. But we were detained so long by the
custom-house officers that we were obliged to shew our letter from
the Captain Bashaw and the firman from the Grand Signior, before we
could prevail on those impudent miscreants to let us depart. As it was
calm, Mr B---, first lieutenant of the *Pearl*, offered us his boats to tow
us out of the harbour, and being extremely impatient to get to Smyrna,
where I expected a great number of letters, not having received any
since I left England, I accepted his kind offer. We were soon towed
beyond the Seraglio point, when a light breeze springing up, we set all
the sail we could carry and soon found ourselves in the Sea of Marmora
(so called from the island of that name), through which we had a very
tedious navigation.

It was not till the evening of 24 December that we anchored off the
Castle of the Dardanelles, on the Asiatic side. The English vice-consul,
for whom we had dispatches from our Ambassador, on hoisting our
colours, came off to us. He gave us to understand that we could not

possibly procure the necessary clearance from the Castle before the next day. We were therefore obliged to submit patiently, though the wind was fair all that night. About twelve o'clock the next day we got under way.

The Castle on the Asiatic side appears to the best advantage in point of strength. The batteries are almost on a level with the water. The cannons are fixed, and some of them throw balls of two and three hundredweight quite across the Strait. These castles are considered by the Turks as the chief defence of Constantinople, nor has this city any other on the side of the Sea of Marmora. Their batteries may very well answer the purpose of preventing merchants' ships from sailing up the Strait before they be visited by the officers of the customs, as they do not choose to expose themselves to the dangers of an attack. But the idea of their obstructing or preventing the passage of an armed naval force! In case a fleet were determined to pass, they might do it very easily without receiving the least injury, according as the winds and currents favoured them. Or they might, in a very short time, not only silence the artillery of the Turks but reduce the castles to a heap of ruins.

We stood this evening with a fair but light wind, close off the Hellespont, weathered the Cape of the Janissaries, formerly called Sigeum, and sailed along the coast of ancient Troy, of whose proud walls and stately edifices not one stone remains, or vestige to point out to the curious traveller where this once renowned city stood! And nothing appears but a few villages scattered along the coast.

One of these villages is called Ghiam Kioz, or the 'Village of the Infidels,' from its being entirely inhabited by Greeks, who on account of their working in the mines belonging to the Grand Signior, are exempted from the *karragio*, or capitation tax, which is annually levied on all the subjects of his dominions. We stood on with a fair wind, and passed the islands of Lemnos and Tenedos, and in the evening made the island of Mitylene, the ancient Lesbos. Here the wind veered round to the north-east, and the captain persisting in his intention of sailing between the island of Mitylene and the continent, instead of keeping to the westward of it, we lost much time in fruitless attempts to effect that purpose, so that we did not make the Gulf of Smyrna before the morning of 27 January.

When we were off the small islands, les files Angloises (for what reason so called, I know not), the wind quite died away, and tho' above five leagues from Smyrna, yet such was our impatience to hear news from England that we took the boat. Off the castle we fell in with our old friend the *London*, Capt. N---, with whom I had sailed to Smyrna. He had waited for us till that morning, and we felt ourselves severely disappointed on finding that he could not wait a moment longer for us, though I offered him £500.

We were received in the most friendly manner by Messrs. Lees, and the female part of the family, who seriously reprimanded us for having made so long a stay at Constantinople. But my anxiety and mortification can neither be imagined or described, when, on enquiring for my letters, I was told there were none for me, tho' three packets had arrived from England since I left Smyrna. My fortitude was not equal to this severe disappointment, which brought on a violent fever. My kind and attentive friend did not leave me one moment during my illness, but had his bed made on the floor in my room.

In about a fortnight every alarming symptom of my illness was removed, and with the assistance of a great deal of bark, and the agreeable company of the ladies, who did me the favour to come and sit in my room every evening, I soon recovered my health, strength and spirits.

As there were at Smyrna several interesting objects, which I had not an opportunity of viewing before, I therefore took advantage of the first moments of convalescence to perambulate the city and examine several beautiful buildings, the most remarkable of which is an immense and majestic Caravansary, which contains a vast number of apartments very well distributed.

We continued our walk to the ancient Circus or Stadium, where a kind of portico is still to be seen, under which, as tradition will have it, the statue of Homer had been placed. This city claims the honour of having given birth to the prince of poets, and to this day the very spot is shewn, on the banks of the Meles, where Critheis, his mother, gave him birth, and the cavern where he is supposed to have retired to compose his immortal works.

Its inhabitants still amount to 100,000; 60,000 of whom are Turks, 20,000 Greeks, 10,000 Jews, and the rest Armenians, or Franks. The latter denomination is applied to Europeans. They all inhabit the Street of the Franks, which much resembles a Christian city, and live very comfortably.

Here are spoken Italian, French, English and Dutch. All religions are tolerated, and the different churches, mosques and temples which present themselves to the view make a very singular appearance.

Difference of religion does not interrupt the harmony which subsists among them. Commerce, that leveller of all ranks and source of all our enjoyments, triumphs over the despotism of Eastern tyrants, and over the still more destructive scourge of fanaticism. All their pursuits are directed towards amassing, with as little labour possible, an easy and competent fortune, and enjoying all the comforts and conveniences of life that a happy climate and a pleasant neighbourhood can afford. Thus the merchants receive all strangers with affability, and vie with each other in shewing every mark of polite attention and hospitality. They all have country-houses, keep dogs and racers, and in short, live in a style of elegance little inferior to that of an English nobleman.

I did not wish to leave Smyrna before I had visited Ephesus, about forty miles south of this town, so famous for its temple of Diana. It is called by the Turks Aja Saluk. It had likewise been the asylum of St Paul and the Virgin Mary after the death of our Saviour. Prodigious heaps of marble, columns, capitals and broken statues, scattered through a most beautiful and fertile plain, seem to attest its ancient splendour. It is now a miserable village, inhabited by thirty or forty Greek families. The fortress, which is upon an eminence, seems to have been the work of the Greek emperors. The Eastern Gate, called the Gate of Persecution, has still three beautiful basso-relievos. The temple of Diana had been turned into a church by the primitive Christians, but nothing now remains of it except the foundations and five or six marble columns, all of one entire piece, sixty feet in length and seven in diameter. Near it, at the foot of the mountain, we saw the Grotto of the Seven Sleepers, so called because it served as a refuge for seven knights persecuted by Diocletian. About four miles further on, we saw the prison of St Paul, a small building on an eminence, where four rooms are still distinguishable.

From hence we had a delightful view of the surrounding plain and the river Meander, whose fantastic serpentine windings, it is supposed, gave Daedalus the idea of building his Labyrinth in Crete.

This recalled to my remembrance the beautiful lines of Ovid:

Non secus ac liquidus Phrygiis Maeander in arvis
Ludit, et ambiguo lapsu refluitque fluitque,
Occurrensque sibi venturas aspicit undas;
Et nunc ad fontes, nunc ad mare versus apertum,
Incertas exercet aquas. Ita Daedalus implet

Innumeras errore vias; vixque ipse reverti
Ad limen potuit, tanta est fallacia tecti.

Our departure from Smyrna was fixed for 3 February. The captain of
the *Heureuse Marie* was to send his boat for us at midnight. I could
not help expressing and really feeling much regret at being obliged to
make so short a stay with Messrs. L--- and their worthy family, from
whom I experienced every kindness and attention that sincere friendship could dictate. After supper we went on board, and by daybreak
found ourselves only off the Castle of Smyrna, as the wind had been
contrary all night, nor did we clear the bay, which is only fifteen leagues
in length, till the evening of 5 February, and during the time we were
obliged to come twice to an anchor and go on shore, where we found
much diversion in shooting swans, of which thousands are to be seen
on the northern side of this gulf.

Towards evening we were forced into the harbour of Fogia Nova, at
the mouth of the Gulf of Smyrna. Here we were detained by a storm
until 9 February. On anchoring here we were the only ship in the
harbour, but before the next morning sixteen sail more were driven
in by the violence of a southerly gale. This town was formerly called
Phocia, it was destroyed last year by the Russians, and exhibits now a
mere heap of ruins, with only a few scattered houses remaining. The
harbour has sufficient water to float the largest ship of the line, but the
entrance is very narrow. On the south side stands a Castle which had
been likewise destroyed by the enemy, but the Turks, considering it of
much importance, have since rebuilt it.

During our stay here we went out every day to shoot, and though
we had no pointers we met with more partridges in one hour than
I had ever seen in any one day of my life. We also shot some hares,
pheasants and quails.

In returning from one of our shooting parties, we were accosted
by a very respectable looking Mahometan, who testified a desire of
accompanying us on board to see our ship. As we intended to return
on shore after dinner, we complied with his request. He seemed much
pleased with our attention to him, and highly praised the flavour of
our bottled porter, to which the Turks in general show no dislike. He
approved much of our English cookery, but when a knife and fork were
presented to him, he appeared a good deal surprised, and in attempting
to use them as we did he betrayed his awkwardness by evident marks

on his mouth and fingers. He then had recourse to his old method, which he found the best, and made a pretty good use of those means of attack which nature has provided; the only weapons, in that kind of warfare, used by the first men in the country and even by the Grand Signior himself.

When dinner was over we offered him some wine, which he refused, but he drank off a whole bottle of rum, and was scarcely satisfied with it. However, as it was scarce with us, I proposed that we should give him some lavender-water: having read in de Tott's Memoirs that the Turks sometimes drink large quantities of this violent spirit. A bottle was brought, accordingly, of which he partook very plentifully, and I really think he would have finished the bottle, if I had not prevented him by strongly representing the dangerous consequences of an immoderate use of such liquids. As the rum and lavender began to operate, I could not help giving way to very serious apprehensions, for when a Turk gets intoxicated he makes no scruple of killing the first Greek or *giaour* he meets, and for this offence he only receives a slight bastinado. I was glad, however, that our guest kept himself quiet, and never attempted to draw his sabre or pistols. We took him on shore and then left him to take care of himself.

## 9 February

We set sail from this place. The wind continued fair till we had weathered Cape Callaburne, and made the island of Spelmadore, when it shifted to the east. We were, however, enabled to sail along the coast of Scio, a beautiful and fertile island. By twelve we were abreast of the town, which is very large and handsome. Much trade is carried on here, particularly in cotton and corn. The former article is exported to Smyrna for the European markets, and the latter to Constantinople for the consumption of that metropolis. Scio is reckoned the richest island in the Archipelago.

For two successive days we experienced contrary winds, and it was with the greatest difficulty we could keep the sea. By 11 February we were off the island of Nicaria, and in the evening we made the islands of Samos and Fournis. At ten at night, the gale increased to such a degree that the captain thought it prudent to run for the island of Patmos. Scarcely had we made the harbour when it blew such a hurricane as would probably have proved fatal had we kept at sea, encircled as we should have been by land on every side. We therefore congratulated each other on being snug in a good harbour, and among the prettiest women of the Archipelago. This is a most beautiful little harbour, in the shape of a horse-shoe and sheltered against every wind.

We walked up to the town, which is built on the highest part of the island, about a mile from the beach. Here, at the door of a mean-look-ing house, I saw the most beautiful woman I ever set my eyes on, and as her husband was a silversmith we had frequent opportunities, under various pretences, of seeing and admiring this exquisitely-finished piece of nature's handywork.

I bought several gold and silver medals of the husband, and finding that the mother-in-law had a particular liking for them, we each of us were favoured with an opportunity of mutual gratification; I in complying with my spirit of generosity, and she in testifying her sense of gratitude.

We went to see a kind of seminary which is established here. It is the only college but one in the Archipelago or the Levant, and to this college or university all the Grecian youths are sent for their educa-tion! What a difference between this and the School of Athens! Here nothing is acquired but bigotry and effeminacy. Nothing now remains of the manly virtues of ancient heroes, so energetically recorded by cotemporary authors, and justly admired by succeeding generations. The present inhabitants are only distinguished for meanness, poverty and ignorance.

One of the youths educated here formed an acquaintance with Pauolo, for the purpose of procuring some bread from me, as the poor lad was nearly starving. I ordered him 500 biscuits, which he said would last him during his stay in the island, as he intended to return to Cyprus, his own country, as soon as he had finished his studies.

Near this college is a cavern in the rock, now converted into a chapel. You are told that St John wrote his gospel in this cave and you are shown the place where he slept, the iron hooks driven into the roof which the superstitious visitors, who in general frequent this place, believe to be really those from which the bed of this man had been suspended.

We afterwards ascended the hill and paid our respects to the Superior of the Convent of St John, which, as we were informed by the friars, had been founded by St John the Evangelist. There is a very ancient chapel within the cloister, in which the saint is buried. They shewed us the coffin which contains his bones. It is placed in one of the niches of the wall, and covered with embroidered purple velvet, fastened on with many silver clasps. This piece of finery was very carefully locked, and I was informed that on particular festivals the coffin was opened and mass celebrated in the chapel in honour of St John.

I wished to have the coffin opened, to satisfy my doubts whether bones could remain after so many ages. But my curiosity could not be gratified without a liberal donation on my part. I therefore opened my purse-strings, and a lusty friar opened the coffin, but not till after he had sprinkled a proper quantity of holy water, crossed himself several times, and prayed upwards of twenty minutes. He then presented to my view a most disgusting spectacle: but most of the bystanders, after uttering a short prayer, kissed these precious relics with the greatest fervour. I was fully convinced that these could not be the bones of St John, but the skeleton of some other person, placed there as his representative, for on some parts of the head, the hair was still remaining. There is no doubt, however, but that this is the spot where St John wrote his gospel, and that he died in this island.

Both the monastery and chapel are very old. They were repaired by Constantine the Great, in the beginning of his reign. There are some very ancient paintings in the chapel, which I suppose were done by a Russian artist, as they appear to have the characteristics of those described by Mr Cox in his Travels, who asserts that painting was first attempted in Russia, and from thence brought into Italy. They are finished on a yellow ground, are gilt, and the outlines very strong and prominent.

The inhabitants of this little island are all Greeks. There is not one Turk resident in Patmos.

The Capitan Bashaw keeps one of his vessels stationed here, for the purpose of collecting the *carragio*, or capitation tax. The taxes laid on the inhabitants are really intolerable, as every individual pays nearly one half of what he possesses. This vessel is also supposed to protect the island from pirates, but the day before we arrived a vessel was plundered in the harbour, and other outrages committed on the inhabitants, without any attempt being made by the Bashaw's men to prevent them. I was assured that, when an opportunity offered, those very protectors turned pirates and plundered with impunity.

We were introduced to a French gentleman who practised physic. We found him truly obliging, and his politeness and friendly attention contributed much to render our situation here agreeable during our stay. He engaged to give us a dance the Sunday following and introduce us to all the prettiest women of this island. To conciliate this useful man's friendship still more, I made him a present of my medicine-chest, with which he had fallen in love, and in return I met, at the doctor's dance, the silversmith's charming wife, dressed out in all her finery.

They have in this island a dance peculiar to themselves, which I did not admire, as it is wholly destitute of meaning. The men take each their particular partners, under the arm, and making a rondeau, they sing as they pursue this circle, in an uninterrupted rotation, while the musician remains standing in the middle. This often continues two hours together.

They have another extraordinary custom: there is a large hole in the fiddler's instrument, and as the dance is going on, if a gentleman wishes to show any particular respect to his fair one, he drops some money into this opening as he passes the musician, which is considered as a mark of profound esteem and admiration. Our complaisant doctor afterwards favoured us with several other pleasant parties, so that we could not help feeling some degree of regret when, on 17 February, a propitious gale suggested the expediency of our departure from this friendly island.

We were but six days on our passage from Patmos to the coast of Syria. The weather being very rough, we were obliged to run for the port of St John De Acre instead of Jaffa, preferring to travel from Acre to Jerusalem by land to remaining any longer at the mercy of the waves. We entered Caiffa Bay and immediately anchored. This is the winter road for ships trading to the coast of Syria, and is about three leagues distant from the town of St John of Acre, which forms the northeast-ern extremity of this vast bay, whilst Mount Carmel forms that to the south-west; and immediately at the foot of this mountain stands the small town of Caiffa Nova, from which the bay takes its name.

A Moor, who lives here and is employed by the vice-consul of Acre in visiting the English ships, very politely offered us his services, and we were soon joined by the consul himself, who very civilly introduced us to his family, by whom we were most graciously received. As we approached the town, on the southern side of which there is a very fine sandy beach, we observed upwards of two hundred of the Bashaw's soldiers exercising on horse-back.

A dinner was prepared for us at the consul's. We did not sit long at table, being desirous to make our respects to Jedzar Bashaw, who holds his Court here, and governs with the most despotic sway. Indeed, we were told that our waiting on him was a duty indispensable with regard to our safety; as providing ourselves with passports from this powerful Turk would much facilitate our progress, and protect us from thence to Jerusalem. We had scarcely dined when a message was brought us from the Bashaw, intimating his desire to see us at his Palace, by the vice-consul, who served us as dragoman on the occasion.

On our arrival at the Palace, we were conducted thro' several spacious apartments, and thence to a gallery of immense length, from whence we descended by a flight of one hundred steps, when we found ourselves in a delightful garden, laid out with much taste, at the end of which we perceived the Bashaw seated under a monstrous magnolia, which with several other evergreens was at that time in full blow.

As we entered the garden, he sent part of the attendants that surrounded him to meet and conduct us to the spot where he chose to give us an audience. He ordered me to be seated on his right hand, my fellow traveller on his left, while the humiliating posture of the vice-consul shocked me. He kneeled before him, and trembled with every limb. I was happy, however, to find that he was only the British consul's deputy, at that time on business at Aleppo.

After the usual compliments, we were served with refreshments of various kinds, differing little from what I had seen at Constantinople. I did not, however, feel so much at ease and was much at a loss how to account for evident marks of terror in the countenance of the kneeling consul.

After partaking of fifty different sorts of sweetmeats, etc., Jedzar began the conversation by asking me if I had not heard of his great power and warlike exploits. I told him I had often heard his name mentioned at Constantinople in terms highly honourable; and could I then foresee that I should land at St John of Acre, I should have provided myself with letters of introduction to his highness. He said these were by no means necessary, that the stranger had always a protector in him, particularly those of my nation, whom he held in much higher estimation than those of any other country in Europe.

He continued the conversation by giving me a full account of his life and adventures, particularly his wars against the unfortunate Ali Bey, a Calif of Egypt, whom he conquered and afterwards put to death. Volney is very accurate in his *History of Egypt* and relates in a most affecting manner the misfortunes of this unhappy prince. But the greatest barbarity exercised by Jedzar in all his conquests happened some years after he had the command of the district of Acre and Nazareth, when his oppression and cruelties became so intolerable to the inhabitants that they were obliged to revolt against the Porte.

Jedzar was ordered by the Sultan to march against the insurgents, and tho' in the first campaign he was rather worsted, owing to the number of the malcontents, yet in the second he so far recovered his loss that, with a force of only 6,000, he defeated 20,000. This battle was fought near Damascus. The Bashaw of that town was killed by Jedzar, and 1,200 prisoners taken, consisting of men, women and children, who were, by his order, sent to Acre, and there, without distinction of age or sex, butchered in cold blood. Jedzar freighted three Venetian vessels and sent the heads of those victims, packed in boxes, to Constantinople – a most acceptable present to his Sultan.

Among the women to be slaughtered on this occasion, there was one of exquisite beauty, she was only fifteen years old. The merchants of Acre, more, I fear, to give the Bashaw a pretext to violate an oath he had taken, 'that all concerned in this rebellion should die,' and that he might add this beautiful girl to his *haram*, than from motives of humanity, petitioned him to spare the life of this unfortunate fair one: but the monster was relentless. He, however, in order to shew the French merchants every possible consideration that could not be construed a violation of his oath, said he would mitigate her sentence, and instead of having her head cut off by the hands of the common executioner, he himself would confer that honour, and accordingly assembled the factory, intimating his desire that all should attend. None dared to disobey, and in the presence of them all, he with some difficulty tied the hands of this beautiful girl behind her back, and drawing his sabre, with one blow severed the head from the body.

It was for this bloody business he was raised to the highest rank among the Turks; and he had the Third Tail sent him on this occasion, from the Porte. He likewise assumed the title of Jedzar, which in Arabic signifies 'butcher'; and surely no title could be more applicable.

He had, at the time of our audience, upwards of three hundred men at work in his garden, who all appeared very attentive to what they were doing, and seldom ventured to raise their eyes from the ground.

One unfortunate fellow, whose crime I could never learn, happened to displease him. He ordered him immediately to be brought before him, and looking at him with eyes inflamed with savage fury, he had him stripped in our presence, and drawing from behind his robe a silver hammer of about four pounds weight was preparing to inflict on the unfortunate victim that punishment I shall now describe, but which I had the heartfelt satisfaction, thro' my intercession, to have mitigated, and a severe bastinadoing expiated his fault. And when the Bashaw's passion cooled a little, I ventured to express a desire of knowing the virtues of this tremendous hammer, and received the following explanation. When Jedzar does not choose to inflict the punishment of death on any of his offending slaves, he orders him to be laid across a bar of wood, with his hands and feet held to the ground; he then, with his hammer, strikes the culprit on the backbone, which immediately brings on a palsy, that ends only with the death of the wretched offender, or, if the blow be very violent, destroys him in a few hours.

While I reflected with indignation on the savage cruelty of this monster, I was suddenly roused by the softest music and the footsteps of many females at the other end of the garden. These were the Bashaw's women: they were two hundred in number, dressed all alike in white, and veiled, as usual, from top to toe. The Bashaw ordered them to walk slowly by him, which ceremony they performed with the most profound silence. This he meant as the greatest compliment he could pay us, but, for my part, I should most willingly have dispensed with this treat. My mind was too much taken up with gloomy reflections on the cruel hammer scene, and the wretched state of servility to which these unfortunate women were doomed, to be gratified with any mark of this Bashaw's favour or complaisance.

I was told by the consul that it was time we should take our leave, and considering that he had been a full hour on his knees, 'tis no wonder he should think so. I desired he would ask the Bashaw when he would be ready to receive some presents I had a wish to make him. He smiled, and appointed that evening. We, therefore, for the present took our leave.

I had not arrived at the consul's when I received a visit from Jedzar's dragoman, accompanied by two slaves. The one brought me a rich furred pelisse, the other presented a handsome pipe and a few pounds of coffee. In return, I waited on the Bashaw, and presented him with a pair of pistols, beautifully ornamented in gold and silver. He could not conceal his admiration of them; they were of the best workmanship and cost 100 guineas. He desired to know if they were as good as they were handsome. I answered in the affirmative, and at his desire loaded them, and having placed a bit of paper, about the size of a crown piece, at twelve yards' distance, he fired and made a pretty good shot. But loading the pistols a second time himself he put in a double charge of powder, which hurt his hand very much and he shot wide of the mark.

This he could not account for, and it was with much difficulty I convinced him that with half the quantity of gunpowder he would shoot better, which, at his request, I proved by hitting the mark three times running, at which he was both pleased and astonished. At length I took my leave and left him in good humour and highly gratified.

This reflection superinduced others, which entirely precluded sleep. I arose at eight, and took my leave of this hospitable bon vivant, fully determined to pass some time with him at my return from Jerusalem.

The following day we were detained a considerable time by those who were to furnish us with mules for our journey, and tho' we had saddles of our own they would not permit us to make use of them: we were forced to ride on large pack-saddles, without a bridle, and the only means we had of directing the animals was to strike them with a stick, sometimes on one side and sometimes on the other. We had no sooner left the strand than we discovered that those Turks who were sent with us as guides were as ignorant as ourselves of the road to Nazareth.

At eleven we stopped to breakfast, and on a sudden found ourselves surrounded by Arabs, to the number of twenty, headed by a chief. They immediately sat themselves down, and before we had time to look about us, devoured our breakfast, everyone seizing whatever fell in his way. This, however, was all the injury they did us, and when they heard we were going to Nazareth, the chief offered us one of his men as a guide.

I acknowledge that I dreaded this man's company, lest he should in the night-time lead us out of our way, and, assisted by other wanderers, rob and plunder us. Pauolo soon dispelled my fears, by assuring me that these were friendly Arabs, and that we had nothing to apprehend till we had passed Nazareth. This Arab was to accompany us as far as that town. As we fell into the right road, about sunset, we determined to stop at the first house that should have the hospitality to receive us.

At nine we arrived at a small village called Scietamor, only twenty miles distant from St John de Acre.

This neighbourhood is famous for its cotton, which is esteemed the best in all Galilee.

We knocked at many doors, but in vain. I could not restrain my indignation, and almost expressed a wish that the words of Christ might be fulfilled on this inhospitable people. After having rambled above an hour, we were at length admitted into the house of a Greek priest, in which we took up our lodgings for the night.

Our landlord was married, had a large family and a small house, containing one room only, where we were to pass the night. The house could afford nothing better than some milk and eggs. After our frugal supper, we spread our mattresses on one side of the fire-place, and our servants lay at our feet. The curé and his wife were opposite to us, and the young ladies of the family lay at some distance. Ludicrous as this scene may appear, it neither discomposed our gravity or prevented us from passing a very comfortable night.

At six in the morning we were again on foot; and after having thanked our hospitable clergyman, we set forward on our journey. We arrived at Nazareth about two, and alighted at the Convent of the Annunciation, so called because the church is built on the very spot where the house of the Holy Virgin stood, and where she was visited by the angel. The country in the environs of Nazareth is very mountainous and wild. It does not answer the description given of this memorable place in the scriptures. The holy fathers of the Convent themselves acknowledge that the entire face of the country must have undergone a considerable change.

The Father-superior and the Procurer-general of the Convent received us in the most friendly and hospitable manner. We had very good beds and comfortable rooms, and every possible attention and respect paid to us. These gentlemen advised us to dismiss those people we had brought with us from Acre, together with our mules, promising that they would furnish us with good mules, experienced conductors and trusty guards, which their intimacy with the Governor of the town would enable them to procure.

Dinner being ready we were conducted by those worthy priests into a great hall, where we found an excellent repast prepared for us, tho' it was then Lent, which is most strictly observed by those Friars.

After dinner they conducted us to the Church of the Annunciation, which fully answered the idea we had formed of it. St Helena, the mother of Constantine the Great, had built a most magnificent temple here, which had been almost destroyed by the Saracens at different periods. It was repaired in 1620 by the Fathers of the Holy Land, who since that time have been constantly making some improvements to it. The whole convent is now surrounded by a thick wall, to protect it against any sudden attack of the Arabs. The church has three aisles, divided by stone pillars; and in the centre is the great altar, dedicated to the angel Gabriel. Behind it is the choir, and underneath the Grotto and Chapel of the Annunciation. The superb staircase, by which you descend to it, consists of fifteen steps of the finest marble, at the foot of which is the place where the gracious message from heaven, announcing the birth of a Saviour, was delivered to the Virgin Mary.

The Altar of the Annunciation is very beautiful, being adorned with a variety of fine marbles, well inlaid. Over the altar is a fine painting, representing the Virgin Mary, and the angel saluting her. On the whole nothing can be more beautiful than this little church, in which all the numberless ceremonies of the greatest Catholic churches and cathedrals in Europe are strictly observed.

From this church we were conducted to the other parts of this convent, which are both spacious and commodious. All the doors are of iron, and the walls are immensely thick and solid. Attached to the convent are the various gardens and offices, kept solely for the entertainment of the pilgrims on their way to and return from the Holy Sepulchre. Their stay is limited to three days and no longer, during which time they are treated in the most hospitable manner without the least expense on their part. There are but fifteen Friars in this convent, though sufficiently endowed, in every respect, for ten times that number. After we had viewed the convent we went to see a Grotto, in which is shewn a stone of an oval form; 3 feet in height by 4 in breadth and 7 in length; on which Jesus Christ is said to have dined with his disciples.

We then visited a church which is said to have been formerly the Synagogue in which our Saviour proved, that in his person was fulfilled the prophecy of Isaiah relating to his mission.

On our return to the convent the Superior proposed that we should visit the Deputy-governor, who resides here. He is under the Bashaw of St John De Acre, collects his revenues, has the care of all his concerns, and the control over all his subjects in the vast district of Nazareth. Though a Greek, he possesses both the legislative and executive power, and holds the inhabitants of this wild country in the most abject subjection, and is by them honoured as their prince.

On entering his palace we were a little disappointed in our expectations, as it had the appearance of a house falling into ruins. This circumstance, however, when the cause was explained to us, raised him in our estimation, and served as a strong proof of his good sense, as it is this uninviting appearance of wretchedness alone, that saves both his head and wealth from the cruelty and avarice of his prince.

We ascended by a stone staircase to an apartment furnished *à la Turque*, with cushions and carpets, where we were presented to Ibrahim Calcussi, who received us very politely. After we were seated, sweet-meats and coffee were introduced, frankincense and perfumes of different kinds succeeded. I was next presented with a large pipe, which I readily accepted, being by this time become an expert smoker.

Our conversation turned chiefly on horses. Ibrahim informed me that the finest horses in all Arabia were bred in this part of the country. I expressed a wish to purchase one to take with me to Europe; but he could not assist me from a dread of incurring the anger of the Bashaw, should it be discovered that he had been instrumental in procuring me one. He accepted a spy-glass which I offered him, and in return gave me a large phial of attar of roses. He regretted that we could not make a longer stay at Nazareth, as he would give us an escort of twenty soldiers, who were then absent on a different service, however, he spared us one of his guards, who, he had no doubt, would prove a sufficient protection till we arrived at Napolosa, the Governor of which town would give us a proper guard, in case of necessity.

Having now returned to the convent, one of the Friars showed us a very excellent collection of medals and antiques which he was forming for the Prince of Asturias. He examined the few I had, and promised me that at my return from Jerusalem he would part with any of those he had to oblige me.

## 26 February

We were on horseback by five o'clock. Our little caravan consisted of a dozen, including Ibrahim's soldier, who was well armed, and equally well mounted. His master had given him letters to the different Governors, both of Genia and Napolosa, where pilgrims pay tribute to the Jaffars, or Arabs, who farm, or take at a certain rate, this branch of the revenue. We were recommended to them in a particular manner, with a request that we should not be detained at either place, or required to pay the tax.

# PART II

# CHAPTER I

Departure from Nazareth – Genia – Its Governor – Napolosa – Its Ruins – Jerusalem – Its History – Conquered by King David – By Nebuchadnezzar – By Cyrus – By Pompey – By Titus – Demolished by Adrian – Who Lays the Foundation of a new City – Jerusalem taken by Omar.

On leaving Nazareth we travelled over an immense plain, the chief product of which was corn and cotton, after which we passed several hills that were rocky and barren. We were astonished at the number of partridges, which appeared like domestic fowl, running quite near us, without shewing the least sign of fear. We also met many foxes and numerous herds of goats, and passed several encampments of wandering Arabs, who seemed to be employed in cultivating the ground and tending their flocks.

Before we arrived at Genia, we desired Ibrahim's soldier to proceed before us and settle everything with the Jaffars before we came up, in order to prevent any unnecessary delay.

On our entering the town, we found him engaged in a debate with the Chief of the Jaffars; who insisted on our paying 15 piastres per head before we were permitted to pass. Our soldier, with whose conduct we had every reason to be well satisfied, espoused our cause very warmly, notwithstanding the virulent abuse to which he exposed himself, by thus taking the part of infidels. I begged of him to comply with their demands but he was determined in his resolution of not submitting to this exaction, declaring that his compliance would be a direct insult to Ibrahim, his master, whose authority he would maintain at the hazard of his life.

The debate still continued without any hope of an accommodation, or concession on either side, when at last we were obliged to have recourse to the Governor's interference. But before we could see him, we found ourselves surrounded by some hundreds of the savage inhabitants, who were now become so violent and determined in their demands, and accompanied them with menaces of such horrid import, as filled us with the most serious apprehensions for our safety and thus did this soldier, in order to preserve his master's honour from insult, expose us to the danger of losing our lives.

On our producing the Grand Signior's firman, the Jaffars did not scruple to say that they totally disregarded it, and we soon perceived that this Governor enjoyed his title without any degree of influence or authority being attached to it. He could not prevail on the people to give up their demands, but they, at last, consented to reduce them to one fourth of the sum they first insisted on and the Governor resigned, with pleasure, his share of the tribute, out of respect to Ibrahim's letter. The people of the town soon became our friends when we paid the money. They persuaded us to proceed no farther this day, lest we should be stopped on the road, and our conductors expressing the same apprehensions, we determined, though reluctantly, to spend the night here.

We had just sat down to supper when a message was brought from the Governor, intimating that he would do us the honour of drinking some wine with us, and soon after his excellency made his appearance. After a few compliments he sat down, and though he declared that he had already supped, he devoured a chicken in a moment and ate the best part of a leg of mutton which we intended to reserve for our breakfast the next day.

Seeing some silver forks, he desired, with earnest curiosity to know their use, which being explained to him he could not help admiring both the ingenuity and assiduity of Christians in promoting whatever tends to the comforts and conveniences of life. This was a very uncommon compliment from a Mahometan but, however deficient he might have been in respect to these accomplishments he so much admired in Christians, he shewed, at least, by his zeal in libations to the rosy god, that he had a taste for the sweets of life. However, feeling the powerful effects of repeated bumpers, and fearing a discovery of the breach of his Prophet's prohibition, he at last got up, and with some difficulty withdrew to his seraglio, which was close to our habitation.

He had not been long gone, when we were alarmed with an unusual outcry and screaming, which we were soon informed was the effect of his excellency's intemperance; for by this time the fumes of the wine he had so copiously swallowed, began to manifest their full power in stimulating him to acts of violence and cruelty towards his unfortunate wives.

The next day we were on horseback by five, and having proceeded a few miles we found ourselves in the midst of the wildest country imaginable. Soon afterwards we passed a castle, built on an eminence, which is said to have been erected by King David. We stopped near a spring to breakfast, but before we had done our soldier, whose vigilance and impatience we had observed while we were eating, advised us to make no longer stay as the place was inhabited by hordes of Arabs, who had sworn vengeance against those of Nazareth, because one of their tribe had been taken in the act of committing a robbery beyond the limits of their district, and was beheaded by the Governor of Nazareth for this encroachment on his exclusive privilege. In such cases blood for blood is the only atonement, and as we did not wish that ours should expiate their crimes we instantly mounted and set forward with all speed.

About one we arrived in safety at Napolosa, the ancient capital of Samaria, mentioned by Herodotus, which we found crowded with people assembled for the purpose of celebrating a victory that the Bashaw of Damascus, just returned from Mecca, had obtained over another Bashaw who had usurped his government during his absence. Knowing that on those occasions the Turks are very insolent, we went immediately to the house of a Greek Catholic to whom we had been recommended by the Superior of the Convent of Nazareth, and at the same time determined not to leave the house until we had made our arrival known to the Governor. We therefore sent our soldier to him and received a very friendly answer, assuring us we might rely on his protection, and at the same time he appointed one of his Guards to accompany us through the town. We then walked out to see the different curiosities that might naturally be expected in this city, once the seat of the kings of Samaria, then called Sichem, the capital of this celebrated country.

There are but a few ruins to attract the notice of the traveller. The most remarkable is a mosque, formerly a magnificent church built by St Helena, and still in some repair. The gateway is of Gothic architecture, supported on beautiful pillars of white marble, it was never decorated with figures of any kind, and though very ancient, is in good preservation, having yet escaped the destructive hands of the Turks. Ruins of temples, numbers of capitals, and fragments of columns lay scattered in different places.

Here our faithful soldier, whom Ibrahim had given us, was to take his leave, and as the most dangerous road was in this neighbourhood, it became necessary for us to strengthen our guard. We therefore applied to the Governor, who directed us to the Sheik, or Chief, of the Arabs. This man was a brave, enterprising fellow, who, on our request being made to him, offered to accompany us himself, but to this the Governor would not consent. He allowed us two of his captains and two other soldiers. When we expressed some uneasiness at the apparent insufficiency of the number, he laid hold of his beard and swore he would be answerable for our safety. This sacred appeal satisfied us, and we determined to set off at sunset, as we were assured by the landlord and other Christians in the town that our surest way to avoid the danger of being attacked in a wood at some leagues' distance was to pass it in the night-time.

At the close of the evening we left the town as silently as possible. Our guides and guards opened the march, M--- and I followed next, and our servants and baggage brought up the rear. By five in the morning of 28 February we found ourselves one mile beyond the dangerous wood. Our entire escort consisted of fourteen men, which I considered equal to double that number of Arabs, as we were all well armed with guns, blunder-busses, and pistols. We had nothing more to fear, and as we ascended to the top of a very high mountain our guards showed us, at some distance behind, the tents of the tribe with whom they were at war, whose custom it is to fall upon their enemies from some ambuscade in the wood through which we had passed an hour before.

We met several other tribes of these wanderers, and though all well armed they did not attempt in the least to molest us. At nine we came to a fountain hewn out of the solid rock, where we halted to breakfast and refreshed our tired mules, after having rode eight hours without stopping, at the rate of four miles an hour, over a most rocky country where scarcely a blade of grass could be seen. The hills in this country have a most singular appearance, being formed of strata of rock so regularly arranged that were it not for their magnitude one might be induced to suppose them the work of art.

About one we arrived at some ruins which we were informed had been one of the country seats of King Solomon. Soon after we passed a very high mountain, from whose summit we saw the Levant near Jaffa. Being informed by some Arabs that we were but a short way from Jerusalem, M--- and I pushed on as fast as our tired mules would permit us, impatient to get a sight of this memorable city, which had been so long the constant subject of our thoughts. All our anxiety and apprehensions now vanished at the transporting prospect of so soon finishing this expedition and again turning our faces homewards.

We were now in sight of the Holy City, which excited in our breasts emotions not to be described, but these soon gave place to a most lively sense of gratitude to that Providence which had protected us from all those dangers incident to the undertaking we had now accomplished. While thus our minds were filled with a mixture of gratitude and pious exultation, the recollection of our European friends crowded on our thoughts, and we would that moment give half the world to have been able to communicate to them a knowledge of our situation.

At half-past three we arrived, and entered Jerusalem by the Gate of Nazareth, and proceeded immediately to the Convent of the Terra Sancta, where we delivered our letters from the Spanish ambassador at Constantinople. The Superior and Procurator of the Convent received us in the politest manner, and showed us into very comfortable apartments, which, thirty years before, had been occupied by a countryman of mine, Mr Smith Barrey.

We afterwards paid our respects to the *Mushelim*, or governor of the town, to whom we had letters of recommendation from the Captain Bashaw, obtained by means of our good friend Sir R A---. The Bashaw was the intimate friend and protector of the Mushelim of Jerusalem, who held this important office through his interest; and, indeed, the politeness with which he received us, and the friendship he, on every occasion, manifested towards us, may be justly considered strong proofs of his gratitude and high esteem for his benefactor. He even offered us apartments in his palace, an honour which, however, we declined, as we were much better *à la Chrétienne* than *à la Turque*: but he insisted on our accepting the use of his horses during our stay, and a guard of janissaries to attend us. We promised to wait on him the following day, when we should be determined with respect to our future plans, and accordingly, portion out our time to the best advantage.

Having intimated a desire of visiting Bethlehem and Sodom we were advised by him not to think of going to Sodom with less than fifty soldiers well armed, as the whole road was infested by robbers, who plundered indiscriminately everyone who fell in their way, and even quarrelled among themselves. We therefore consulted our honest Superior, who confirmed the truth of these terrifying accounts by declaring that though he had been in the Convent upwards of forty years he had never yet ventured to go to Sodom, though but eight hours' ride from Jerusalem. He acknowledged indeed that the place, by all accounts, was well worth seeing, but at the same time would deem it the highest degree of temerity to encounter the many dangers and difficulties that stood in the way to this gratification. We therefore thought it prudent to yield to these reasonings, and rest satisfied with such curiosities as we should find at Jerusalem and at Bethlehem.

We set out with the dragoman of the Convent and two janissaries, and first stopped at the Temple of Solomon, which through so many ages has been celebrated for its grandeur and magnificence. As no Christian, since the Turks came into the possession of Jerusalem, has ever been admitted into it, we could not expect to be peculiarly favoured in this respect, except on condition of abjuring our faith and being banished for ever from our country and friends. We therefore contented ourselves with viewing the outside only of this stupendous and almost divinely magnificent monument of art.

I shall not enter into a circumstantial account of events or long historical detail, but merely confine myself to the principal revolutions it has undergone since its first foundation.

King David, after he had conquered Jerusalem, AM 2988, and built many superb edifices, formed the design of erecting a magnificent temple to the Lord, in which he proposed to place the Ark. The prophet Nathan told him that his intentions were acceptable in the sight of God, but that his son Solomon was the person whom the Lord had chosen to fulfil them. David, however, began to collect materials, in order to facilitate the work for Solomon, but was interrupted by one of his sons, Absalom, who took the city in the year 3009. Absalom being killed by Joab the city became again subject to David, who died in the year 3021.

Solomon soon rebuilt the walls of Jerusalem, and filled up with what remained of the rubbish the little valley between the hills Bozeta and Mona that he might have a proper place for the Temple. He began this great building in the twentieth year of his age, four years after the death of his father, and in seven years completed this stupendous work, which for its structure and the riches it contained became the admiration of surrounding nations.

The Temple being ready for the Ark it was brought from Mount Sion, then called the City of David, where it had remained under a magnificent Tabernacle, and was deposited in this Sanctuary. Solomon consecrated the Temple at the same time, and on this occasion offered a peace-offering of 22,000 oxen and 120,000 sheep. This happened at the time of the Jewish Festival, which commonly lasted seven days, but on account of this solemnization the tabernacles were kept open fourteen days, and on the fifteenth day the people, who had assembled to the number of 700,000, left the city. Solomon reigned peaceably forty years after, and died in the sixtieth year of his age, AM 3061. The wealth and splendour of Solomon's court, as mentioned in the Bible, exceeds everything of the kind ever known or recorded. He likewise built a palace for himself, which was the work of fourteen years, not having the materials collected beforehand as his father had for the Temple.

About the year 3436 Nebuchadnezzar took Jerusalem for the third time. It is from this period we may date the seventy years' captivity. He sent the king, his mother, wives and children, all the great men of his court, and 10,000 men captives into Babylon. He pillaged the Temple of all its treasures, and carried with him the sacred vessels which Solomon had made in the Temple of the Lord.

About a century after, Cyrus, king of Persia, conquered the kingdoms of Assyria and Babylon. He restored to the Jews the sacred vases of the Temple, which they were permitted to rebuild as the foundations only remained. This memorable event was foretold by Jeremiah the prophet. The Jews returned in crowds to Jerusalem and began to rebuild the Temple in the year 3517, according to certain dimensions given by Cyrus and afterwards by Darius the son of Hystaspes. They met with many impediments which were thrown in their way by the Samaritans, their neighbours and enemies.

In 3991 Pompey laid siege to Jerusalem, on the inhabitants refusing to pay a certain tribute which he demanded. He took the city and entered the Temple – even the Holy of Holies – but did not touch any of its treasures. This event took place in the consulship of Caius Antonius and M.T. Cicero.

In 4045 Herod the Great, who had considerably repaired and improved the city, added greatly to the Temple, which had been erected after the return of the Jews from captivity; and this he completed in eight years.

In the year of our Lord 70, Titus, who was the emperor Vespasian's Lieutenant in Syria, besieged Jerusalem at a time when it was rent by various desperate factions. The partisans of the two adverse factions meeting in the Temple, a dreadful conflict ensued, in which the sacred place was defiled with the blood of the inhabitants. After an obstinate resistance, from 14 April to 10 August, during which time the besieged underwent the severest hardships, the Romans entered the city, but met with such determined opposition that the Jews were not finally subdued till 2 September, in the year 71 of our Lord, and thirty-eight years after his crucifixion. The city was sacked by the Roman soldiery and the Temple a second time destroyed, an event which furnishes an awful attestation of the divine mission of our Saviour, as the actual accomplishment of his solemn prediction of those miseries which were to befall that ungrateful city, and the destruction of the Temple. The walls were entirely demolished, except at the western side, which Titus suffered to remain as a monument of the power of the Roman arms. The massy golden ornaments of the Temple were conveyed to Rome to grace the triumph of Titus, who entered the city in great pomp, and on that occasion received the title of Caesar.

Many Jews, however, still remained in Jerusalem, which in the year 118 rebelled under the reign of the emperor Trajan, and again under Adrian, who entirely destroyed the town and thus finally verified what the Lord had said 'There shall not be left here one stone upon another that shall not be thrown down'.

In 119 Adrian laid the foundations of a new city, which he called Aelia, from his name of Aelius Adrianus. On the spot where the Temple formerly stood he caused another to be built, dedicated to Jupiter Capitolinus. Thence the city was called Aelia Capitolina. The Jews were not allowed to enter it till the year 363, when Julian allowed them to rebuild the Temple. They crowded from all places to engage in this pleasing enterprise, but scarcely had they began it than all their materials were destroyed by an earthquake, which made them abandon the attempt, and give some credit to the prophecy of Daniel, 'He shall make it desolate, even unto the Consummation'.

However, in the year 643, Omar, Caliph of the Saracens and one of the successors of Mahomet, after having taken Jerusalem, began to build a superb mosque on the very spot where the Temple of Solomon once stood, and erected his building over the foundations of the other.

# CHAPTER II

Jerusalem continued – The Temple of the
Resurrection – The Holy Sepulchre – The House of
Pontius Pilate – The House of Herod – The Armenian
Convent – Mount of Olives – The Fountain of Silva
– Journey to Bethlehem – The Valley of the Giants
– Fons Signatus – The Convent of Terra Sancta –
Basilica di Santa Maria – The Street of the Cross.

From the Temple of Solomon we returned to the Convent and, accompanied by one of the friars, visited the Temple of the Resurrection, in the centre of which is the Holy Sepulchre of our Saviour.

This temple is a magnificent building, founded by the emperor Constantine, who delivered this sacred spot from the hands of the infidels. He wrote to all the Eastern Provinces to demand contributions, sent a priest from Constantinople to act as architect, and St Helena, his mother, undertook the journey to superintend this pious work. This great fabric was finished in nine years. The prodigious quantities of gold and silver ornaments which the emperor sent were the wonder of those times.

Many and various are the vicissitudes which this church has undergone from the different governments to which the city has been subjected since that time. When the Saracens under Saladin took Jerusalem, the Temple of the Resurrection was plundered of all its riches, but the building received no damage. On examining its walls they are found to be of white calcareous stone, which abounds throughout Palestine, and is capable of a polish little inferior to marble.

> HIC IACET INCLITVS
> DVX GODEFRIDVS DE
> BVLLON QVI TOTAN.
> ^
> AQVISIVIT TERRAM
> ISTAM. CVLTVI
> X̄P̄IANO CVI ANIMA
> REGNET CVM X̄P̄O AMEN.

Here lies the famous captain Godfrey de Bouillon, who won all this land for the Christian faith. May his soul reign with Christ. Amen.

In that part of the church called the Chapel of Adam are two very ancient tombs of bad workmanship. The inscriptions are in ancient characters, and scarcely legible they set forth that Godfrey and Baldwin, two brothers and kings of Jerusalem, were buried there. I copied the writing exactly as it was on the stone:

It was under this Prince's reign that the order of the Knights Templars was first instituted, as well as that of the Knights Hospitalers. The latter, whose number rapidly increased, took up arms, as much to escort and protect the pilgrims who came from all parts to visit the holy places, as to assist the Christian kings in the wars against the infidels. The success of the Hospitalers encouraged some French gentlemen to enrol themselves under their banner. The chief of these were Hugues de Payan and Godfrey of St Admer, or St Omer.

King Godfrey died Anno Domini 1100, and his brother in 1118, the former at Jerusalem and the latter at Larissa, where he was embalmed and afterwards sent to Jerusalem to be interred.

The following inscription, in characters of the twelfth century, is under a picture of St Paul, and now almost illegible:

*Ego gratia Dei sum id quod sum, et gratia ejus in me vacua non fuit.*

After having seen the remainder of the church, which is divided into four different chapels – the Catholic, Greek, Armenian, and Copt – we were conducted to the Holy Sepulchre, built in the centre of the church immediately under the great cupola and though, as the Scripture says, 'hewn out of a rock', is itself a church in miniature, having a cupola and all the external appearance of a chapel. The entrance to it is by a very small door, from which you descend by a few steps, and first enter a narrow apartment, at the bottom of which are two perpendicular holes that lead to a small cavern in the rock, on which the little chapel is erected. This is the burial place of two of our Saviour's disciples. Proceeding a little further you pass, by a very small door, into the Holy Sepulchre itself.

It is nine feet in length, by about six feet and a half wide. On one side is the Tomb of our Saviour, raised about four feet from the floor, it is of white marble and fixed against the wall. This little cavern is lighted by a number of silver lamps suspended from the ceiling, which cause so great a heat that it is difficult to remain long in this awful place.

Though we remained here near a quarter of an hour yet we were so wrapped up in meditation that not a word was uttered. On entering this Holy Shrine I was struck with reverential awe, and felt a kind of pleasing agitation of mind which no language can express, nor do I think it possible for even the most hardy freethinker to set his foot on this hallowed spot without feeling at least a momentary conviction of his dangerous error. As there were many people waiting to succeed us, we withdrew and went to see the place of crucifixion.

I shall not attempt to describe all the remarkable places in this church.

While we were in the Greek Church a priest was delivering a sermon. He spoke with much vehemence and energy, and seemed to command the attention of a very large assembly, composed mostly of women. They were all veiled, as the Turks will not permit even the Greek women to appear abroad with their faces uncovered. The concourse of people, always formed at this church, gives it more the appearance of a court of justice than the sacred place of divine worship. The number of different sects, too, which we saw here is really surprising, the Jews only are forbidden to enter the Temple. A little before my arrival a Jew was found secreting himself in the church during the procession of the pilgrims; he was instantly dragged into the square before the Temple and in a few moments torn to pieces.

The Porte receives so great a revenue from the taxes laid on the pilgrims visiting the Holy Sepulchre that it is deemed expedient to preserve them from every kind of molestation and interruption. The Turks of Jerusalem, whenever they enter the Temple, conduct themselves with the greatest propriety, being convinced that the slightest offence on their part, being represented by any of the priests, would subject them to the severest punishment.

From the Temple of the Resurrection, we went to see the Seraglio of the Governor, who resides in the same house where Pontius Pilate dwelt when our Saviour was crucified. The small room where the crown of thorns was platted is now the chamber where the Governor's soldiers mount guard. The great council-chamber was also shewn us, in which Pilate, to appease the multitude, passed sentence on our Lord, and also the great hall in which the soldiers afterwards took him, and mocked him by putting on him the scarlet robe and the crown of thorns.

We afterwards went to the house in which Herod resided when Pilate sent our Saviour to him, and passed under a very large arch called *ecce homo* Arch, from Pilate having stood there when Jesus came forth with the purple robe and crown of thorns, and said to the people, *ecce homo*.

There is a pillar yet standing in the town from which it is said that the sentence was made public after being passed on Jesus. We were also shewn the house of Jairus, and many other memorable places, where our Saviour performed those miracles recorded in the sacred writings.

From thence we went to the Armenian Convent, and were politely received. This is the richest and most extensive in Jerusalem. Its Superior is a bishop and vested with great powers.

He informed me that he had at times lodged one thousand pilgrims in the Convent, but that of late years, the impositions to which they were subjected on the roads thro' Arabia were such that many had been obliged to relinquish their pious intentions of visiting the Holy Sepulchre, and consequently that the number of pilgrims was greatly diminished.

There are many ill-executed paintings in the church of this convent, among which is one representing the Devil with our Saviour, on a pinnacle of the Temple, tempting him, and another frightful piece, of an extraordinary size, representing the Day of Judgment.

We were also shewn within a white marble sepulchre, in a glass case, the head or skull of St John the Baptist. This is held as the greatest curiosity of the Holy Land, and in a manner worshipped by the Catholics.

I shall leave to those gentlemen, whose pursuits give them a peculiar claim to the character of a natural philosopher, to determine, how far it may be possible to preserve a skull, for a period little short of eighteen hundred years. For my own part, I would rather subject myself, for ever, to the imputation of weakness, or even superstition, than for a moment to lose sight of those exalted views, and pleasing hopes, with which faith, or a belief of the revealed truths of religion, fill the mind of man.

In the evening we walked out of the town by the Gate of St Stephen, and viewed with admiration its ancient walls. At a little distance we were shewn the Sepulchres of Absalom and King Manasseh, which are close to each other in the valley of Jehoshaphat. Absalom died one thousand and twenty-three years before Christ, and though the City, since that period, has been destroyed more than fifty times, yet his tomb remains still unmolested, and may be considered the oldest piece of masonry in the world.

A little further on we saw the memorable Mount of Olives mentioned in the gospel, and the spot on which Jesus kneeled and prayed, when the angel appeared to strengthen him, is distinguished by a kind of building erected over it.

About a stone's throw from hence is Gethsemane, where Jesus, after rising from prayer, found his disciples asleep and you are also shewn the place where Jesus was taken by the high priests and elders, and where Peter, drawing the sword, cut off the ear of the servant of the high priest.

Returning another way to the City, we were shown the Fountain of Silva where the blind received their sight, and a natural grotto where the disciples concealed themselves after Jesus was taken, another grotto to which Peter retired to weep after he had denied our Saviour; and the place where St Stephen was stoned.

From this place we went to the Chapel of the Virgin Mary. To the right you see the Sepulchre of Joseph, and opposite to it that of Anna, the mother of the Holy Virgin. Lower down in a little chapel is the sepulchre of the Virgin Mary, which has an altar hung with lamps and richly decorated. At the bottom of the stairs to the left there is a very fine well, the water of which is said to cure all diseases and work many miracles. On returning to the City by the Valley of Jehoshaphat, you are shown the ruins of the palace where Solomon kept his concubines; and which you are taught to believe was once surrounded by extensive gardens, displaying all the beauties of exquisite taste and luxuriant fertility but at present, this place, as well as the whole country round Jerusalem, exhibits nothing but sterility and indigence.

On entering the City we examined a castle where the Turks regularly mount guard; and which, on account of its antiquity (being erected by King David), is well worth seeing. It is almost the only building that has escaped the ravages of the successive wars that have taken place. It was from a window in this castle that King David first saw the fair Bathsheba, as she was bathing in a fountain, which is overlooked by the tower. There is a terrace on the top with embrasures, but it has only a few dismounted and useless guns which have remained here since the time of the Crusades.

In an apartment at the top of the castle we saw a great number of coats of mail, helmets, breast- and shoulder-plates, old spears and some shields, brought hither by Richard Coeur de Lion at the time he undertook to take the City from the Saracens and reduce it under the power of the Christians.

This tower is surrounded by a very deep ditch, has a draw-bridge, and is defended below by a few pieces of ordnance. And were it not for local disadvantages it might, from the thickness and strength of its walls, be a safe place of retreat in time of danger.

Night coming on we returned to the Convent, where our friend the Governor always had a good bowl of punch à l'Angloise ready for us. We acquainted him with our intention of visiting Bethlehem the following day, in consequence of which he gave orders to have mules and janissaries ready for the journey.

Accordingly, we set out at six in the morning, and our guides shewed us the most remarkable places on our way to Bethlehem.

On the south-west of Jerusalem there is a valley, called the Valley of the Giants, or of Raphaim, famous for the defeat of the Philistines, who were twice over-thrown here by David. At a little distance to the left is a small eminence with some ruins on it. It is called Mons Mali Consulii from the first council having met here to deliberate on taking and putting to death our Saviour. Near this is the valley where the angel of the Lord slew, in one night, 185,000 soldiers of the army of Sennacherib King of Assyria, who came in the reign of Hezekiah to take the City of Jerusalem.

In this valley are still the ruins of the tower in which Simon lived, who received Jesus when a child from the arms of the Virgin Mary, in the Temple of Jerusalem. We passed the valley called Terebinthus, and were shown the spot where Mary sat down under the Terebinthus tree, when she was carrying Jesus from Bethlehem to the Temple. We saw in the environs the ruins of the house where Joseph was warned by the angel to 'arise and take the young child and his mother and flee into Egypt'.

Being now within a mile of Bethlehem, we determined on examining its environs before we went to the Convent. We therefore turned to the right, and stopped at a place called Fons Signatus, the entrance to which is a narrow cave, through which a man can with difficulty make his way. After having descended, you find two chambers in the rock, vaulted over with square stones. One of them is 48 by 27 feet, the other 42 by 27. On the western side are three grottos, from each of which runs a small stream of pure water, which unite in one channel of about six feet wide and six feet deep, they again separate, and one flows into a fountain, the second follows the inclination to the Fishponds or Cisterns erected by Solomon, and the third is conveyed by an aqueduct to the City of Jerusalem.

Not far from the Fans Sitnatus is a castle, the lower part of the walls of which are of Solomon's time, but the superstructure is of a much later date. Close to it is the first of the Cisterns, 190 yards long, and 108 broad. The second, somewhat lower, is 229 yards in length, and 139 in breadth. And the third, which is still lower, measures 286 by 123 yards. These were formerly constantly full, but the Fons Sitnatus, from which they were supplied, does not at present yield sufficient water. Their depth is from forty to fifty feet. They have been cut out of the solid rock, and their sides are covered with a cement of a substance so hard, that it has withstood the force of water for so many centuries.

These extraordinary basins are situated in the centre of a valley one below the other; so that the overflowings of the first are received by the second, and afterwards by the third successively. They are not level at the bottom, but cut out or indented like steps from the sides to the centre.

This wonderful work is reckoned among those great undertakings which distinguish the reign of the richest and wisest of monarchs, and the Ponds are the same that are mentioned in Ecclesiastes Chapter 2, Verses 5 and 6.

After a quarter of an hour's ride from the Ponds, in the same valley, you arrive at a place called Hortus Conclusus, mentioned in the Psalms. Near the Cisterns is the source of an aqueduct, which receiving a part of the waters of Fons Signatus conveys it for upwards of ten miles, through various winding passages, to the City of Jerusalem.

About eleven o'clock we arrived at the ancient town of Bethlehem of Judea, so called to distinguish it from another Bethlehem in Galilee, in the tribe of Zebulon.

It first came into the hands of the Christians in the year 1099, when Tancred was detached from the army of Godfroy de Bouillon to take it. After the loss of Jerusalem in 1187 it was again abandoned by them, and has since been under the Saracen or Turkish government but has always been inhabited by Christians.

We alighted at the Convent of the Terra Sancta, and the Padre Guardiano received us with politeness and paid us the most friendly attention.

As you approach the town, the Convent presents the appearance of a most venerable ruin. You pass through a gate-way, which is at present in its last stage of ruin though originally of immense thickness. From the gate-way, you go along a large terrace, on which formerly stood a magnificent piazza supported by marble column.

You afterwards arrive at the church, which has three doors, chiefly built as a security against the Arabs, the centre, or middle door, is an aperture through which one person only can enter at a time. This opening is secured by an iron door of great thickness, capable of resisting any force but that of gunpowder. It leads you to a great hall with two doors, one opening to the Armenian Convent, and the other to the church called Basilica di Santa Maria. On entering this church the traveller is struck with surprise to find himself in a noble edifice of exquisite workmanship.

It is divided into five aisles by four rows of superb columns of white marble with red veins, the produce of the neighbouring hills of Judea. Their capitals are of statuary marble, of the Corinthian order, executed in the most masterly manner. The beams which rest on the columns and support the superstructure are of the cedar of Mount Lebanus, of immense dimensions, and astonishingly well preserved. The roof has suffered much at different periods, but most of the cedar beams have remained entire since the death of our Lord, and the whole roof is now covered with lead. The altar is in the centre, and raised some steps above the floor of the church behind the altar you descend by semicircular steps to the grotto where our Saviour was born. There are three altars in this cavern, now a church, the Great Altar, the Altar of the Wise Men, and the Altar of the Circumcision of our Lord.

The walls were formerly ornamented with inlaid slabs of the finest marble, but a Sultan of Egypt tore them down and carried them to Cairo to adorn his seraglio. The floor was likewise finished with the same ornamental slabs as the sides, but now consists only of the uneven rock. At the eastern extremity is a small grotto, the spot where our Saviour was born.

This place, which was once a stable, is now superbly ornamented with different coloured marbles. In the centre is the Table of the Altar, and under it you are shewed the spot where the child was found, which still resembles a manger or stone basin. There is a star in it, whose centre is porphyry, surrounded with rays of silver, and studded with precious stones as a memorial of the star which conducted the Wise Men to the place where Jesus lay. Under it is written the following motto:

Hic de Virgine Maria
Jesus Christus natus eSt
MDCCXXIX

The surface of the altar is an ancient table representing the birth of our Saviour. Joseph and the Virgin are in the attitude of kneeling and worshipping him while he lies smiling on a bundle of straw. In the clouds is seen a group of angels, holding a scroll in their hands, on which is written 'Gloria in excelsis Deo.' In the back ground is the angel announcing the birth to the Shepherds.

The religionists of the Holy Land had the exclusive right of resorting to this sanctuary, but for some years past the Greeks have been allowed the same privilege. Near the Altar of the Manger is a painting representing the Magi offering their gifts. This grotto is of an irregular form, and is about ten feet every way. The length of the other from the eastern extremity to the western door is upwards of fifty feet. In the centre of the ceiling are hung a row of lamps, the gifts of different European Catholic princes. This place is held in very high estimation by the Mahometans, who profess the greatest veneration for our Saviour and for the Virgin Mary. And though they do not acknowledge Jesus Christ to be the Son of God, yet they allow him to be the greatest Prophet of all prophets, conceived by the breath of God in the womb of the Virgin Mary. They acknowledge his miracles, adding that he foretold the coming of Mahomet.

They believe that in the day of the resurrection we shall be judged in the presence of God by three persons, namely Moses, Jesus Christ and Mahomet; and that each of them will judge his own sectaries.

The Mahometans are permitted to come here to pray, which they have been known to do in cases of extreme distress, or in times of public calamity. When they enter the sanctuary they uncover their heads and proceed barefooted, with apparent awe and veneration.

The Emperor Adrian, when he had reduced Judea to a Roman Province, placed images of the heathen gods in all those places which the Christians held most sacred, supposing that after having been polluted by idols, they never would renew their worship there. He placed the image of Venus in the spot where our Saviour was born.

These subterraneous grottos branch out into different parts which have been dedicated to various persons buried here. You descend by five steps into the Cave of the Innocents, from whence there is a narrow passage leading to a chasm in the rock, into which it is said the bodies of the children were thrown after they had been put to death by order of Herod.

There is a very large terrace on the top of the Convent, from which you have a most extensive view of the surrounding country. On a clear day the Dead Sea may be discovered. I expressed my desire to the Superior of visiting it, and other places in the neighbourhood, but he only corroborated the opinion of the Holy Fathers of Jerusalem, by pointing out the insurmountable difficulties that stood in the way. All which I should have braved, were I not circumscribed in respect to time. I was bound, by my contract with the captain of our ship at St John De Acre, to be back in twelve days from the day I left the ship, under a very heavy penalty. I assured the Superior, that ere long I would pay him another visit, and should then be prepared, with a strong guard to proceed to Sodom and Gomorrah, which is only twenty miles from Bethlehem.

There are some very large Cisterns under the Convent, constructed by King David, and the whole monastery is surrounded by a very strong wall. From the manner in which it is built, it resembles a fortified place, and in certain cases might hold out a long siege.

The town of Bethlehem is built on the southern side of a most barren mountain, and at present only consists of a few houses.

The inhabitants are all Christians or at least call themselves so. They are supposed to be the bravest race of people in the Holy Land, and have twice repulsed the Turks.

A few years ago, the Bashaw of Acre having sent a little army to carry off the heads of all the inhabitants, the people of the town assembled to the number of about 500 and made so brave a defence that the greater part of the Bashaw's soldiers were cut to pieces.

These people are very poor, and the country is nothing but rocks and stones, so that they could not possibly subsist, were it not for a manufactory of beads and crosses which they sell as relics to the Catholic countries of Europe. These relics are made of mother-of-pearl, which is found in great quantities in the sea near Acre, and of a sort of hard red wood.

We were attended all the morning by these innocent men, and at one an excellent dinner was prepared for us, consisting of at least thirty dishes. These good friars left us to enjoy it, and retired to sing hymns before they sat down to their scanty meal; it being Lent time, which they observe very strictly. After dinner we went to see the different cells and other inhabited parts of the Convent, all which are kept very neat and in excellent repair.

Before we returned to Jerusalem, I promised my spyglass to the Superior, as a small token of the high sense I entertained of his politeness and attention; and though he at first refused it, it was evident that he felt happier in accepting it than if I had given him the finest Arabian horse.

In two hours we found ourselves back again at Jerusalem, and heartily thanked the Superior for the friendly reception he had procured for us at Bethlehem.

The next day we had several remarkable places to examine. On leaving the Convent, we were shewn the spot where the house of Zebedee, the father of St John, once stood. It is now a Greek church. The Virgin Mary and St John the Evangelist remained here during the Crucifixion of our Saviour.

We afterwards went to the Church of St James, which belongs to the Armenians. It is lighted by a very beautiful dome, and is said to be the place where St James was beheaded. Three very remarkable stones are seen here. The first is that against which Moses broke the twelve Tables, the second, that which was on Mount Tabor at the Transfiguration of Jesus Christ, and the third was in the River Jordan at the place where John baptized our Lord.

We passed through the Gate of Mount Sion, or Gate of David, where we saw the foundations of the house where the Virgin Mary died, after having lived there fourteen years. The two venerable priests who accompanied us spoke of those places with such profound veneration as shewed how implicitly they believed what they had related of them to us.

Near it is the Church of Mount Sion, now a mosque, built before the place where the Holy Ghost descended on the apostles, and where Jesus Christ administered the sacrament to his disciples and washed their feet.

At a little distance is the house of Caiaphas, where St Peter denied his Master. Part of the pedestal on which the cock crew is still remaining, and a marble cock placed on it.

We re-entered the City and went to see the Temple of the Dedication, so called because it was here our Lord was dedicated to God, and Simon took him up in his arms, and said 'Lord now lettest thou thy Servant depart in peace, according to thy word', etc. There is here a column of vast dimensions in full preservation, which, I think, is one of the most curious pieces of antiquity in Jerusalem.

From thence we went to see the Hospital of St Helena, which has been preserved entire, and is still used as an hospital for the poor Turks.

The following day we began our excursion through the Street of the Cross. We saw the spot where our Saviour was whipped, which formerly was part of the House of Pilate.

Near this is the arch where Pilate produced Jesus to the people with his body lacerated, saying, *Ecce homo*. This arch extends from one side of the street to the other, under which are written these words, *'Tolle, Tolle, Crucifige Eum.'*

Farther on is a little door, thro' which the Virgin Mary saw her Son pass, carrying the cross, and the place where he fell under its weight, when it was placed on the shoulders of Simon the Cyrenean.

The place was afterwards shewed us where the house of the poor man Lazarus stood, as also the palace of the rich man. We were likewise shewed the spot where stood the house of Veronica, on whose handkerchief the image of Christ was imprinted when she wiped the sweat from his brow. Lastly we saw the Door of Condemnation, through which Christ was led to Mount Calvary to be crucified. In the middle of this door the column still remains on which his sentence was stuck up. Here ends the Street of the Cross, which is about 1,000 paces from the House of Pilate.

Having now seen and examined all the antiquities and curiosities of Jerusalem, we did not wish to delay our departure one moment. The Superior was much affected, and actually shed tears on hearing our determination to set out for St John De Acre that very night, nor did he give up his arguments and entreaties to induce us to spend a few days more with him, until I explained to him the agreement between me and the captain of our ship. Upon which he immediately gave orders that we should be furnished with a sufficiency of provisions for our journey.

He had heard, he said, that I was making a collection of medals, and at the same time shewed me several, which excited my admiration, and I felt a mixture of pleasure and surprise when he insisted that I should accept them. They consisted of ten gold ones, and several of silver and brass. He assured me that he had been thirty years collecting his medals, and that these he gave me were the best he met with. In return for which, I presented him with a very costly spy-glass, and a curious case of pistols, which with much difficulty I persuaded him to accept.

I had now some very material business to settle with this good gentleman before I took my final leave, and therefore took this opportunity of requesting that he would give me a certificate, properly drawn up, signed and witnessed, stating the time of our arrival at Jerusalem as a proof of my having visited that celebrated City, to be produced to my friends in Ireland.

This innocent man never inquired further into the motives of this particular request, but soon after delivered me a paper which contained a certificate, that I had visited Jerusalem, *religionis gratia*. I really was pleased at the opinion this worthy man entertained of us, and felt a little inward shame, from a consciousness of demerit in this respect. He wished us every happiness this world could bestow; and hoped that the Almighty would further strengthen our pious resolution of revisiting the Holy Land. We received the Reverend Father's benediction with becoming humility and gratitude, and two hours after sunset began to proceed on our way to Napolosa, which is fifteen hours' ride from Jerusalem.

COPY OF THE SUPERIOR'S CERTIFICATE.

Ego infrascriptus Guardianus hujus Conventns S. Mariae fidem facio omnibus et singulis has literas inspecturis, D. D. Thomasum Whaley et Hugh Moore fuisse, et habitasse duabus vicibus in hac Civitate Nazareh spatio trium dierum. in quorum fide etc.

Datum in eadem Civitate Nazareh.

Die 5to, Martis, A.D. 1789.

F. Archangelus ab Interaq. guar et supr.

I, the undersigned Guardian of this Convent of St Mary, certify to all and singular who may read these presents, that Messrs. Thomas Whaley and Hugh Moore have, on two occasions, been present and resided in this City of Nazareth for the space of three days, in witness whereof-

Given in the City of Nazareth,

5 March 1789.

Brother Archangel of Entraigues, Guardian and Superior.

# CHAPTER III

Departure from Jerusalem – Attacked by Arabs
– Napolosa – Its Governor – Its Various Names and
Revolutions – Origin of the Samaritans – Difficulties
in Leaving Napolosa – Character of the Arabs – Arrival
at St John of Acre – Caiffa.

He only, who has encountered dangers and difficulties, and groaned under the pressure of hunger and fatigue, may be said to know the inestimable blessings of personal security, ease and comfort. This, and the like reflections, filled my mind for a considerable time after I had turned my back to Jerusalem. The idea of having now accomplished what appeared to most of my friends insuperable, gave an unusual flow to my spirits, which was still increased by the cheerfulness and vivacity of my friend and fellow traveller, Mr M---, whose sympathizing soul participated my felicity.

The day was remarkably warm, the country around us delightful and the road good, and we travelled at our ease, without interruption till we got within six miles of Napolosa. It was about two in the afternoon, and not supposing we had anything to fear at this hour, M--- and I had advanced with our two Arabian chiefs, leaving servants and conductors, six in number, behind together with our baggage.

We had not proceeded half a mile farther, when we were saluted by twenty Arabs, who appeared much better armed than they usually are. We did not suspect them for any hostile intentions towards us, but in less than ten minutes after they had passed us, we had reason to alter our opinion of them. For on hearing Pauolo suddenly set up his Persian warwhoop, we looked about, and to our astonishment saw, at the distance of half a mile, some of the Arabs leading our two camels away, while others were beating our guides most unmercifully. Pauolo, armed with a blunderbuss and a case of pistols, wisely contented himself with acting on the defensive till we came up.

We made all possible haste to his assistance. Our two Arabs, who were better mounted than M--- or myself, arrived first, and rushed into the middle of the band, desiring us on no account to fire, or advance nearer to the robbers, who, when they saw us approaching, sent ten of their gang to surround us.

This they did so effectually as to leave us no way of escaping. They still continued advancing till they were within four yards of us, when the Chief ordered us to lay down our arms, menacing instant death to every individual of us, in case of refusal or hesitation. Thus situated, opposition on our part would bespeak the highest degree of temerity. For, though we might, in case of a rencounter, kill and wound many of them, and even make our escape from the field; yet, from the great superiority of their number to ours, we must have fallen a sacrifice to them in the end. Therefore, with hearts burning with stifled indignation, we submitted to our fate and obeyed the imperious command.

The advanced party still kept us closely hemmed. I had three guns levelled at my breast and M--- as many; all the rest of our party, except our two chiefs, were severely bastinadoed. At length, our chiefs, after some altercation with the captain of the robbers, prevailed on him to restore us one of our camels; and fortunately for us, the robber chose for himself the one that was heavier laden, which carried only our provisions and kitchen utensils.

Having thus escaped without personal injury, or the loss of our valuables, we proceeded to Napolosa as fast as we could, in hopes that the Governor would send a party of soldiers after the robbers, and take them before they got at too great a distance.

This city, now called Napolosa was the ancient and celebrated city of Sichem, which is particularly noticed in Holy Writ. It was here Simeon and Levi, sons of Jacob, massacred in one night all the male inhabitants of the city, with Emer their King and Sichem his son, at a time when they were all suffering under a severe indisposition, from circumcision. This they did to be revenged on Sichem for having violated their sister Dinah. Some centuries after, this city was totally destroyed by

Abimelech, the natural son of Gideon. It was afterwards rebuilt by Jeroboam, and called Mamorta, afterwards Naples, and since Napolosa. It is situated in the Province of Samaria, which took its name from the Assyrian colonies which Sennacherib, a king of the Chaldeans sent thither to keep the Jews in subjection.

These tribes were afterwards called Samaritans, which signifies guardians, and the Jews, ignorant of the true meaning of the word, when they wished to calumniate Jesus Christ, called him Samaritan, not knowing that it implied 'guardian' or 'keeper'. Our Saviour replied that he did not deny he was a Samaritan and the true keeper of the faithful.

The gallop we had given our mules had so tired them that we did not reach the town in less than two hours. We immediately waited on the Governor, told him our disaster, and sued for redress. He seemed struck with astonishment; changed colour several times, and instantly ordered all the Sheiks and Chiefs of the different tribes to be called together and addressed them in our presence in a short but energetic speech, pointing out the enormity of the crime, emphatically observing that we were Englishmen, the best of the Christian race, the only men of that persuasion who kept their word and did not worship images. He said that we were the friends of the Grand Signior, and that our king wished well to the Turks. He concluded by assuring the Sheiks that total destruction awaited their town if our goods were not found and restored before sunset, adding that the Bashaw of St John of Acre would be glad of this pretext to send an army of 20,000 to pillage and lay waste the town and neighbourhood.

This speech had the desired effect, for one of the Sheiks advanced and informed the Governor that the people who robbed us belonged to him, and pledged his beard that he would have our effects restored in a few hours, at the same time swearing by Mahomet that if they did not he would destroy every man, woman, and child in the village. After this he ordered several of his followers to prepare themselves, and almost in an instant appeared on horseback, at the head of a little troop, well armed with lances and pistols.

As we were in great haste, we proposed to leave some of our conductors behind to wait for the camel, while we went on in the cool of the evening. But the Governor advised us by no means to attempt it; observing, that these people were so much afraid of our complaining to Jedzar Bashaw of Acre, that in order to prevent it, they would follow us, and put every man of us to death.

This information alarmed us very much, so that we now wished, from our hearts, that we had tacitly submitted to the trifling loss we had sustained, rather than by seeking redress to excite the malignity of our enemies. But if the Governor's remonstrance had alarmed us, what must be our consternation, when, at our return to our lodging, we were informed by our host, that the people of the town, who had heard of our being robbed, and of the vast treasure contained in the hampers we had lost, now, finding that all were to be restored to us, felt so much disappointed and chagrined at the loss of such a booty, that they had vowed vengeance against us, and sworn that they would waylay us and that nothing but our lives and property should satisfy them.

We were still more alarmed at this intelligence on recollecting that in the year 1785 a Dutch gentleman and his suite had been cut to pieces in this very neighbourhood, after being robbed of every species of property he had then on him, which was of immense value and we were given to understand that in the general opinion of those plunderers, our treasure fell little short of the unfortunate Dutch gentleman's.

We expressed our apprehensions to the Governor, assuring him that we had no treasure, but at the same time declared that in case of a second attack, we should prove to our enemies that no Arab regarded less his life than we did, and that we were determined to sell ours at the dearest rate.

He replied that he entertained no doubt of the courage of the English, who, next to the Arabs, were the most warlike and courageous nation, and he highly commended the recent instance of our cool and steady conduct, in forbearing to fire on the robbers, for had we acted otherwise, and they could reach the town before us, it would be impossible to protect us from the fury of their numerous and powerful tribe.

We were obliged to remain here till about noon the following day, when the Sheik returned successful from his expedition, having brought with him our camel and all our effects; even the provisions were returned untouched, as they found a ham among them, of which the Arabs are, by their doctrine, strictly forbidden to eat. Strange! And unaccountable, that any doctrine or precept should influence the conduct of vile wretches who deemed it no crime to plunder us, or even to take away our lives, if they could have done it with impunity.

Nothing remained now to be done but to deliberate and determine on what should appear to us the best mode of making our escape from this diabolical country. We endeavoured to convince the Governor as well as the Arabs, that so far from possessing a treasure, we had no more money about us than what was barely sufficient to take us to St John of Acre, and yet little as it was, that we would part with it only with our lives. To shew that this was our determination, we loaded our arms afresh, and also thought it prudent to conceal from our enemies the time we had fixed for our departure, to which end we openly declared our intention of setting out at six the next morning, but privately made our arrangements so as to depart by midnight, which we could do unobserved, as it fortunately happened our lodging was close to the Gate of the town.

The Governor gave us two of his men to accompany us, and pledged his life that they would defend us to the last drop of their blood. We therefore set out at twelve from this inhospitable and dangerous town, expecting that by this plan we should give them the slip. We sent Pauolo before us to reconnoitre, and having met with no interruption we were in a few minutes beyond the precincts of Napolosa.

The night, for the first two hours, was remarkably serene, and we made the most of our time, riding at the rate of about four miles an hour. Our Napolosa men rode in front, next came M——— and I, and our servants and guides followed us with our baggage. But at half-past two the night in a moment became so dark that we could scarcely see each other; fortunately one of our guides rode a grey mule, and this circumstance enabled me to distinguish and keep close to him. Immediately the rain began to pour in such torrents that we were soon wet to the skin. In addition to our distress and perplexity we found that we had lost our way and one of our guides.

The loss or absence of our guide at this critical moment was not only severely felt, but also created in our minds the strongest suspicions of treachery on his part, and that he had thus absconded for the purpose of joining his accomplices and putting in execution some premeditated plan for our destruction.

My passion in a short time overcame my fears, and riding up to the guide, who spoke Italian, I desired him to tell the Napolosa guard that as his companion had so shamefully deserted, I was convinced they meant to betray us. That should we be stopped, I was determined to risk my life in the contest, but that before the rencounter, I should certainly have the pleasure of blowing his brains out.

The poor fellow declared his innocence, and that he would answer for his companion. He swore that he would sooner lose his head than betray us, and only wished for an opportunity of shewing me his steadiness and bravery in my defence in case of an attack. This somewhat pacified me, but I by no means wished him such an opportunity of testifying his fidelity.

The darkness seemed still to increase, and for some time we remained in a dreadful sort of suspense. The dread of losing our way, if we still continued our dreary march, was succeeded by apprehensions no less terrifying for our safety, in case we attempted to halt. In this hopeless situation, what could equal our joy on hearing, at some distance, the barking of dogs, which naturally led us to conclude that we were not far from some house or village.

It was unanimously agreed, that we should endeavour to direct our course towards the place from whence the cheering signal was heard, and in order to induce a repetition of it, I desired Pauolo to sing one of his war songs. His melancholy ditty had the desired effect and the dogs thus continuing their harmonious accompaniment, directed our steps to a small village, where we were glad to rest our weary limbs for a couple of hours.

We took shelter in a most miserable hut. The land-lord informed us that, about a league farther on, there was an encampment of a wandering savage tribe, who, had we fallen into their hands, would have plundered us of everything; and not only taken our mules, but stripped us quite naked. In our way to Jerusalem we narrowly escaped those very plunderers, through the vigilance of the honest soldier of Ibrahim, who having previously informed himself of every danger incidental to the journey, took us by another road to avoid them, and the same precaution was now, on our part, absolutely necessary.

Less than half an hour after our arrival at this place we were joined by our lost guide. His disappearing from us was merely accidental, he and his horse having fallen into a pond or pit full of water, out of which he with much difficulty extricated himself, and hearing the barking of dogs, was almost instinctively led to follow our steps to the village.

We remained in the house of this friendly Arab till six in the morning, when we again mounted, and pursued our journey. I gave him three piastres for our two hours lodging, during which we were obliged to sleep in our wet clothes, and were assailed on all sides by a species of Arabian vermin, resembling those on European sheep, and full as large.

By nine we were in the district of Nazareth, where the people, owing to Ibrahim's good government, seem to regulate their conduct on the principles of true honour and integrity. Here we dismissed our Napolosa men, and at twelve arrived at Nazareth, but so exhausted with fatigue and anxiety that we found ourselves quite incapable of proceeding on our journey, and therefore yielded to the solicitations of the Friars to spend the remainder of the day with them and to set off early the next morning for St John of Acre, whither the Procurator, who had some business to transact with the Bashaw, Jedzar, promised to accompany us.

In the evening the Governor paid us a visit, and favoured us with his company for upwards of two hours during which the conversation turned on various subjects, on each of which he delivered his sentiments with perspicuity and judgment.

He promised me his assistance in getting the finest Arabian horse he knew, in respect of pedigree: but that his price was enormous, being set at no less than 10,000 piastres. He himself would willingly give eight, but his friend would not part with him for less than ten. I took the address of the man who possessed this valuable horse, who proved to be the Governor of Caiffa, where I resolved to go immediately after my arrival at Acre.

The conversation then turned from the horses to their masters. Jedzar Bashaw was the principal subject. Ibrahim informed us that this man had more authority in this country than the Grand Signior had in Constantinople. Indeed, from his account, I may venture to say that in ancient or modern history we do not meet with a more despotic prince, or one who has so unfeelingly exercised every species of tyranny, cruelty and injustice over his fellow creatures.

Ibrahim pays the Governor of St John, in annual taxes, the enormous sum of 15,000 purses or £1,000,000. He spoke to us in the most open and unreserved manner, respecting the character of his countrymen, a sketch of which may not appear wholly uninteresting to my readers.

The Arabs in general are by no means so ferocious or barbarous as they are represented to us. There are many very estimable characters among them. The Bedouins, or Arabs of Arabia Deserta, have no fixed habitation. They live under tents, which they carry from one place to another, according to the wants of their flocks, which consist of sheep and goats. They pride themselves so much on their nobility, that they hold the exercise of all mechanical arts in the utmost contempt, and prefer predatory excursions on horseback. In summer they live on the heights, in order to be able to discover the travellers, whom they intend to rob. In winter they direct their course towards the south as far as Cesarea. Their tents are made of goat's hair, woven together and dyed in black.

Their principal chiefs are called Emirs, next in rank are the Sheiks, whose authority extends over a smaller number of Arabs. These people, though living chiefly by plunder, are neither cruel or wicked, on the contrary they are known to exercise the most generous acts of hospitality and benevolence to those who fall in their way, and whose distress seems to claim their protection.

They follow the religion of Mahomet, are, or at least affect to be, more devout than the Turks, and are much more superstitious. If an Arab kills another Arab, all friendship is at an end between the two families and their posterity, until the injury be expiated by the blood of one of the offending family, or a reconciliation obtained by the payment of a large sum of money.

They respect their beards almost to adoration, the wives kiss those of their husbands, and the men mutually kiss each other's beards in token of friendship and esteem. They are passionately fond of horses, and manifest their pride and ostentation in keeping the finest and dearest.

The Bedouins, as well as the Turks, are not allowed to wear green in any part of their apparel. They have in general very forbidding countenances; and in all my journey through this part of Arabia, I did not meet with even one handsome woman.

We felt ourselves much obliged to Ibrahim for his kind and instructive conversation, and took our leave, with professions of friendship, gratitude and esteem. The good Friars of the Convent kept us company till evening, and persuaded me to accept of several valuable presents, with some very curious antiques and Grecian and Egyptian medals.

The following day we were very early on the road, accompanied by the reverend father and our guides. We had a most agreeable ride, and arrived at St John of Acre by four in the afternoon. We took up our lodgings at the Chan, which is a very large square building of four stories, divided into numerous apartments. The first story is used as warehouses and the second is occupied by Europeans, most of whom are French.

The next day, we waited on the Governor, who received us with all that kind of politeness and pompous ceremony peculiar to Asiatic grandees. After a short audience we withdrew, and took a nearer view of the city. It was formerly called Ptolemais, from the name of Ptolemy, king of Egypt, who is supposed to have been its founder. It was then one of the most considerable towns of all the East, nothing now remains but a few houses, and some very curious ruins. I took a sketch of the one that most attracted my attention: it is of Gothic architecture and appears to have been once a temple. At a distance you discover Mount Carmel, the Convent of the Carmelites on the opposite side, and the village of Caiffa near the sea-shore.

Caiffa, which the Turks and Arabs know by the name of Kaffas, being only three leagues distant from hence, and the time which our captain had granted us not being expired, I determined to go there the next day in order to get a view of the fine horse so much extolled by Ibrahim. In short I was determined, if possible, to purchase this admirable quadruped, not only for my own gratification; but chiefly with a view of improving our breed of horses in Ireland.

On our arrival at Caiffa I sent Pauolo to the Governor to know if I would be permitted to see the horse he meant to dispose of, to which he returned me a very polite answer, assuring me I should have an opportunity of seeing and examining him as often as I pleased, before I had finally determined on being the purchaser.

I was accordingly conducted to the place where this rare animal stood, and truly nothing but the pencil of Apelles could do him justice. His price was 10,000 piastres, and it would be a kind of insult to offer less to this inflexible Turk. I therefore gave him a letter of exchange on Smyrna, and sent the horse to Acre with orders to have him put on board my vessel there.

Caiffa is situated to the north of Mount Carmel and was once a celebrated place. The grottos cut in the solid rock where the Prophets Elisha and Elias used to live, are still shewn. This mountain is likewise distinguished for the many petrifications of melons and other fruits, as well as oysters, which have been found on it.

# CHAPTER IV

## Departure from Acre – Cyprus – Its General History – Character of its present inhabitants, etc.

Immediately on our return to Acre, I told the captain that I was ready to go on board, and accordingly, on the day following, we set sail with a fair wind, and bid an eternal adieu to Palestine, highly gratified with the idea of having seen a Country so eminently distinguished above all others for memorable and truly interesting events. But the wind soon changing, with every appearance of an impending storm, I persuaded the captain to put in at the island of Cyprus, where according to Anacreontic writers, Venus took refuge, and surrounded by the Zephyrs and Graces kept her court.

This island is about 150 miles in length by 66 in breadth, lying in 35 degrees of north latitude. It is forty-one leagues from the coast of Syria, and next to Sicily is the largest island of the Mediterranean. It is of a triangular shape, has several capes and promontories, few, if any good harbours, but very good anchorage, particularly in the bay of Sharnaca. Here we landed at a small neat village of the same name, and were conducted by my faithful Pauolo to the country-house of Mr D---, the British Consul. His villa is at some distance from the town, delightfully situated. The house is one of the best I have seen in Asia, and is shaded by a profusion of cedars and myrtles, which seem to vie with each other for beauty and supereminence.

Mr D---, who holds the office of Consul at Acre and Aleppo as well as in this island, was at this time from home, having set out a few days before our arrival to settle some business of importance at Aleppo where he mostly resides, though, not from choice, as I have

been told, but because the duties of his office require his presence more
at Aleppo than at either of the two other places. He has a deputy, or
vice-consul, at Acre as well as in this island, from whom we received
every mark politeness and generous hospitality. We dined at Mr D---'s
and spent the evening very pleasantly in the company of some agreeable
Cypriotes, whom the vice-consul, to contribute as much as possible to
our entertainment, had invited. One of these ladies gave me a letter to
a female friend of hers, resident at Nicosi, the capital of the island of
whose hospitality I shall speak hereafter

The town of Sharnaca lies low, and in the summer months is one of
the most unhealthy parts of the island. The town itself is neatly built and
the streets are clean and well paved. In its vicinity there are some ruins,
of which the foundations only are worth notice. These extend in large
caverns under the town, but what the building was originally I could
not learn, and must therefore trust to my own observations, which lead
me to suppose that it was once a castle of great extent and strength.

Early the next day we hired mules and guides and set out to visit the
remains of the temple of Apollo, situated near the village of Piscopi,
where there are some ruins to be seen, and the country for many miles
round presents every appearance of fertility and cultivation. The sacred
wood, which we are told was dedicated to Apollo, appears to have been
metamorphosed into a beautiful plain.

We spent the day at this village and were tolerably well entertained
at the house of a Greek priest to whom Pauolo had got letters of
recommendation. He gave us some rare wine, which he averred was
one hundred years in his family.

Having now seen as much of the temple of Apollo as deserved
the attention of a philosophic traveller, and converted the temple of
the Greek priest into that of Bacchus, we mounted our mules and
proceeded on our journey at nine o'clock the next day, intending to
visit the temple of Venus, situated twenty miles to the westward of the
village of Piscopi.

The day being uncommonly hot we did not arrive here till noon.
The ruins of this temple may be justly considered as monuments of its
ancient splendour. They are of vast extent, and for many miles round
there are columns of exquisite workmanship, and fragments of capitals
lying promiscuously.

At six o'clock we left the temple of Venus, and proceeded along
the banks of a beautiful rivulet, on each side of which we observed

herds of goats browsing on the arbutus and other flowering shrubs. At nine o'clock we entered the village of Achicis, where we took up our lodging for the night. It is situated on the river Muosi, and consists of only a few straggling houses, inhabited by wretches whose appearance bespoke their poverty and inattention to cleanliness. Here, after much importuning we procured some rice and goat's milk, on which having supped, we lay down on some clean straw, and being fatigued with travelling and the excessive heat of the day, we enjoyed under the roof of this homely cot that soft refreshing repose so often denied to those who sleep on beds of the softest down.

Before we set out this morning for Nicosi, the capital of the island, we were informed that it would be absolutely necessary to provide ourselves with provisions for this day's ride, as no refreshment of any kind could be had on the way. We therefore dispatched our trusty Pauolo, who seldom or never failed in any expedition, and my friend and I went to a cellar at some distance from our hotel to purchase some Falernian. At our return we found Pauolo very busy, roasting a turkey and a couple of brace of partridges, which when fit, were carefully packed up with our wine, and having made a hearty breakfast on some coffee and eggs, we mounted our mules and proceeded on our journey towards Nicosi distant about seven leagues from this village.

We stopped at a place called Tritmetusa, which is about midway between Nicosi and Achici, and having refreshed ourselves and mules, we proceeded on our way, and at nine o'clock arrived at the capital.

I had almost forgotten to mention a circumstance that occurred in our journey this day, which, had we time to delay on the road, we might have turned to some advantage.

At the little village of Patarsa, through which we were about to pass without stopping, Pauolo was accosted by a tall elderly woman, who inquired of him we were, and being informed that we were Englishmen, just returning from the holy Sepulchre, she immediately deemed us proper persons for her purpose and having next inquired if any of us understood physic and being answered in the affirmative, she earnestly entreated us to accompany her to her house, to see her daughter who lay sick of a fever.

Pauolo instantly took the alarm, and with evident marks of solicitude and serious apprehensions, entreated me not to go with her, swearing that nothing less dreadful than my taking the plague would be the consequence. But all entreaties and remonstrances were in vain. I had now been nine months in Turkey and had learned to think of infection with as much indifference as the best Mahometan, and having about me some papers of James's Powders, I resolved to try their efficacy in this case, therefore desired the woman to conduct me to her dwelling.

I found the child's pulse very high, and immediately ordered her half a paper. She appeared to be about twelve years old, and was attended by all the young persons of her own sex in the village. I gave directions that this dose should be repeated, if in the course of an hour some change for the better did not appear; and leaving a few papers with proper directions, I took my leave, and felt myself amply recompensed for this act of humanity by the grateful acknowledgments of the afflicted mother, and the prayers of those lovely innocent attendants, who surrounded the bed of the little sufferer, and seemed to consider me as the restorer of their dear companion. But in passing through the village, I found that we had not only acquired the character of men skilled in physic but also that of magicians.

We travelled for the last six miles along the banks of the Pedicus, where we met plenty of all sorts of game, particularly the red partridge, and bevies of quails. In this day's ride we also observed many eagles and vultures, very tame and daring. I fired several shots at them, and though within the common distance of a gun-shot, did not kill any, owing, I suppose, to the smallness of the shot.

Near the village of Scurlo are still to be seen the remains of an arch, said to have been raised to Alexander the Great, near to which are several broken pillars, on some of which hieroglyphics are still discernible. From all that fell under my observations in examining these monuments it appeared to me that the Corinthian order prevailed throughout.

On our arrival at Nicosi, we found ourselves so much tired from the journey that we held a council, whether we should dress or go to bed. In the meantime I sent Pauolo to inquire for the lady to whom I had got a letter of introduction from my fair friend at Sharnaca. I was informed that her residence was almost a league distant from the town. But in a short time, I saw, to my great surprise, this fair incognita, accompanied by several ladies and gentlemen, conducted by Pauolo to our hotel. This unexpected visit threw my friend and me into the greatest confusion, which was not much lessened when Madame, for whom I had the letter, expressed her regret that we should stop at a miserable gargette, as she called it, insisting at the same time that we should immediately accompany her to her brother's. As we saw, with extreme concern, that we had already given offence by setting up at this coffee-house, we at once determined, half-dressed as we were, to make some atonement by our prompt obedience to her commands.

On our way to this lady's brother, she addressed herself to Pauolo in Greek, and endeavoured to learn from him the particulars of my history; in the detail of which, as he afterwards informed me, he made her believe that I was son to the King of Ireland.

After a quarter of an hour's walk we passed the eastern extremity of the town, and soon after arrived at the residence of Madam E---'s brother, to whom she most graciously introduced us.

This gentleman appeared to be about thirty-five years of age, and had, according to his own account, seen more of the eastern world than any of his contemporaries. His principal residence was at Aleppo, and he came here in the summer months for his recreation, when he made liberal offerings at the shrine of Venus.

His adventures were much of a piece with those of Sinbad, in the Arabian Nights: one time the persecuted victim of divine wrath; at another the distinguished favourite of a most benign Providence.

He had been taken in the early part of his life by a tribe of wandering Arabs, who defeated a caravan to which he belonged on their route from Aleppo to Damascus. Every soul was put to the sword, except himself, and he was spared merely on account of his personal beauty: And indeed it must be owned that in this respect he seemed the distinguished favourite of nature, so that he might be justly styled the Adonis of the island.

He made his escape from these Arabs and got safe to Tripoli, where he embarked on board a Venetian ship, bound for Cyprus, but unfortunately falling in with an Algerine corsair, he with the rest of the crew was carried into slavery. Shortly after he was sold to the Dey of Tunis, and during a captivity of six years encountered such a variety of dangers and difficulties as perhaps never fell to the lot of any man before him, and in addition to his wayward fate, that beauty which was once the means of saving his life, now served only to increase the dangers of his hopeless situation. At length, having disguised himself in female attire, after many adventures he escaped to St John of Acre, where he again embarked on board a Venetian ship bound for Scandaroon, from whence he got safe back to Aleppo.

This gentleman, in addition to the beauty of his person, possessed, in an eminent degree, those mental accomplishments which distinguish the philosopher and the man of refined taste. His sister was also very handsome; had a charming voice, which she had the complacency to exert for our entertainment, in several fine Italian and Persian airs, whilst her brother accompanied her with the German flute or the guitar, both of which he played admirably well.

After supper, which was very sumptuous, we walked in the garden till midnight. It contained upwards of ten acres, planted with fruit-trees of every kind; the mulberry, the pomegranate, the date and the orange, all in full blow.

This delightful garden was laid out with great taste. The walks were spacious and tiled in the neatest manner. The mulberry trees planted on each side, and kept closely clipped, formed a shade impenetrable even to the rays of the meridian sun.

Our party consisted of half a dozen, of both sexes. Singing, dancing, and playing at hide and seek, with a variety of other childish amusements, beguiled the hours till past midnight, when our admirable hostess proposed that we should return to the saloon and take some refreshment before we retired for the night. The company obeyed, I believe, with reluctance. For my own part, I was so delighted with our garden scene, that no change could afford me a higher gratification.

Soon after twelve we were all in the saloon, and having taken coffee and sweetmeats, every one retired to his apartment for the night.

I found myself little disposed to rest, and therefore having waited impatiently for the morning, I eagerly returned to the garden, where I met my charming E---. Once more I was entertained with her captivating voice, which she accompanied with her mandoline. But, at nine, our tête-á-tête was interrupted by the appearance of the rest of the company, who now assembled to breakfast in the garden, and propose some new entertainment for the day.

The scenes of the preceding day and night furnished abundant matter for conversation during breakfast, which consisted of a cold collation of meats and game, among the latter was the *beca tigue*, which is reckoned the greatest delicacy: Fruits of all kinds were likewise served up.

It appeared to me that the company at this early hour were more inclined to drink than to eat; and for the first time I saw wine supply the place of tea. It was the best I drank in the island, and with respect to age exceeded that of the priest of Piscopi's by one hundred years. After such a breakfast, 'tis natural to suppose our spirits were equal to any enterprise, and our generous host, finding we were fond of the chase, proposed that of the wild boar but the ladies appearing terrified and disappointed at the idea of this kind of sport, it was at once given up, and the greyhound, pointers and guns were unanimously preferred.

At ten o'clock we sallied forth and the ladies, notwithstanding the heat of the day, partook of our sport, which ended about twelve o'clock, and short as the time may appear, to a keen or sanguinary sportsman, he must indeed carry his ideas of sporting or destroying game to a most unreasonable degree if he should not be satisfied with the spoils which each of us brought from the field.

Before I take my leave of Nicosi, I think it necessary to say something of its situation, strength and extent. It appears, from the most authentic records, that it has always been the capital of this island, and at so early a period as 420 years before Christ was deemed a place of considerable strength. It is situated near the river Pedicus, and commands an extensive prospect over a rich and fertile country. It is surrounded with a strong wall and a deep trench, and had formerly several towers, of which four only are now standing, and even these are bordering on ruin. It is said to have once contained 50,000 inhabitants, but at present its population falls very short of that number. The best wine is made here, of which the inhabitants drink very freely.

There is a small convent in the town, which for some years past has not been inhabited. The people are mostly employed in rolling silk, of which there is here great abundance, so that large quantities of the raw material are sent to the markets of Smyrna and Aleppo.

The women in this part of the island are remarkable for their beauty and voluptuousness: they generally marry at the age of thirteen or fourteen, and scarcely retain any vestige of their beauty after thirty. Having arrived at that period, they no longer play the coquette; but endeavour to become the accomplished matron, and by their exemplary conduct to render themselves useful to their juvenile friends.

Having now made our little arrangements, we took leave of our hospitable and truly amiable friends with much regret, and at six in the evening set out on our journey towards Famagousta. The air was still warm to a degree that induced both lassitude and languor; and we were much annoyed by the mosquitoes. For two hours we continued our ride along the banks of the Pedicus and then crossed it. The country on both sides of this river appeared to be cultivated with much judgment, and, as far as the naked eye could see, abounded mostly with Indian corn. The mulberry tree is cultivated with the utmost care, for on its leaves are fed the silk-worms, the principal source of the wealth of the island at the present day.

At half-past nine o'clock we arrived at a small neat village, situated on the banks of a lake where, I was told, salt was found in great abundance. We had procured a letter to a Greek, who possessed this branch of commerce at a certain rent; he received us with marks of politeness and friendship; and it is but barely doing him justice to say that in point of hospitality he seemed to possess the soul of a true Hibernian. After a good substantial supper, and a copious libation to the rosy god, we reeled to bed, and slept till eight the next morning.

Finding now that the day was too far advanced for us to make any progress in our journey before the meridian heat came on, we accepted the kind invitation of our generous host to dine with him, and in the cool of the evening to proceed towards the town of Famagousta. It was likewise necessary to send a messenger to acquaint the Governor of our intention of paying him a visit, and to provide ourselves with a firman for that purpose, as strangers, particularly if they be Christians, are not permitted to enter the town without the imperial passport.

At three o'clock we took leave of our Greek friend and set out, accompanied by his nephew. In our way we saw the ruins of a town said to have been built by Pompey. We observed this evening a great number of serpents of the green spotted kind, and many large lizards running among the grass.

At five o'clock we found ourselves again on the banks of the Pedicus, along which we pursued our road for several miles, and discovered many superb remains of antiquity. In this neighbourhood our young guide shewed us the temple of Adonis, of whose ancient grandeur and magnificence there is still remaining enough to excite the traveller's admiration.

There are vast subterraneous caverns here, which we did not enter on account of the air, at the very entrance, being extremely fetid, and we also had every reason to apprehend that they were infested with noxious animals.

In many places I observed scattered among these ruins blocks of verde antico and pillars of granite and porphyry, mingling with common rubbish.

A thought instantly came into my mind, of applying to the Governor for leave to take some of these inestimable remains to Europe, but in this I failed, as will appear hereafter.

I should willingly have remained here the rest of the day; but was told by our young companion that it was time to pursue our journey. I followed his advice without inquiring his reasons, and at ten o'clock we arrived at the small bourg called Trapesa, where we delivered our letter, and were tolerably well accommodated for the night in this village, which is about two miles distant from Famagousta. My firman was entrusted to the care of Pauolo, who set off with it at daybreak to demand permission from the Governor, under its authority, to enter the town and pay our respects to his excellency.

He was kept waiting so long at the gates that I began to grow impatient and uneasy about him, but at length he returned with a favourable answer, and we immediately proceeded towards the town.

We were met at the outer gate by some soldiers on horseback, who insisted on our mules being left outside the town, and that we should also leave our boots behind.

On hearing this injunction a violent dispute arose between Pauolo and one of the soldiers, which probably would have ended very seriously, had I not prevailed on one of these Janissaries, by means of a small bribe, to go to the Governor for instructions, and this I did merely to satisfy Pauolo, as it really was a matter of indifference to me whether I walked into town in slippers, or made my entrance in the equestrian style, with my red boots.

The janissary returned soon after accompanied by the Governor's dragoman, who was instructed to grant us the indulgence of making our appearance in boots, leaving our mules and baggage behind, which he promised should be immediately brought after us. To this we readily complied, and soon after were introduced to the Governor to whom I delivered my credentials, and was most graciously received and hospitably entertained in his palace.

Our dinner was sumptuous in the highest degree, and for variety and number of dishes far exceeded anything of the kind I had ever seen before, and to complete our felicity, we had the peculiar honour of the Governor's company at this splendid entertainment – a singular instance of hospitality and condescension from a proud Turk!

The Turks, as I have already observed, never use a fork: the Governor therefore laughed heartily on seeing our method of eating, while we inwardly reprobated his disgusting practice of every moment putting his hand into the dish; thence to his mouth until he was satisfied.

There is a rule strictly observed by these people, which is that the cook, at every entertainment, is ordered to taste of every dish, in the presence of the company, in order to satisfy the guests that they may eat of any with safety. Sherbet was the only beverage used at this entertainment, nor did I observe any of the Turks drink of any kind of liquid till they had finished their repast.

The entertainment being now at an end, ablutions were again repeated, and after a short prayer the meeting broke up.

I made this worthy Governor many presents, which he received with the most gracious acknowledgments, and in return gave me a curious bow, with some poisoned arrows.

In the evening we went, accompanied by the dragoman, to the most curious places in the town, but we soon found it necessary to return to the palace and provide ourselves with an escort of soldiers to protect us from violence or insult, as the boys had already begun to pelt us with stones, which coming to the Governor's ears, he was filled with indignation, and vowed that the first who would attempt to interrupt or offer us the least injury should be instantly strangled. This denunciation had the desired effect; for, during three days residence in this town, we met with no molestation or insult whatever.

The Town of Famagousta is situated on the east of the island, between the capes of St Andrew and Greek Cape, and is pretty much in the form of an irregular square. Its walls are washed by the sea, and it was formerly a place of great strength, having stood many desperate sieges in the time of the Crusades, when it was defended by the Christians against the Turks. It is surrounded by a deep ditch, of very great breadth, which can be occasionally filled with water. Its walls are, at present, in a very ruinous state. It had once thirteen towers and a bastion, built by Henry, in the year 1293, since which time it has been well fortified by the Venetians, who built another bastion on the northern side, but since it fell into the hands of the Turks, its fortifications have been entirely neglected.

This town took its name from the famous battle of Actium, where Augustus Caesar triumphed over Mark Antony and Cleopatra, though it is probable the name has been corrupted by the Greeks. It was originally Fama-augusta, afterwards Famagousta, and latterly Amoskousta, which signifies 'buried in sand', as the town from its situation really appears to be.

The harbour, which is about a mile in circumference, is the best in the island. Vessels may ride there in perfect safety, let the wind blow from what quarter it will. The entrance, however, is both narrow and shallow, so that none but small vessels can enter it without much difficulty. An iron chain across the entrance and a tower, on which are mounted some pieces of ordnance, are at present its only defence.

About the year 1160, Richard Coeur de Lion, returning from Palestine after the Crusades, was overtaken by a violent storm and his fleet dispersed. One of his ships and two galleys were wrecked on the western coast of this island. Richard, however, with the principal part of his fleet, had the good fortune to make the harbour of Rhodes, where he learned that those ships which were driven on shore in the island were seized, and his people barbarously murdered by order of Isaac Courmene, nephew to the Emperor of that name, who sent him to take charge of the government; against whom Isaac rebelled, and usurped the government of the island.

Richard also learned, with indignation, that Isaac had the barbarity even to refuse his sister Jane, wife to the king of Sicily, leave to land on his coast in the midst of the tempest, and accordingly having refitted his fleet he sailed from Rhodes, fully determined to land in Cyprus and severely punish Isaac for his cruel barbarity.

His descent was opposed with vigour, and many lives were lost on the occasion, but after many obstinate battles he effected a landing and took this inhuman and perfidious Greek prisoner, whom he loaded with chains, and although historians affirm these chains were of gold, yet they were not the less galling.

Richard having now made himself master of the island, had himself crowned king of Cyprus; and thus this island, after having remained a duchy for many ages under the Greek emperors, was now changed into a kingdom.

The next thing done by this monarch was to appoint a nobleman of the name of Robert Truhare his viceroy: and having put the island in a state of defence, he sailed from Lernacha to fulfil a vow he had made to assist Philip of France in his wars against the Turks. He therefore repaired to join this Prince at Ptolomaise, which town Philip was then besieging.     Richard arrived before this place, loaded with the glory of conquest and the treasures of Cyprus. Ancient writers mention this island under a variety of names, owing, I suppose, to its having fallen under the dominion of so many different nations, attracted by the mildness of the climate, the fertility of the soil, and, above all, by the advantages of its situation, which renders it the centre of communication and commerce between Asia Minor, Syria, Phenicia, and Egypt.

The whole island may be very properly divided into three distinct parts, differing in outward appearance and in the quality of the soil. The first is composed of high mountains, running from Cape St Andrew, at the east, to Cape Cormachiti in the west, being for the most part covered with wood.

The second manifests itself in fertile hills and delightful valleys at the foot of these mountains, watered with rivulets and four rivers which take their source from Mount Olympus.

The third part of the island is a vast, beautiful plain, extending from the south-east to the north-west of the island, and is about 16 leagues in length, and in many places from 8 to 10 in breadth. This plain has, from its richness and fertility, acquired the appellation of Messaire. It produces corn, cotton, and the most nutritive vegetables of every kind, in abundance, as also silk.

Formerly there were fifteen large cities, besides several villages in this island, of which nine cities were the capitals of as many distinct kingdoms, each having a separate government from the other.

At the present day little more remains than the ruins of these cities; whereof only a few deserve the notice of the traveller, as the towns of Nicosi, which is the capital, in the centre of the island, Famagousta on the banks of the Pedicus, opposite to Syria, which is built on the ruins of ancient Salamis or Ceraunia, on the northern side, and Paphos on the southern. The two last are very inconsiderable, and only remarkable for being at present the episcopal seats of the Greek Churches.

Besides these cities, there are also the ruins of many castles, which from their situation are almost inaccessible.

The revolutions which have happened in this island are indeed aston-ishing, particularly since the time of Dion Cassius, who wrote the Life of the Emperor Trajan.

He tells us that at that time the Jews revolted against the Romans, and possessed themselves of the island in the reign of this monarch, and in the space of a few days massacred 240,000 persons in hopes of shaking off the Roman yoke. But Trajan made them pay dearly for this act of barbarity, for having defeated their army in Syria, he sent one of his captains named Lucius into Cyprus, with a sufficient force to drive the Jews out of the island, and passed a decree that none of their race should ever after be allowed to settle in Cyprus, which decree was not only observed as long as the Romans possessed the island, but likewise by all those princes under whose dominion it has fallen, and even at this day it is observed under the Ottoman authority.

The mines of gold, copper etc., which, according to Strabo and other ancient writers, were formerly found in this island, are not now to be met with.

With respect to precious stones, which the same authors assert were also found here in abundance, the same [may] be said as of their gold mines, etc. The only gem found at present in any part of the island is an inferior kind of onyx.

With respect to the salt of this island, from which such great revenues formerly arose, the same advantages may still be derived from it if duly attended to. It may be had in great quantities at little expense from a lake situated near the sea, between the bourg of Lernacha, and Ptomolasa. This lake is about three leagues in circumference. It is a mixture of sea and rain-water, which being exposed to the influence of a very hot sun, a coherency of the salt particles is effected.

The sugar-cane was formerly planted in this island, but has been long discontinued, and the cotton-tree and a mulberry are substituted, the latter furnishes food for the silk-worm, which is certainly preferable to the sugar-cane.

The island also produces corn of every kind in abundance, of which great quantities are annually exported into Syria, Greece, and all the islands.

The wine of Cyprus has been justly celebrated, both by ancient and modern writers. Solomon himself speaks particularly of it. This wine is in the highest perfection when it is a hundred years old, and acquires, by this time, such smoothness and potency as renders it a perfect cordial. It is even said to be an antidote against poison, and of wonderful efficacy in all nervous affections.

There is a custom, handed down from time immemorial, still kept up in Cyprus, according to which every bridegroom, on the night of his nuptials, is to fill a large jar of this wine and bury it under ground, where it is to remain till the joyful event of his first child's marriage, and this they very properly call *vin de noce*, the nuptial wine. As it often happens that the children die before the wished-for period, the wine thus buried has been often known to lie untouched for two or three generations, particularly in the wealthy families who had no occasion to use it till the intended occasion offered. And by this means it was first discovered that Cyprus wine could not be too long kept.

When in the island, I purchased a ton of this *vino del amore*, which I was assured had been made thirty years. I carried it with me to

Marseilles, and sent it from thence to England, and though I have some of it still by me, yet I could never prevail on myself to put it under ground.

The island produces two sorts of wine, both in equal estimation, but one will not keep as long as the other, that which so wonderfully improves by age is by much the dearest, and costs about 2 shillings a bottle on the spot

The Egyptians have at all times given the preference to this wine: and even at the present day large quantities are annually exported to that country, which of itself does not produce wine of any kind.

The island of Cyprus is not less remarkable for its excellent olive oil, besides rape oil, which among the natives, is more in use than the former. This oil is certainly much better and less rancid than that made in Europe.

This island likewise produces honey of a superior quality, also saffron, capers, laudanum, mandrake, vermilion, and a great variety of aromatic and medicinal herbs.

The island is not so famous for its horses as its mules, which though not so large as those of Spain are nevertheless preferred, particularly on account of their gentleness and tractability.

Every species of domestic fowl known in Europe may be met with here, and with respect to game, no island can surpass it. There are several small birds in very high estimation in this island, among which may be reckoned the *ortolan* and *becque figue*; the latter is accounted the greatest delicacy both in the island and in all parts of Europe. They are preserved in Cyprus wine mixed with vinegar, and sent in great quantity to Venice, where they are in the highest estimation among the nobility.

The greyhounds of Cyprus are said to surpass in swiftness those of any other country: As to the truth of this assertion, I can only say that at Nicosi I had an opportunity of seeing repeated trials of their agility and speed, and were I to form my judgment from the shortness of the time in which they ran down a hare, I must certainly decide in their favour. The cats of this island are very beautiful, and exceed in shape and size those of Angora. They have a peculiarity which is not to be found in any of the feline kind yet discovered, and that is their mortal hatred to serpents, which they destroy and persecute with the same degree of implacable fury and malignity which the whole race manifest towards rats and mice.

Chameleons are to be met with in great numbers, in the mulberry gardens, and vineyards. I had one of these inoffensive animals for many months, and carried to Marseilles in my bosom, which place it seldom left, except when provoked by injury, or pinched by hunger. Its passion, in either case, to which it is very subject, is always expressed by a change of colour, and so quick is the succession of these changes, that one of those curious creatures will display no less than fifty different colours in the space of a few minutes. This I had many opportunities of observing, when I could not procure for my little favourite what he usually fed upon, namely flies. And again, after it had eaten a sufficiency, should I not immediately receive it into my bosom, its anger would instantly appear in the same variety of colours.

This little animal, notwithstanding all my care, died in the lazaretto whilst I performed quarantine at Marseilles.

The air, in some parts of this island, during the summer and part of the autumn, is rendered extremely unwholesome by the excessive heats which prevail at those seasons of the year. The grass is burnt up, and malignant fevers rage; particularly in the country around Lernacha and Famagousta. But all these inconveniences may be avoided by retiring at the approach of those baneful heats to the cantons of Soli, Nicosi, Lapatros, Carpasso, or Piscopi, in all which places the air is found to be as temperate and salutary as in any part of France.

And bad as the air is in those maritime places I have mentioned, I think the inhabitants may in some measure prevent, or guard against its noxious influence, by building their dwelling-houses at least two stories high instead of one. This improvement would at least secure them from the incessant attacks of the mosquito and other troublesome insects, to which they are always exposed by lying on the ground.

It is asserted by most authors who have given or attempted a general history of this island, that it is watered only by the torrents caused by the heavy rains during the winter. But this is certainly a mistake, and shews that those writers were entirely unacquainted with the interior parts of the country. It must indeed be owned that the island cannot boast any large rivers, but there are many pretty rivulets and streams that never dry up.

The only river that deserves the name of one is the Pedicus, which I have had occasion to mention before. This river divides into two considerable branches, traversing all the plains of Messaria, and passes through the town of Nicosi. It sometimes overflows, and in this case produces the same happy effects on its neighbouring plains that the river Nile does in Egypt.

There are also many springs of excellent water, and four or five rivulets gushing from Mount Olympus, and the neighbouring mountains. One of these waters the delightful country in the neighbourhood of Piscopi, also the lordship of Colossi, formerly the benefice belonging to the Knights Templars and Hospitalers, to whom this famous benefice was granted after the extinction of the former.

There is another beautiful spring of limpid water above the bourg Chitrie. This source, after furnishing sufficient water for thirty-six miles, serves the inhabitants of Palecitro to water a very great extent of gardens. Hence it must appear that the accounts of some authors, respecting a want of water in this island, are totally unfounded. It sometimes happens, as I was informed, that there is no fall of rain in any part of the island for three months together. To guard against this calamity, the islanders sink deep wells in proper places, and by means of machines made for the purpose, in imitation of the Egyptians, they supply themselves from these wells.

I have already observed that this island produces silk in abundance, which in the opinion of most silk buyers has more substance in it than any that is to be met with in other countries, and is therefore preferred to all other, both in France and England, for particular uses, such as fringe, and in stuffs where embroidery is introduced.

Their cotton trade is not less important than their silk, and its superior quality is so well known that it always meets a preference in the European markets.

There are still many parts of the island in a state of nature, which produce olives in great abundance spontaneously. These uncultivated tracts are principally to be found in the cantons of Carpasso, which from the fertility of the soil, if duly attended to, would yield an immense increase to the revenues of the island.

Cyprus is not the only country on this part of the globe where, from the want of inhabitants, the finest soil lies uncultivated. The greater part of the Ottoman empire appears in this primeval state, as their population bears no proportion to their extent of territory.

The amazing fertility of this island, and the little labour and expense in procuring here not only the necessaries but also the luxuries of life in abundance, serves only to render the inhabitants sensual, indolent, and effeminate. Their whole time is devoted to adorning their persons, feasting, dancing, and the like amusements.

The women are in general of the middle size, and much inferior to the English ladies in point of figure. Their complexion is rather dark, but their fine expressive black eyes and good teeth make up, in a great measure, for the want of those beautiful tints of fair and red which characterize our British and Hibernian ladies. They are not only warm in their attachment, but violent to the greatest degree; ever ready to make any sacrifice, or encounter any difficulty to promote and secure the happiness of the object of their choice. But let the happy man beware of betraying any appearance of coolness or indifference on his part, and above all, let him take care how he ventures to withdraw himself from a Cypriot.

The men are treacherous, and so cowardly and lost to a sense of honour that they will not dare to smell gunpowder, even in defence or vindication of the honour of a sister or a wife.

Before I take my final leave of this beautiful island, I shall take notice of the variety of names under which it has been known at different periods.

The Greeks call it 'Kupros,' as appears from the works of Homer and Hesiod, as well as many other poets. The name or epithet 'Kypris' or 'Koupris' given to Venus is, in the opinion of many writers a proof that she was first worshipped in this island. The Greeks have not agreed upon the origin of the word 'Kupros', but they have endeavoured to remove the difficulty in their usual way by supposing that a hero had given his name to the island. Others ascribe it to a plant which grows spontaneously in many parts of the island. This plant resembles the pomegranate in its branches and leaves, and flowers somewhat like the vine. Its blossoms have an odoriferous smell, and as Strabo relates, were much used for medicinal purposes by the physicians of his day.

The Turkish women, and some of the inhabitants of the islands of Chio and Patmos, stain their nails and hair with a juice extracted from this flower, or blossom, which is considered by them as a great beauty.

Having now made our little arrangements, we journeyed back with all possible expedition to Lernacha, where my ship was waiting to take me back to Europe. On our return to Lernacha, we immediately waited on our good friend the vice-consul, to whom we were indebted for the very favourable reception we met with at the different places we visited in our tour through this island, particularly at Nicosi, and I was not a little surprised on receiving a letter from the truly amiable and charming Madame E---, by the hands of her confidential friend, which breathed such warm professions of inviolable attachment, disinterested friendship and esteem, as would have induced any man but myself to settle for life in this paradisiacal island. But to the mind of a man, such as I then was, the slave of passion and the votary of licentiousness, such an idea would be no less horrible than that of self-destruction.

However, I said every thing that could tend to reconcile her to a temporary separation, as I termed it, assuring her that I was only going to pay my respects to Sir R A--- at Constantinople, and would return very shortly from thence to Cyprus.

# CHAPTER V

Departure from Cyprus – Character and Manners of the Modern Greeks – Crete – Arrival at Marseilles – The Lazaretto – Paris – Dublin – Brighton – English Blacklegs – A Scuffle with Opposition – The French Revolution, etc. – A French Gambling-house – King's Return from Varenne, etc.- Reflections on Gaming, etc.

Before I leave the country of ancient heroes and demi-gods, I must beg permission to make a few observations respecting what I have seen and heard of the character and manners of the modern Greeks.

Ancient Greece, which once presented to the admiring world so many noble and flourishing cities, and gave birth to so many distinguished warriors, poets and orators, now appears a desolate and ruined country where the hand of despotism has levelled to the ground the monuments of its former grandeur; extinguished the fire of genius and destroyed the energy of its inhabitants.

The wretched descendants of those renowned heroes are at the present day distinguished only for low cunning, baseness, ferocity and the grossest superstition. The abject state of slavery and humiliation to which they are reduced has rendered them mean and dastardly.

But I must not omit to observe that such of the inhabitants as are at a small distance from the seat of empire seem still to preserve a portion of hereditary spirit, particularly those of the Tagget mountains, who maintain that they are the true descendants of the ancient Spartans. These people could never be subdued, but in order to preserve what they call their independence, they pay to this moment a tribute to the Porte.

The Greeks differ very little from the Turks in their manners, but fall infinitely short of them in point of sincerity and fidelity. The only difference in their dress is that the Greeks are not permitted to wear green, or yellow. The Greeks very often give their daughters in marriage to Turks, but it must be on condition that the children of these Grecian ladies shall be brought up in the Mahometan religion.

The marriage ceremony is always performed in the presence of a priest, and is held a sacrament, but the union is not considered as indissoluble, and accordingly a divorce is obtained on merely applying for it, and the parties are at liberty to marry as soon after as they may think proper.

The brilliant torch of Hymen, so celebrated by the ancient poets, is not forgotten by the modern Greeks. It is placed in the nuptial room, and remains there till it be consumed. As soon as the bride arrives at the house of her husband, she is obliged to walk over a cribble placed on the carpet for that purpose, and should she not break it, the husband, without further proof, would give way to suspicions of the most unfavourable kind, therefore great care is taken that those cribbles should be of a very fine texture.

It is the custom always to burn a lamp in their bedrooms – the rich from habit, the poor from devotion – and this lamp is placed before an image.

The women are intolerably proud, though not so handsome as they are represented by many travellers. The most beautiful are in the island of Chio. They all paint their eyebrows with a preparation of antimony and gall-nuts. They are not allowed to live with a Frank without having previously obtained permission from the Cadi. The Grecian ladies never appear in public without a numerous suite, and at public ceremonies they are always on horseback.

The wind, for the first part of our voyage, was pretty fair, and after a navigation of ten days we discovered the island of Candia, formerly called Crete, so celebrated in ancient history and mythology. This island is about 200 miles long and 50 broad, and is at present chiefly inhabited by Greeks, who are said to pay the strictest regard to social and moral duties. The island produces plenty of excellent wine, corn, oil, silk and hemp, and is covered with olive-trees as large and flourishing as those of Toulon and Seville. The capital, of the same name, which was formerly so populous, is now almost desolate; it is, however, the see of a Greek archbishop, and its walls are still standing.

At the extremity of the town is a small rivulet, supposed to be the river Lethe of the ancients. Mount Ida, so famous in history, is nothing but a sharp pointed eminence, or craggy ridge, which divides this island. This mountain, however, must not be confounded with mount Ida in the neighbourhood of Troy, where the shepherd Paris adjudged the prize of beauty to the goddess Venus.

The Labyrinth so famed in Classic history, built by Daedalus in imitation of that in Egypt, extends for upwards of two miles under a hill at the foot of Mount Ida.

The next day we descried the island of Cythera, now called Cerigo, forty miles distant from the island of Candia. It was sacred to Venus, with a very ancient temple of that goddess, who was supposed to have emerged from the sea near its coasts.

We now continued our course for several days without interruption, till, within three leagues of the island of Malta, we discovered a vessel which our captain thought bore a suspicious appearance. Having examined her with my glass, I perceived that she had no guns, but was full of men armed with sabres and pistols.

Our fears subsided a little on her nearer approach, as we saw that she carried Tunisian colours, and those states were then at peace with France, to which nation our vessel belonged. Having no boat on board, they made us a signal to hoist out ours and when within hail they ordered our captain to go on board and carry with him some brandy, a chart and a compass, which having obtained, they permitted us to proceed without even returning us thanks, judging, perhaps rightly, that they owed their acquisition more to our fears than any friendly disposition towards them.

A few days after we made Cape Bona, on the Barbary Coast, and soon after discovered Sardinia on our starboard. At length, in thirty-seven days after our departure from Cyprus, we came to an anchor in the port of Marseilles.

The captain went on shore to deliver his letters at a particular place appointed for that purpose, as all vessels coming from the Levant are obliged to perform quarantine at the lazaretto, or Pest-house, of Marseilles. If in the space of those forty days none of the crew fall sick, they are enlarged and permitted to enter the pales of society; otherwise the quarantine recommences until they are all in perfect health.

The lazaretto is one of the best establishments I have seen for strict order and regularity.

The building, which is very extensive, is situated on the sea-side and surrounded by high walls, within which are several large squares, for the purpose of airing the merchandise, lest they might retain infection. The crew of every vessel is separately guarded, and should any person who had nearly performed his quarantine touch any one who was just entering on it, he becomes, ipso facto, re-involved in the same necessity of probation with the other. If even a friend comes to visit him, he must not approach nearer than two yards from the grated door: and should he be so imprudent as to touch him, he is subject to the same painful confinement.

This excellent institution is regulated by the Board of Trade, who every year appoint twelve merchants under the title of Superintendents of Health, with unlimited authority in everything that regards the establishment.

Having passed thirty days in this retreat, as we had letters of health from our Consul, we were at length judged fit once more to become members of society, an intelligence which I received with inexpressible joy and satisfaction, and resolved to make ample amends for the long abstinence and self-denial I had undergone.

On my first visit to Marseilles I became acquainted with a young officer of Infantry, who had distinguished himself as a spendthrift, a gambler and a self-sufficient blockhead. He possessed all the volubility and vain boasting of his countrymen, without any of their agreeable qualifications. This worthy gentleman often came to see me while I was in the lazaretto, and as soon as the auspicious day was announced, I commissioned him to make every necessary preparation to celebrate the joyful event of my deliverance from this tedious and irksome confinement; as it was my wish that nothing should be wanting, as far as money, wine and the fair votaries of the Cyprian goddess, with whom this happy city abounds, could contribute to the entertainment of a select party.

This was a charge which he undertook with the greatest readiness, and acquitted himself entirely to the satisfaction of his friends. Everything was *comme il faut*. But as usual on these occasions, the lot fell upon Jonas, for besides the extravagant charges of the entertainment I lost 300 louis d'ors at play to complete the happiness and hilarity of these good-natured friends.

After I had rested a fortnight at Marseilles, I set out for Paris, and amused myself there and in its environs for about three weeks. I had the honour of being introduced to a lady of high rank, who was the particular favourite of a great personage, and who has since ended her career in a manner, at that time little expected, which may be justly considered one of the most extraordinary events of this extraordinary age.

This unfortunate victim, to whom every heart and every court in Europe was then paying homage, could not afterwards find one individual resolute enough to risk his life for her deliverance. She shone then a bright star in all the splendour of royalty

Coming one evening to this lady's house, she honoured me with particular attentions and entered into a long conversation with me on the subject of my travels, in the course of which she made such observations as proved her a lady of brilliant wit and much information.

Soon after this conference, I quitted Paris for London, where I did not remain long, being impatient to receive the reward of my dangerous expedition.

When I arrived in Dublin I produced such incontestable proofs of having accomplished my arduous undertaking, and fulfilled my engagement, that my friends, who had staked their money on the supposed impracticability of the journey, were obliged reluctantly to pay me £15,000.

The expenses of my journey to Jerusalem amounted to £8,000, so that I cleared £7,000 by this expedition; the only instance in all my life before, in which any of my projects turned out to my advantage.

On leaving London, I committed my fine Arabian horse to the care of my groom. All the amateurs and knowing ones of London flocked to see him.

One of them offered me 1,000 guineas for the horse, but as I had no intention of parting with him for any sum, the offer was of course rejected. In a few days after I received, with inexpressible grief and vexation, the news of his death. It was the general opinion that some scoundrel, under the malign influence of envy, had poisoned this incomparable quadruped; and though I could never discover the author, yet I have not the smallest doubt of the fact.

I remained in Dublin upwards of two years, during which time I addicted myself to play with unabating eagerness, and with various success, but upon the close, the balance was considerably against me.

It was at that period I happily formed an acquaintance with a lady of exquisite taste and sensibility from whom I have never since separated.

She has been a consolation to me in all my troubles – her persuasive mildness has been a constant check on the impetuosity of my temper and at this moment constitutes, in my retirement, the principal source of all my felicity.

When I had gone the round of all the amusements which my own country could afford, I panted after something new, and as I never had a fixed establishment in London, I thought this scheme offered an opportunity of gratifying my volatility. With that rapidity which marked all my actions, I took a house in London; bought horses and carriages; subscribed to all the fashionable clubs and was in a short time a complete man of the town at the West End of the Town.

I had the honour of being presented at Court, and was particularly introduced to his Royal Highness the Prince of Wales, who honoured me with every mark of polite attention, for which this Prince is so eminently distinguished.

After having for some time enjoyed the pleasures of the metropolis, I went to the races at Brighton. One evening, after having had the honour of dining with HRH at the Pavilion, we repaired to the ball-room, where he did me the honour of introducing me to the Duchess of C--- .

The wine I had drank, joined to the habit I had acquired abroad, of behaving with very little ceremony to ladies, made me behave with so little respect and decorum towards the duchess, that had I met with my real deserts, I should have been kicked out of the ball-room. I shall never be able to suppress the reproaches of my heart for my unwarrantable behaviour in addressing this lady in too familiar and unbecoming a manner. But she good-naturedly imputed my conduct to the effects of wine – the only excuse our poor countrymen can make for their various absurdities and errors in all parts of the world.

After the Ball, I took a walk with two of my friends upon the Steyn, and as we were returning we heard the voices of many people in a house, which we had no sooner entered than we discovered several of our friends, surrounded by some of the most noted blacklegs in England, deeply engaged at play. Though I knew the character of those I had to deal with, yet such was my blind attachment to play that I could not resist the opportunity; and according to the proverb, embraced the evil in order to avoid the temptation.

Whether my adversaries meant to draw me in by encouraging me at first, or that the dice ran unusually in my favour, certain it is that I was, in a little time, a gainer of more than 500 guineas, whereupon one of the blacklegs, vexed at his ill-luck, vented his chagrin in such impertinent language to me, that I was provoked to give him a most hearty thrashing, which broke up the party for the night.

The next evening I returned to the scene of action, and not only lost what I had won the preceding night, but a considerable sum beside.

When I came home, Mr C--- my fellow-lodger and companion in affliction, asked me if I did not perceive that we had been most egregiously cheated? I answered no, and that I believed our losses were owing merely to ill-luck. 'I am convinced to the contrary,' replied he, 'and that Rascal Major G---, I have no doubt, is the principal agent in the business'. 'Impossible', said I; 'a man of his fortune and connections could not descend to such meanness.' 'Well then', added Mr C--- 'are you willing to put it to the proof? If so, I will undertake this night, to convict this man of fortune and high connections, of using false dice, which, on my honour, I believe he conceals in the hollow of his hand, to be produced whenever a fit occasion offers'.

I immediately expressed my approbation of my friend's proposal, and having fixed our plan, we repaired to the place appointed, accompanied by Col.-Sgt L--- and the Abbé St F---, both of whom quitted the room soon after our arrival. We found nearly the same company as the evening before. It was then about midnight; and the better to carry on our scheme we affected to be much intoxicated, an appearance which the Major likewise assumed, though for a very different purpose.

After some throws of the dice the Major's turn came. We staked very large sums, which were eagerly accepted. At the moment of throwing my friend gave the signal, and instantly seized on the Major's hand. I flew to his assistance, calling at the same time to the rest of the company for their interference, asserting that the Major had false dice and that we were ready to stake our lives upon the issue of a strict examination.

Not a soul interfered in the dispute; so that we were left to contend with our adversary, who exerted all his strength to withhold from us the proof of his villainy. After a severe scuffle, the violence of our exertions at length brought us all to the ground near the sideboard, from whence I snatched a knife and threatened the Major, that if he did not instantly disclose what he had in his hand I would cut it open. Finding it vain to contend any longer, he at last complied, and we, with a mixture of indignation and astonishment, discovered the object of our search, namely a pair of dice, while those with which the company played remained on the table.

Upon examination we found them to be so contrived as never to throw seven; a main which the Major constantly called, so that whatever chance he brought, though apparently against him, was in fact in his favour. He took all the odds that were offered him and of course could never lose.

We now found it as difficult to protect the Major from the rage of the company as we had before to procure assistance against him. The majority were for throwing him out of the window, and indeed the poor devil himself, almost dead with apprehension, seemed to expect nothing but instant destruction. He pressed my hand and begged for mercy. My compassion was moved, which at once suppressed my resentment, and he was through my intercession, joined by that of my friend, at length suffered to depart, after I had given him a glass of wine to raise his drooping spirits and enable him to find his way home.

That which generally happens at all gaming-tables in consequence of a scuffle was precisely the case at ours, for not only all the money which the Major had won and lay before him on the table disappeared, but every individual of the company complained of having been either cheated or robbed – for the truth of which I can vouch with respect to one of the company, as on my return home I found myself literally penniless.

I took care to get the false and the fair dice sealed up by the groom-porter, in whose possession they were left till the next day, when he had orders to deliver them into the hands of Sir Charles B---, the Steward of the Course, who produced them at the Jockey Club, of which I was a member, and it happened that the Prince of Wales dined with us that day. The implements were handed about and every one had a fling at the unfortunate Major, for among gamblers as well as among women, reputation is of the most tender nature, and consequently is injured, or perhaps utterly lost, by the smallest stain or imputation.

The Prince highly commended our conduct, but at the same time observed that had we failed in our attempt to wrest from the Major the incontrovertible proof of his fraudulent practice, we should probably have cause to repent our enterprise.

The Major, as we afterwards learned, set off, in about a quarter of an hour after he had left us, for Falmouth, where he embarked for Jamaica, in hopes of arriving there in time to sell his property before his disgrace should be known in that quarter of the globe. But notwithstanding all his caution and expedition, the story got the start of him, and to his utter ruin, had even reached the ears of his relation, Admiral G---, who would not admit him into his presence.

Thus disgraced and disappointed, he re-embarked for England and died, as was generally supposed, through excessive grief and vexation, on his passage.

The races being now over at which, contrary to my usual custom, I met with some success, and having made some necessary arrangements, I returned to London and soon resumed my former course of life.

My next trip was to Newmarket, a glorious arena in which I had an opportunity of entering the lists against Mr F---, though not in a political discussion or a trial of oratorical powers. In these I might have made some proficiency, had I availed myself of the very favourable opportunities that presented themselves to me on my first setting out in life, having been returned a Member in the Irish Parliament at the early age of eighteen, a circumstance which induced me to apply myself for some time to the study of the constitution, laws and commerce of the country, with that degree of attention and assiduity, which so important and arduous a pursuit required. But the dissipated life into which I afterwards plunged, soon put a period to this and every other serious and laudable application.

But to return to Mr F---, there is not among his most devoted friends a greater admirer of his genius, talents and manly eloquence than I am, yet at that time, his abilities as a statesman were not less conspicuous than the dissipation of his manners. He could sit up a whole night at a gaming table, and the next day make the Treasury Bench shake by the force of arguments. In our contest I paid a compliment of 2,000 guineas to his superior skill, and 6,000 to several others of the same party: among whom was HRH the Duke of Y---, so that the opposition was completely triumphant, and levied a pretty severe fine on my purse.

Of all the severe losses I ever sustained, this was the one I least regretted, as I had not the most remote idea of suspecting the honour or integrity of my antagonists.

The French Revolution, at this time, began to make some noise in the world. All Europe had their attention on the National Assembly. Our nation was particularly respected by the French, and the Constitution of England was looked upon as the best model for their intended fabric.

This was the shield under which the Orleans faction covered their designs, and concealed the horrors and wide-spreading evils they were then preparing for their ill-fated country.

Under the pretext of reformation they drew to their party all those whose notions of liberty were perfectly consistent with principles of the very best constitution, whilst the populace were enticed by the abolition of titles and the sacrifice of a few privileges which the faction could easily resume when their power was once established. By these means they concentrated the whole force of the kingdom, and at one blow, overturned a monarchy which had stood the test of so many ages.

Amongst the many whom curiosity led to this wonderful scene of action, I repaired to Paris in the year 1791. On this occasion, and two more visits which I afterwards paid to France, I was enabled to make some observations on the infatuated people of that vast and once flourishing empire.

With a considerable sum of money in my pocket, I arrived at Paris, that epitome of the world, where greatness and meanness, riches and poverty, wisdom and folly, are all to be met with in their highest degree.

This immense city has at all times been the rendezvous and asylum of all the intriguers and desperadoes of Europe. It was likewise the abode of the most celebrated artists, as well as the most learned, the most opulent and most profligate of mankind.

Every person I saw wore, in some shape or other, the tri-coloured riband as the symbol of Liberty. Through all the provinces I observed a general fermentation among the people, but Paris was the focus whence emanated all the rays of enthusiasm to the most distant parts of the empire.

The Palais Royal was the general rendezvous of the conspirators, of whom its proprietor was the chief. Here was laid the plan, and the hour fixed, for an insurrection which was to be regulated by a signal from the Water-works. In every part of the garden were groups of men, each group, or separate body, had their particular orator, thundering forth downfall and destruction to royalty.

This may be justly termed the volcano, from whose baneful crater issued all the lava that desolated the finest provinces in France; and might with equal justice be called the Academy of Sedition and Irreligion, where pupils were taught to deny their God and disobey their king.

Any person resolute enough to combat these doctrines was sure of meeting with the grossest insults, and may think himself peculiarly fortunate if he escaped with life.

Chairs, tables and stools were converted into rostrums from whence the Apostles of Sedition harangued their tumultuous auditors, and here I cannot help expressing my astonishment, that in such a nation as France then was, a few thousands of incendiaries should be permitted thus to deliberate on the subversion of the existing government, and meditate the destruction of all those who were inimical to their system.

My heart was wrung on beholding in the Tuileries the illustrious but unfortunate Royal family, who were doomed soon to be the victims of this popular effervescence.

When the most renowned monarch that ever governed France erected that edifice, he little imagined that it should one day become the prison of the best and mildest of his descendants, and that its doors should be guarded by a band of miscreants many of whom had tasted largely of the bounty of their august prisoners.

I often attended the sittings of the National Convention, where I could discover nothing of that sober dignity that might be expected from the representatives of a great nation. On the contrary the most violent and sanguinary measures were proposed and heard with rapture, and the promoter of these measures applauded as one of the best and wisest legislators.

Mirabeau and the Abbé Maury were the two great political combatants on this prize-fighting stage. A French writer very justly remarks on the former 'that he was more famous than celebrated, more original than eloquent, and equally actuated by avarice and ambition.' Totally lost to a sense of morality, he wanted even that suavity of manners which might give a sort of gloss to his vices, and throughout his whole conduct manifested a degree of savage fierceness and audacity never known in any character before him.

He generally had the majority on his side, as the violence of his doctrine was well adapted to the character of his auditors, mostly composed of the Orleans faction.

But the Club of the Jacobins was the place where the whole contents of Pandora's Box seemed concentrated. Here the goddess of Liberty presided – not the mild beneficent deity, under whose protecting arm and salutary influence are experienced all those blessings and rational enjoyments which man can reasonably expect or wish for in a state of civil society – but a strumpet assuming her name, and glorying in her attributes, in order to give a sanction to her votaries for pillage, massacre and every species of atrocity without control.

It is impossible to conceive an institution more afflictive or more disgraceful to human nature than that which had acquired for its title the Jacobin Club. An assemblage of worthless wretches, who acknowledged no God but Voltaire, no religious code but that of the visionary Rousseau, no system of morality but that of the apostate Raynal, nor political jurisdiction but that of an assassin.

With these principles they made and are still making war against all regular governments, and proscribing without scruple all who are eminent for probity, virtue or talents.

That such a mass of corruption should have been able to erect itself without control, into a supreme tribunal within the metropolis of a vast empire; that its members should have established societies of their own order, in almost all the large cities of Europe, organized bands of robbers, prisoners and assassins, and shaken the thrones of sovereigns to their very foundations, that they should have murdered their own King, his Royal Consort and sister, and poisoned the young and innocent offspring of sixty-six kings, in fine, that they should have been tamely suffered to imprison, banish, pillage and massacre all those who dared to oppose them, can only be accounted for by supposing the most extraordinary resignation on the one hand, and the most unparalleled audacity on the other.

In this pandemonium I was desired to observe a little man about five feet high, whose very aspect bespoke him the arch-fiend of the diabolic assembly – this Marat!

Before the Revolution, he had no other way of subsistence than that of vending herbs, which he affirmed to be the production of certain mountains in Switzerland, and, according to his account, possessed, in the most eminent degree, all those sanative qualities ascribed to our modern patent medicines. This man certainly had a most daring mind, and an unblushing front. He was not to be disconcerted by rebuffs, or intimidated by danger; in the prosecution of his designs no compunctions of humanity ever obtruded themselves to impede his progress.

From this infernal mansion I was impatient to depart, and again to visit the haunts of men. I was soon introduced to a society of a very different stamp, where I met with agreeable women, good cheer and deep play. This was the Pavillon d'Hanovre, built by Maréchal de Richelieu on his return from his campaigns in Germany. It was then occupied by the Viscount C---, whose vices and immorality were as conspicuous as his rank.

To this distinguished apostate I was introduced, and as he had previously received some information concerning me, he regulated his motions accordingly.

I was received with the highest degree of affability and respect, and as he spoke English tolerably well we conversed for some time in that language, after which he introduced me to the ladies who were all expert at their trade, and perfect mistresses of the art of seduction.

'Has milord been long in France?' said one. 'Does he propose to make any stay in it?' says another. 'It cannot be for the purpose of learning the language,' observed a third, 'as he already speaks it with greater purity than we do ourselves.'

The men too, played off all the artillery of their wit and politeness. They were all *soi-disant* men of fashion, and talked much of their influence at court, but I afterwards learned that they were a set of rascals, hired for the same purpose as the women.

The only victims present were a counsellor of the Parliament and myself, though the company consisted of at least thirty. The counsellor was, according to the phrase, entirely done up, having lost his whole fortune left him by his father, a *fermier-générale*, which amounted to upwards of £300,000.

The dinner was served up with a display of profusion and elegance, while the lively conversation of the ladies gave the highest zest to our entertainment, for it must be granted that the French ladies surpass those of any other nation in their agreeable manner of conversing and their lively turns of imagination, and in this opinion I am convinced all my countrymen who have visited France will concur.

With the French, the manner is all in all, and provided a thing be done with a good grace, the merits of it form but a secondary consideration. A Frenchman offers you his house, his table, his horses, and even his wife, and the last article is, perhaps, the only one he means you should accept.

In France fashion governs everything, and the spirit of intrigue prevails so much among them that a man of the town would be as much ashamed of even the appearance of an attachment to his wife, as if he were detected in any improper or dishonourable act. In other respects the French character, unsophisticated by the 'Rights of Man,' is truly respectable. They are warm in friendship, brave, generous and loyal to excess.

The good cheer and conviviality that prevailed at the viscount's table was entirely to my taste. The first day I played but little nor indeed was

I much pressed or solicited, for as they saw that I nibbled at the bait, they entertained no doubt but that I would soon swallow the hook, nor were they deceived; as in a few days after I returned to the lure and in two sittings they contrived to ease me of 3,000 louis. This obliged me to pay another visit to Ireland in order to recruit my purse.

The evening before I quitted Paris I was present at the return of the King, after having been stopped at Varennes, by the order of Romoeuf at that time his aide-de-camp.

Romoeuf on that day decided the fate of France, and the emigrants in London had the mortification of seeing in that very city, for upwards of two years, the villain who had the audacity to arrest his king and lead him to prison, from whence he was never brought but to meet the regicide judges and ascend the scaffold.

When the King's flight was known at Paris, a universal consternation prevailed throughout the city. Each party was apprehensive of some ill consequences from the event, though Garat in his Memoirs positively asserts that the whole was previously known, and either forwarded or connived at by all.

At three o'clock in the afternoon, I procured by the help of a few louis d'ors, a seat in a sort of theatre, built for the purpose at the Gate of the Tuileries.

A general order was issued that a profound silence should be observed, and that no person, on any pretence, should take off his hat. The King's carriage was surrounded by National Guards, who formed an impenetrable mass against bands of assassins said to be employed by Orleans, and his subsequent conduct proved that there was just ground for this conjecture.

La Fayette encouraged the mob in the grossest insults against the Royal family, and often repeated the order that no one should uncover. This, however, did not prevent me from lifting my hat as the King passed, for which I should have paid dearly were it not for one of the National Guards, who persuaded the sans-culottes to do me no injury by assuring them I was a mad Irishman.

There were in the carriage with the Royal family two of the commissaries, Barnave and Petion. The latter had the Dauphin on his knee during the whole procession. La Tour Maubourg, the third commissary, was in another carriage. On the box of the King's coach were seated the two *Gardes du Corps*, young men of family and fortune. They had their hands tied like the vilest criminal, and their faces exposed to the

scorching sun, encountering wherever they turned their eyes the ferocious countenances of a set of miscreants who were ready to tear them
piecemeal for their attachment and fidelity to the best of Kings.

One of these *Gardes*, as *avant coureur*, had got some miles beyond
Varennes when he heard of the King's arrest, and though he might have
made his escape, yet he could not for a moment entertain the idea of
abandoning his Royal master. His name was Vallory, and I feel much
pleasure in having it in my power to rescue from oblivion this act of
generous loyalty in this young man.

The King's return restored a temporary tranquillity to the metropolis,
and I gladly availed myself of this calm, to demand my passport, which
was immediately granted.

In a short time after my arrival in Dublin I sold an estate which
produced me £25,000, and having paid some debts and made a few
necessary purchases, I returned to Paris with £14,000 in my pocket.

I found this city in a state of greater tumult than when I left it. The
hirelings of faction grew every day bolder and less restrained in their
insults to the King. It was at this time that a horde of regicides, headed
by St Huruge and Barras, broke into the palace, and though they did
not effect the horrid purpose for which there is every reason to believe
they were employed, yet every outrage, short of murder, was committed
against this unfortunate family.

I shall not attempt to describe the heartrending scene to which I
myself was an eye-witness, nor would any language express the different sensations which alternately took possession of my soul. Pity,
rage, and loyalty forced from me a torrent of tears, which a regard to
self-preservation should have induced me to suppress.

I beheld the unfortunate King full of mildness and majesty, pity-
ing and still loving his deluded subjects. He was obliged to drink the
health of those who sought his blood, assassinated his amiable family,
overturned his throne, and deluged his fair kingdom with the blood
of its most noble inhabitants.

At length Petion, the Mayor of Paris, arrived, and having harangued
these brave citizens and applauded their conduct, he had sufficient
influence over them to persuade them immediately to retire. Nor is
this to be wondered at, as he was the very person who had planned
the proceedings of that memorable day. But what renders this man's
character odious in the highest degree, is that a few days before the
tumult he had a conference with the King, and received a large sum of

money to induce him to use his influence and authority in preventing any outrage that may be attempted against the Royal family.

The next day I observed, in a print shop, a caricature representing the Duke of Orleans playing at picquet with the King. The Duke wore the bonnet rouge, and the King appeared endeavouring to prevent his crown from falling off his head. A label from the King's mouth contained these words: 'I have discarded the Hearts – He has all the Spades'. In French 'Piques' means both 'Spades' at cards and 'Pikes' as a weapon. 'I've lost the Game', it went on to say.

While I was reflecting on this severe sarcasm, I recognized a person whom I had often seen at Marseilles and London. He once possessed a very considerable fortune, which in early youth he squandered, and was now reduced to the necessity of living on the fruits of an experience dearly bought, of which he so well availed himself that he supported the appearance and, what is much more extraordinary, the character of a gentleman, having never been known, by any voluntary act, to incur the imputation of meanness or dishonesty. In the course of my acquaintance with him, I had many opportunities of proving the sincerity of his friendship and the strictness of his principles as a man of true honour and integrity.

His knowledge of mankind was extensive, and as he was admitted into all societies, he was equally conversant in the tricks and frauds practised by adventurers both in high and low life.

After some general conversation, he asked how long I had been at Paris. Upon which I told him I was just returned from Dublin, and related to him the cause of my journey. 'It was very unlucky', said he, 'that I happened not to be in Paris at the time, or I might have prevented your falling into the hands of the Philistines, but', continued he, 'pardon me the expression, you seem born to be continually a dupe – I shall prove it to you whenever you please – and it is vain to contend with fate'.

'That may very well be,' replied I, 'but at all events come and breakfast with me to-morrow morning.' We parted for the present, and in the morning my friend was announced before I was out of bed.

After breakfast the subject of our conversation the preceding day was resumed, and I detailed to him the several severe losses I had sustained at the Pavilion of Hanover.

'My dear W---' he exclaimed, 'it is astonishing that you are yet to learn that within these ten years the practice of knavery has been reduced into a regular science. That it has infected all societies and that you cannot go into any house of high or low degree without meeting with swarms of adventurers whose whole study, day and night, is how they may plunder their neighbours with impunity. I know them all by their names, titles and degree of proficiency. I may easily guard you against their different modes of deception. You must consider that in Paris you cannot find deep play, unless it be at a very great disadvantage.

The games which are generally introduced in polite circles are *pharo* and *rouge et noir*, at which the holders of the bank have so great an advantage that it is impossible but that a punter must be a loser in the course of a month, let him play with ever so much caution and even apparent success.'

'If that be the case', then said I, "tis astonishing that there are so many players at a game so decidedly against them.'

'You are to consider', replied my friend, 'that it is not every person who can command a sufficient capital to set up a bank, and many who can are deterred by the greatness of the stake, as it requires no less than five or 6,000 pounds, not considering that they lose little by little, as punters, what would be sufficient to establish a bank.

Besides, there are various motives and many inducements to gaming. Some enter into it from a natural inclination, without once considering whether the chances are for or against them. Others out of indolence, not knowing how else to employ their time, and many whose affairs are deranged or fortunes ruined, hope by some lucky run to retrieve their affairs. You will likewise find great numbers who frequent these places merely for the good cheer that is to be found in them, though they might regale themselves on much more reasonable terms at any tavern in town – all these can only be punters.

The ostensible holders of the bank are generally low fellows; gamblers by profession and adepts in their art. They are of obscure family, and most of them have obtained by swindling the very capital which constitutes their sole establishment.

With these swindlers people of property have of late years associated themselves, thinking it an excellent method to let their money out to advantage.'

'You seem', said I, 'to have a complete knowledge of the business, but if the advantage be so great, why do not you yourself hold a bank?'

'For a very good reason: the want of means', answered he. I told him that I had a capital more than sufficient for the purpose, and that

I would readily embark in it, if I thought it would succeed. He said he would answer for the success but that it would be necessary, in case of such an establishment, to have a confidential person whose business it would be to watch with the strictest attention over those who deal and play. 'For you must know', continued he, 'that it is not here as in London, where people of rank and character undertake that office.

In Paris, a gentleman would think himself disgraced by such an employment. The bank holders are therefore under the necessity of employing poor wretches for this purpose, who are paid a couple of louis a night for their trouble, and as they are fellows devoid of the principles of honour and integrity they are often bribed by sharpers to cheat their employers. But if you be determined to put your design into execution, I shall take care to guard against them, as I am perfectly well acquainted with all their tricks.

The ancient chancellery of the Duke of Orleans is now to be let, a most commodious situation for our purpose, and you will find there an excellent cook, a character of no small importance in our household, for the votaries in these temples pay the most devout homage to those altars where the richest *morceaux* and the most delicate viands abound.'

After this disquisition I gave him unlimited powers to arrange every thing relative to the business, and assured him that the money should be forthcoming when required.

Thus empowered my friend set to work, and in a few days we made every necessary arrangement and opened shop, nor were we long without customers – the increase and continuance of which the skill of our cook contributed not a little.

I received, for two months, the genteelest and most numerous company ever met with in Paris on such occasions, and gained by this speculation about £15,000, part of which was expended in entertainments.

# CHAPTER VI

A Journey to Switzerland – Lausanne – The Glaciers – Mr B--- – Some Observations on the Swiss – Their Candour – Their Bravery – Their Honesty – National Honour – Public Justice – Geneva – Milan – Florence – Rome – Some Reflections on Italy.

The troubles in Paris increasing daily, and the season for going to Switzerland approaching, our punters fell off by degrees, many of whom went to join the emigrant princes. I therefore determined to visit Switzerland, and accordingly mounted my carriage. I had, besides, four others that followed me, with an immense retinue, not forgetting my cook and thirty led horses.

My purse was considerably diminished, notwithstanding the success of my bank.

'Tis true there was due to me £25,000, a shilling of which, in all probability, I shall never touch – thanks to the Revolution, which deprived my debtors of the means of payment.

On my route I was often stopped and examined by the sans-culottes, who were now the supreme rulers, but at length I arrived without any accident at Lausanne, the general rendezvous of foreigners who visit Switzerland. At that time it was full of genteel company, and though I did not stake a single crown at play, I contrived to amuse myself tolerably well.

My first object was to set my French cook to work, whose rare talents I did not suffer to remain unemployed, as I kept open table for strangers in general, but more particularly for my own countrymen.

Scarce an evening passed but we had a tea-party and a ball, at which was always present a number of beautiful and accomplished women, many of whom were of the first quality. Among those who honoured me with their presence were the Princess Loubomeski, formerly the favourite of the King of Poland, and the Princess Joseph de Monaco, both of whom have since been guillotined at Paris, whither they went contrary to the advice and remonstrances of all their friends.

Besides these, I was often visited by the Russian Princess Bellouski, with her intimate friend Miss Cassenove, and Miss de'Apraxim, who had been accused and convicted of polygamy. But when the Duchess of D--- honoured those assemblies with her presence, she at once attracted the attention and admiration of the company by the beauty of her person and her mental accomplishments.

From this charming society I separated with reluctance, in consequence of a resolution I had formed of making a tour round the glaciers and of endeavouring, if possible, to ascend Mont Blanc. In my route I had the pleasure of meeting Lord Charles T--- and Mr B---, the former of whom has since lost his life in a manner peculiarly unfortunate, an event which I can never remember but with extreme concern, having conceived for him a most sincere friendship and esteem, founded upon a knowledge of his merit and distinguished virtues.

I shall not attempt a description of the glaciers and Mount Blanc; but refer my readers to the account given by Monsieur de Saussure, who expended a considerable part of his fortune in the most dangerous attempts to discover whatever was rare or worthy of observation in those grand wonders of nature. He has composed a scientific work about the Alps, in which he gives their altitude, describes the immense masses of snow which cover them with some learned conjectures about their probable duration, ascertains the weight of the air and gives a minute account of the fossils and metals contained in the bowels of those vast mountains.

He is the only man who has acquired the glory of attaining the Summit of Mount Blanc, where he has left a bottle containing a paper with his name inscribed on it.

The reading of his work filled my mind with a desire of doing the same and of paying homage to this great man by placing my name next to this bottle. But whether it was not the proper season, or that the weather was unusually severe, we had not proceeded above two-thirds of the ascent when, owing to a violent shower of hail, a mass of snow detached itself from the mountain and killed two of our guides, which so intimidated the rest that it was impossible to prevail on them to proceed one step farther, as they affirmed that the snow would soon fall in such masses as would inevitably overwhelm us all. I was now left alone with Lord Charles, and after some deliberation we determined to join our cowardly attendants, as any attempt to proceed without them would be vain.

We therefore returned to Lausanne, and the next day I received an invitation to a ball given by the Princess B---. Besides the pleasure I took in dancing, I found myself induced, by another motive of a more powerful ascendancy, to accept this invitation. Miss E--- the friend and companion of the Princess, was rich only in the gifts of nature, improved by accomplishments, the chief of which were music and painting, in which she eminently excelled. With these natural and acquired advantages, she began her career of conquests, in hopes of procuring a husband who might make amends for her only deficiency.

It is natural to suppose that a young man of my turn could not long remain insensible to so many attractions, and I made no scruple of telling her so. My assiduities were not rejected. I ventured a love-declaration in writing, to which she vouchsafed such an answer as induced a regular correspondence highly pleasing to me. But all my endeavours to procure a private interview were ineffectual, as I never could see her but in the company of her patroness, and I could plainly perceive that both of them meant I should be indebted to Hymen for what I hoped to obtain by means of love alone.

However, I still continued my assiduities in hopes of turning to my advantage the first favourable opportunity. But as none offered, I gave up the pursuit, nor did I suffer much pain from the disappointment.

At Evian, a small town of Savoy on the borders of the lake, lived at that time an English gentleman, remarkable for his literary talents, his immense fortune, and still more so by the imputation of a crime which has been alleged against him, of a nature so horrible, that I wish to draw a veil over it, scarcely believing it possible that a man so amiable in every respect could ever have been so depraved.

The bare accusation, however, has obliged him to quit his native country, where such a crime is looked upon with a degree of abhorrence equal to its enormity. I shall not hazard any farther opinion respecting this extraordinary charge against him, but merely relate a conversation that passed between him and a friend of mine who was on a very intimate footing with him.

William Beckford (1759-1844), author of Vathek, and other works.

One day in a tête-à-tête my friend ventured to touch on the awful subject, or the suspicion entertained by the world against him. Mr B--- solemnly declared that it was nothing but mere suspicion, and that he would not exist an hour under a consciousness of having wilfully given cause or grounds for such a suspicion, and hoped that time would manifest to the world a much clearer proof of his innocence than ever was adduced of his guilt. But to return to the ball. After a few country dances, the Princess proposed that the whole party, consisting of the Princess L---, the family of the Apraxims, the two Princes Camille, Jules and the writer of these memoirs, should pay a visit to Mr B---, which was unanimously agreed to, and accordingly the next morning we all embarked to cross the lake, and after two hours' pleasant navigation arrived at Evian. The Prince Camille, who was very intimate with Mr B---, introduced us severally. And I do not think that I ever saw a man of a more captivating exterior than our host nor did he appear less indebted to nature for the endowments of his mind, for during the twenty-four hours that we passed with him, we were constantly entertained with something new and interesting in his conversation.

The dinner was sumptuous, and served with the utmost taste and elegance. During the repast we were entertained with a concert, performed by a select band of twenty-four musicians, which he keeps constantly in his pay. When we had taken our coffee, Mr B--- gave us several airs of his own composition on the pianoforte, which he touched with masterly execution and exquisite taste.

Afterwards the carriages were announced, the whole company were conveyed in coaches-and-four and on about twenty saddle-horses to the distance of about four miles, where we arrived at a most delightful wood, in the midst of which was a garden laid out in the English taste, adorned with statues, and here and there with clumps of the most odoriferous flowering shrubs.

Here, while we sauntered, our ears were often unexpectedly struck with the softest music, the performers of which were to us invisible, and the sounds were reverberated, with ravishing melody, by the echoing mountains which surrounded us, so that the whole appeared the effect of enchantment.

On our return to the house we were presented with tea and sweetmeats, the whole concluding with a ball at which this admirable exile shewed himself as great an adept in dancing as he had before done in music. Our amusements continued till morning, when we all reembarked on our return to Lausanne after taking leave of our kind host, who expressed his hopes that we would often favour him with our company in his retirement.

During our passage across the lake, nothing was talked of but this modern Anacreontic Lucullus.

The ladies were very lavish in his praise, not knowing, or seeming to know, anything of the cause which brought him to his present abode. They all agreed that the woman who could inspire him with love must be the envy of her sex, while each perhaps, fancied herself the only one who stood a chance for such a distinction.

One young lady in particular seemed to be of that opinion, but she laid her snares with so little caution and address that Mr B--, who was a wary bird, easily escaped being entangled, and he proved to her by his very particular attention and cold civilities, that marriage was not so attracting a lure as the young lady expected.

The next morning I paid a visit to the Duchess of D---, accompanied by two of the ladies who were of the party the preceding day; where I found a large company and close to her ladyship, as usual, her two faithful attendants. I cannot pass over what appeared to me a peculiarity in this distinguished lady, which is, that she gives to all persons introduced to her a gracious reception, nor can she by any coldness of manners or sarcastic mode of civility drive any one from her presence, however disagreeable in manners or conversation.

Of this weakness, and an amiable weakness it must surely be allowed, two old gentlemen, and both conspicuous characters, took advantage, and were as constant at her levee as her attendants. When I entered the room and saw her thus attended, it instantly brought to my mind the picture of Susanna between the two elders.

The one was a Swiss physician, in his person the very transcript of Don Quixote, and a Thomas Diafoirus in his conversation. He had raised his reputation a little by the publication of a sort of medical nomenclature though in his own practice he prescribed but one remedy for all diseases, and as his patients were of the *beau monde*, whose disorders were, for the most part, imaginary, he was tolerably successful.

The other was the most renowned and most voluminous historian of our age, but whatever pleasure the reading of his works may afford, it was more than counterbalanced by the insipidity of his conversation.

Some of the company made inquiries concerning our expedition to Evian, and when I had related the particulars the historian observed, with a truly pedantic air, that it was astonishing any Englishman would visit a man who lay under such ah imputation as Mr B--- did: that even supposing him innocent still some regard was due to the opinion of the world; and he would venture to say that I was the only one among my countrymen who had ever paid that man the smallest attention since his banishment. The only reply I made to his impertinent animadversion was that I did not look upon this little piece of history as any way deserving the attention of so great a man.

The Duchess complacently smiled, the rest of the company looked grave, my pedant was dumb, and I took my leave.

The season for enjoying Switzerland being nearly over, I prepared for my departure. But before I quit it I shall take the liberty of saying a few words concerning the character of that nation described by so many authors, and this I do because the observations I have made differ so materially from all the accounts I have read.

It is certain that at present no trace can be discovered of the contemporaries of William Tell. All those who have given any account of Switzerland are lavish in their descriptions of the beauties of the country, where nature is permitted to indulge herself in all her native grandeur and majesty, unrestrained by the intrusive hand of art.

The inhabitants are represented as candid, brave and laborious, faithful and steady in their friendship, and always ready to sacrifice their lives in support of their country's honour. The women are said to be handsome, domestic, virtuous, without any propensity to expensive pleasures.

I confess that I had not penetration enough to discover these rare perfections during my residence among them. And as to their frankness and candour, they appeared to me rather boorish, except when they have any point to carry and then they are all civility and complaisance, but not in the least degree more candid on that account. And since the Canton of Berne has taken upon itself to regulate the others, whatever degree of candour they might have possessed before is considerably diminished, owing to the electioneering intrigues carried on previous to the nomination of magistrates.

They are said to be brave − true, if a sort of mechanical courage, hired out to the best bidder, can be called bravery. But I never saw in them any instance of that true courage, which consists in a jealous sense of honour and a congenial warmth in the cause of friendship. When they fight among themselves it is with sticks, and as they never engage upon equal terms, the contest is soon decided by the weak yielding to the strong. The peasants and mechanics spend half the day in eating and their nights at the tavern. In fact, none among them can be justly called laborious but the women. They indeed are never idle, and seem only to hold the place of upper servants in the family.

I have heard the Swiss praised for their honesty. To this I shall only say that upon entering Switzerland, I was particularly cautioned to beware of the roguery of servants, which salutary advice I did not attend to, and suffered accordingly.

As to the sacrifices they are always ready to make in support of the honour of their country, the French Revolution affords a sufficient answer. Never was a people so degraded and insulted as the Swiss were upon that occasion. It cannot be forgotten that the regiment of Wallwill was disarmed at Aix in Provence by the National Guard, and shamefully driven home − a direct infringement of the rights of treaties and the laws of nations. And when the Swiss Guards were massacred at Paris, and the brave Major Bachman executed on a public scaffold, the silence of the thirteen Cantons upon these events convinced the revolutionists that they might have effected any attempt they pleased against that nation with impunity.

That Switzerland, after the efforts she had made to shake off the imperial yoke and erect herself into a republic, should not have turned her arms against France, while pursuing a similar object, is in no way surprising. On the contrary, it was rather to be expected that she would rather have assisted, from motives of religion and policy, in bringing about the Revolution. But that any regular government should tamely submit to the grossest insults without making one attempt to obtain redress, exceeds credibility, and is not to be paralleled in ancient or modern history.

They have even gone further: they have received into their States an ambassador from the Jacobins, citizen Barthelemy, a political chameleon, who has successively dictated to them the orders he received either from Orleans or Brissot, Collot de Herbois or Robespierre, Madame Tallien or the Five Kings; and they have constantly bent with the most abject submission under the yoke of those tyrants. Some individuals have even given up their crosses of the order of St Lewis, in direct violation of the oath they had taken on receiving it.

Their strict administration of justice has been much extolled – the following instance will shew how justly. In travelling through the country, I stopped at Schaffhausen to spend the night. Our supper, for two, consisted of milk porridge, four eggs, some middling kind of bread, and a pint of excellent wine. Our chamber and beds every way corresponded with this delicious fare. In the morning our conscientious host made no scruple of charging 36 livres for our supper and beds. The charge was truly exorbitant; yet to avoid any sort of altercation, I threw a louis on the table, declaring that I would pay no more. But as he still persisted in demanding the full amount of his charge, I at length said to him, 'Surely, my friend, there is justice to be had in this country. I insist upon going immediately to the magistrate.' 'You need not go far, then', said my host dryly, 'I am the magistrate, and if you once oblige me to assume the magisterial character I shall make you pay double for your contumacy'. In fact, it was the burgomaster of the town I had to deal with, and I was under the necessity of satisfying his rapacity as an innkeeper to escape his injustice as a magistrate.

I read in the public papers that the French had violated the territory of the Grisons, by which circumstance the Cantons became at the mercy of the French Republic, the first consequence of which was an order to banish all French emigrants out of the country. These people had never been a burden to the Swiss: on the contrary, they had expended considerable sums of money among them, and to this alone they were indebted for the favourable reception they met with.

As to the women, they are much the same in Switzerland as in other places. At Berne, Zurich and Soleure, you see them all dressed in the English or French fashions. In love intrigues they are in no way inferior to their neighbours, and the readiest way to gain your point with a Swiss lady is by splendid entertainments or presents. When a young lady in Switzerland, as is often the case, becomes a mother before she is a wife, the lover is obliged to pay a certain sum of money unless he chooses to marry, which effectually seals up the lips of her relations and in some degree patches up her tattered reputation.

I cannot conclude these observations without briefly mentioning an establishment called the *Matte*, which is sanctioned by Government. This consists of public baths, where prostitutes are hired out at stated fares like our hackney coaches. A State that encourages such an institution certainly cannot boast much of its attention to the morals of youth.

For the present we shall take leave of the Helvetic States and turn our attention to Geneva, whose restless disposition has produced a number of revolutions in a very short space of time.

These revolutions were set on foot by foreign powers, in hopes of gaining possession of that rich and industrious city, and seconded by bribed incendiaries within. On my entrance into the town, I was struck with a scene truly afflicting.

As the French had just entered Chambery, about five or six thousand emigrants, French and Savoyards, had taken refuge in Geneva. Among these were numbers of priests, women, and children, covered with mud and miserably drenched in rain, having been exposed to all the inclemency of a most tempestuous night.

These poor wretches stood shivering in the streets, and not one dared to afford them the least shelter or relief, neither could they pursue their journey by land to Switzerland, as the little town of Versoix was at that time garrisoned by the French. They had therefore no way or means of arriving there but by crossing the lake, which was attended by many difficulties, as there were but few boats and for these the Genevese charged most exorbitant prices, well knowing these unfortunate people were entirely at their mercy.

Chambery being then in the hands of the French, which prevented me from passing over Mt. Cenis, I hired a large boat to take me across the lake back again to Lausanne, from whence it was my intention to pass through the Tyrolese into Italy.

We had scarcely proceeded a quarter of a league when we perceived a dozen boats coming out of the port of Versoix, forming a sort of line across the lake and at the same time, saw a small one approaching us from Geneva, upon which we lay to till she came up alongside. In this I met two friends, who advised me by no means to continue my voyage, as the French whom I saw were a banditti determined to pillage all who fell in their way.

As I had a number of emigrants with me, to whom I had granted a passage, and knew that my danger would be increased by having them on board, I determined to return and risk going by land to Lausanne, which I at last accomplished after having been stopped at Versoix, but upon producing my passport I was suffered to proceed.

When I arrived at Lausanne I learned that Mr B--- had quitted his retirement at Evian, not choosing to reside in any place occupied by the French, and had hired a house for three months at Lausanne, but the very day of his arrival he was given to understand by a peremptory message from Monsieur L. Baron de E---, then Bailiff of the town, that he must immediately depart, and that if he or any of his people were to be found there by seven the morning following, they should be taken into custody.

An order so severe, and conveyed in such harsh terms, excited much surprise, but Mr B--- thought it most prudent to obey. The reason alleged for this extraordinary conduct was that Mr B--- was suspected of having, by means of a considerable sum of money, favoured the escape of a prisoner, who had been confined upwards of twenty years on conviction of being the chief in forming a conspiracy at Rolles, the object of which was that of detaching this bailiwick from its dependence on Berne and of delivering it into the hands of the French.

It is certain that the prisoner made his escape at that time, but I cannot persuade myself that Mr B--- took any part in the business, as he must be convinced that nothing could result from his interference in that affair but the hatred and animosity of those very people among whom he meant to fix his residence. But what surprises me the most is that Mr B--- never made any application to our court for redress against so gross an insult offered to a British subject. But probably he conceived that an application of that sort would be attended with so much trouble and humiliation that his proud and independent spirit could not stoop to hazard the attempt.

I now bade my last adieu to Switzerland, and after having visited the famous Waterfall of the Rhine, about half a league from Schaffhausen, I continued my route through the Tyrolese as far as Milan, without making any stop except at Trent, situated at the foot of the Alps, famous for the general Council called the Council of Trent, which lasted eighteen years and whose decision forms the basis on which the principal tenets of the Popish religion are founded.

At Milan I spent three weeks in admiring one of the largest and most magnificent cities of Italy. The metropolitan church particularly engaged my attention, an undertaking so stupendous that it is not yet finished, though workmen are continually employed in the prosecution of it.

This city has been long very populous, and is now become the residence of some of the first families in the country. They have lately completed a most superb promenade, which commands prospects far surpassing, in point of elegance and variety any I ever saw.

From Milan I proceeded to Bologna, where I remained some days wholly occupied in viewing the works of the most eminent masters in painting and sculpture, and at length reached Florence with an intention of spending some time with my friend Lord H---, then ambassador at the Court of Tuscany.

On my arrival I lost no time in waiting upon his lordship, who received me with all the cordiality of an old friend, and as such introduced me to his lady, one of the most amiable and accomplished of her sex. Here I had the good fortune of meeting again the Duchess of D---, who had the goodness to remember that she had formerly done me the honour of admitting me into her society at Lausanne.

In this charming society I passed my time in the most agreeable manner. The mornings I generally devoted to visiting every object that appeared most worthy of observation, the chief of which is certainly the Meridian at the Cathedral, one of the finest pieces of mechanism in the world. My evenings I constantly passed in the charming and fascinating society I met at our ambassador's.

But in pursuance of my itinerant plan I was obliged to quit them, though with extreme regret. Previous to my departure, I sold my carriages and horses to Lord H--- for £2,200, on condition that I should be paid at the death of his father. The father, however, is still living and the son dead, so that if the surviving brother who was then at Florence and knows the whole transaction, should not think proper to pay me at the stipulated time, I must add this to the list of my bad bargains which, considering my present circumstances, is already by much too long.

After having visited and taken leave of all my friends, I set out for Rome.

There have been so many accounts of this famous and ancient city, and every thing it contains so minutely described by writers of the first distinction, that I shall not take up the reader's time with any observations of my own upon it, but merely intimate that, for the two months I remained there, I always found something new to admire, though I generally spent eight hours every day in viewing whatever was worthy the notice of a traveller.

From Rome it was my intention to go to Naples, when I received a letter from my attorney at Paris, with whom I had left an account of what was due to me, amounting to £25,000, as I have already mentioned. He informed me that if I did not use the utmost expedition, I should probably lose the whole, as the time limited for the creditors of emigrants to lay in their claims was nearly expired. I therefore made what speed I could to Leghorn, where I embarked in an open boat, not finding any better conveyance.

In quitting the Italian coast some reflections involuntarily occurred to me on the present inhabitants of a country so renowned for the arts, the eminent men it has produced, and the number of its revolutions. Their language, once so copious and sublime, which formed the standard of perfection throughout the known world, is now frittered into a mere sing-song, and the ancient Romans, who by their bravery and wisdom gave laws to Europe, who were both fertile in imagining and quick in executing the most arduous and wonderful undertakings, are now succeeded by a race of effeminate, cowardly and superstitious bigots.

Everything in Italy is tinctured with superstition; it pervades their palaces, the chambers of their Coquettes, the lectures of their pretended philosophers, and stalks broad in their streets and on their highways, polluting he fountain of true and sacred religion.

The Italian women are by nature coquettes, and of course intriguing and inconstant. They do not think themselves truly beloved unless the

gallant be ready and willing to commit the most atrocious crime for
their sake. Far different from the English and French in this respect, the
former content themselves with laying their lovers under contribution,
and in France he is most likely to succeed who can play the fop, or
man of the world, with the best grace.

We had scarce sailed fifteen miles when we were overtaken by a violent storm, which obliged us to take shelter in the port of Spezzia, one
of the largest and finest in the world. It is so large that five fleets of two
or three hundred sail each may ride in it with safety and convenience.
The observation that a storm is succeeded by a calm was verified with
us; we took advantage of it, and with the help of our oars arrived safely
at Antibes. Here I quitted the vessel, and travelled on through Nice, to
Marseilles, from whence I proceeded directly to Paris.

# CHAPTER VII

My Return to Paris – The Valois Club – The King's
Trial – His Death – The Duke of Orleans – A Duel
– *Egalité* – Lisle – Brussels – The Theatre – Calais
– A Journey to Ostend – to Dover – to London
– Conclusion.

The morning after my arrival O--- T--- entered my room and informed
my companion and me that there was much danger in walking the
streets, and advised us to be upon our guard. As I thought it would be
an imputation on my courage to keep within doors on that account, I
was determined not to regard his injunctions, be the consequence what
it might. This was the very point he wished to gain. Danger there was
indeed, but not of the nature he represented.

After we had dined and drank pretty freely, we went together to
the Valois Club, where I found the Count A--- D---, general of the
sans-culottes, G---, a Spanish count, then Commissary-at-War, both
of whom have been since guillotined, and the Chevalier de St M--.
This party prevailed on me to play at hazard, and in the course of the
evening I lost 2,000 louis d'ors in ready money, and 2,000 more on
my parole.

At six o'clock in the morning I found my way home, perplexed
and stupefied with my losses, and cursing that infatuation, which was
continually involving me in new distresses.

My situation was certainly as deplorable as could be imagined – in a
city where no person could be secure for a moment, and deprived of
every means of quitting it. But what still increased my apprehensions

and embarrassment was that a war was on the eve of breaking out between England and France. In this emergency I determined on sending my fair friend to England to procure me some money, if possible. It was agreed that she should turn into cash what jewels she had, part of which would bear her expenses to England, and the remainder was to be left with me.

Everything being settled according to this plan, she departed accompanied only by her servant, leaving with me our little boy Tom, who had been my companion in all my travels, and a footman. I then threw myself on the bed and remained some time overwhelmed with grief and vexation, during which an accident happened to her which proved the danger of appearing at that time in the streets of Paris.

Mrs W--- had scarce left me and prepared to get into the carriage when a rascal who had been my *valet de chambre*, and whom I had dismissed from my service for having robbed me, and to whom I did not owe a sixpence, instantly raised a mob around her by exclaiming that she was an aristocrat, and that her motive for absconding was to evade paying him 50 louis due of his wages.

Had he accused her of being a thief or a murderer, she might in all probability, have passed unmolested, but to be an aristocrat precluded all chance of mercy, and she must inevitably have been torn to pieces, if fortunately, a member of the National Assembly had not passed by at that moment and rescued her from the hands of those furies. This, however, he could not effect till he had paid the 50 louis to the villain who had excited the tumult, after which he conducted her safe to her carriage and took his leave.

I endeavoured to find out who the generous person was to whom I was so much indebted, and discharge at least the pecuniary part of the obligation, but I could never discover him. Since my return to England I learned that his name is Monsieur de Naublanc, now a member of the Council of Five Hundred, and who has lately so eminently distinguished himself by pleading the cause of the oppressed and unfortunate.

The next morning I received a letter from A--- D---, in which he proposed that if it was not in my power to pay the 2,000 louis d'ors I had lost to him, he would content himself with my note of hand payable in three months, to which I replied that as I had sent to England for money, and I hoped to pay him before the expiration of that time, any such engagement appeared to me totally useless and unnecessary.

At that time Paris was in a state of the most dreadful consternation. The trial of the King had commenced, and all minds were intent upon the issue, but no one dare communicate his thoughts to another. All was distrust and gloomy silence, in a city once the seat of mirth and noisy festivity. But though the anxiety as to the event of the trial was universal, yet the motives that actuated each party were very different. Good men were struck with the horror of what they had but too much reason to apprehend, and bloodthirsty miscreants feared that their rage might be disappointed.

At length the regicide Assembly passed the horrible decree and doomed the unfortunate Louis to an ignominious death. I saw Garat, the Minister of Justice, Le Brun, Minister for Foreign Affairs, and Gourvelle, Secretary of the Council, mount the carriage pale and trembling, like so many culprits, charged with the awful commission of announcing to the King a sentence which was at once a mockery of justice and a disgrace to human nature.

I shall pass over everything relative to what happened within the walls of the temple, of which so many contradictory accounts have been given, and confine myself to what fell within my own observation.

After I had seen, with heartfelt indignation, the three wretches depart on their mission, I went to an appointment I had made with one of my friends at the Café de Foix. I had scarce entered the room when I saw two men approach, armed with sabres and pistols, exclaiming and repeating many times 'Let all join with us who wish to save our unfortunate monarch'. To this no answer was made, and while I was reflecting on so strange an occurrence, my friend arrived and we soon retired to our hotel.

The next day was the memorable twenty-first of January, 1793. At nine in the morning, habited like a true sans-culotte, I repaired to the Place Louis Quinze, now the Place of the Revolution. All the streets were lined with armed men, and cannon placed at the entrances. The concourse of people was prodigious. I pushed my way through with much difficulty, so as to get near the scaffold, which was erected between the pedestal of the statue and the Elysian Fields.

But when I came to the fatal spot, my resolution failed me, and fully convinced that there was not the smallest prospect of rescuing the unfortunate victim from the hands of his murderers, and I fled with as much precipitancy from this scene of slaughter, this deed of blood by which human nature was so woefully outraged, as I had used before in approaching it.

At ten a large body of soldiers, both horse and foot, made their appearance. They were followed by a coach drawn by two black horses, in which were the royal victim, his confessor, a municipal officer, two officers of the National Guards, J. Roux and P. Bernard, and two municipal priests. Before the coach rode Berruyer, pensioner of the King, and the infamous Santerre.

When arrived at the foot of the scaffold, the King alighted, pulled off his coat, which was of a grey colour, and ascended the scaffold with a firm step and tranquil aspect, while he benignly cast his eyes on the surrounding multitude. He then advanced, and would have addressed the people, but the noise of the drums, which were then ordered to be beat, drowned his voice, so that these words only could be distinctly heard: 'I die innocent. I forgive my enemies, and Heaven grant that France – ' here, on a signal from Santerre, the executioner seized the King and tied him to the plank. In this position he raised his head and once more gazed on the multitude. It was at this instant that his confessor, kneeling close to his face, pronounced with an emphatic tone 'Son of St Louis, ascend to Heaven', when the fatal axe immediately fell, and this faithful adherent was besprinkled with the blood of his royal master.

The falling of the guillotine did not immediately separate the head from the body; but upon a pressure of the iron it fell into a casket placed for the purpose.

One of the executioners, who was said to be a tavern-keeper, and had been clerk to a wine-merchant of Rheims, took up his head and, walking round the scaffold, exposed it to the people. A few voices, and but few, exclaimed, *'Vive la nation, vive la République'.*

During the whole proceeding, the soldiers observed the most profound silence. All expressions of pity were suppressed by terror; and after the execution a deathlike stillness prevailed throughout, which gave additional horror to the scene.

I was told that the Duke of Orleans was on the Pont Louis, seated in a cabriolet, and calmly beholding the murder in which he bore so principal a part.

He stayed till the body was removed, and drove afterwards to his palace, where an elegant carriage drawn by six bays waited to convey him to Rincy, one of his country seats a few miles from Paris, where he had invited Robespierre, Collot d'Herbois, Cambon, and some other conspirators to dine with him and to celebrate the death of their royal master.

I have before mentioned that my feelings could not endure this bloody spectacle. The relation I have given of it is, however, but too correct. I had not returned many minutes from this fatal spot, my mind tortured with the most afflicting sensations, and with the dreadful consequences likely to ensue, when Oh! Shame on the perversion of every best principle – Oh! Shame upon those degraded Englishmen! – No, can I call them by that dignified name? – Some of my country-men entered the coffee-room, and with an air of self-complacency and grim satisfaction displayed to my view their handkerchiefs, stained with drops of the blood of the mild and beneficent Louis.

My own blood curdled at the sight, and with a sternness produced by a kind of sensation I had never felt before, I boldly rebuked them for the savage pleasure they testified and the mean part they had acted.

'These are accursed spots', exclaimed I, with the liveliest emotion, 'which not all the waters of the Thames or the Seine can wash away'.

On the following day I did not go out till it was late, and on the Pont Neuf I met my friend Colonel Wall, a most loyal though unfortunate man, to whom I related my adventure with Arthur D---. He was clearly of opinion that I had been cheated, and advised me by no means to pay the 2,000 louis, which I had lost upon my parole, or give him any security for that sum.

I remained for eight days without hearing any thing from him, when one morning O--- entered my apartment. I immediately charged him with being in league with the set who had plundered me, and threat-ened to chastise him on the spot: upon which he burst into tears, and confessed that he was an accomplice in their villainous transactions; but solemnly protested that he had not touched a sol of the ready money, and that his share of the spoil was to be 500 louis out of the 2,000 due, provided he could find means to recover it. He then declared that if I would give him the 500, he would not only discover to me how I had been cheated but avow it openly to their faces.

I told him that I felt infinitely more hurt at the idea of being injured by him, who must be sensible how much I had been his friend, than by being betrayed by those to whom I was a perfect stranger. He acknowledged that his conduct was reprehensible in the highest degree, and that he deserved nothing from me but the severest reproaches, but at the same time observed, by way of justification of his conduct, that as he saw I was plundered by every one he thought he had as good a right to a share of the spoil as any other. He concluded by repeating his offer of disclosing the villainy on condition of being recompensed with 500 louis, to which I made no other return than that of kicking him out of doors.

Two days after I had another message from A. D---, in consequence of which I went to him accompanied by my friend W---. There we found D--- and G--- with pistols lying on the table. This apparatus did not prevent me from telling D--- what I thought of his behaviour, or signifying my determination not to pay him, as I was convinced I had been cheated, which I could prove by the evidence of one of his associates.

W--- supported my charge, and the two friends of D--- ranged themselves on his side.

It was impossible that a dispute of this kind could end amicably, and accordingly D--- demanded satisfaction, which I readily agreed to grant, notwithstanding the advice of W--- to the contrary. We appointed the following evening to meet at six o'clock in the Elysian Fields – we were to begin with pistols and, should these take no effect, the contest was to be decided by the sword.

W--- and I were punctual to the time and place appointed, but we waited near half an hour before D--- appeared. At last we saw him advancing, accompanied by G--- and two others, who were entire strangers to us.

W--- who had no sword, perceiving that G---, second to Dillon, had one by his side, desired him instantly to quit it, threatening, in case of refusal, to lodge the contents of his pistols in his body. This demand G--- thought proper to comply with, and no further obstacle remaining, I took my station. W--- called on D--- to do the same; but he expressed a wish to speak to G---, to which my friend would by no means consent, having some suspicion of foul play.

While this matter was in agitation, the man who held our horses came speedily to inform us that a troop of National Guards was coming towards us, which I perceived to be really the case. I had scarcely time to mount my horse, and apprise W--- of our danger, when the horsemen came close upon us. We immediately set off full gallop. D--- pursued us till we were out of hearing, uttering all the invectives and opprobrious language he could think of.

By the excellence of our horses, however, we escaped our pursuers, and in about an hour arrived at Nanterre, a little village three leagues from Paris. Here we stopped for the night, and in the morning sent a person on whose fidelity we could depend to make inquiries concerning the general opinion entertained of our adventure.

From this faithful emissary we learned that D--- exerted all his influence with the Jacobin Club to get me imprisoned.

At that time, there was from the prison to the guillotine but a regular step, and the interval very short between the one and the other.

Notwithstanding this alarming information, I returned to Paris the same day, and remained there for three weeks, skulking about like a thief; never sleeping two nights in succession in the same place, to evade the domiciliary visits that were made almost every night.

Harassed with fatigue, exposed to every kind of danger, and feeling the greatest solicitude for my little boy, for whose safety I entertained a thousand fears, receiving no intelligence from his mother, whom I had dispatched to England, and finding from the information of my friends that D--- had laid a plan to assassinate me, or at least to intimidate me so as to extort payment of the debt he claimed, I determined to leave this wretched capital and repair to Brussels, but the difficulty was how to obtain a passport, all the avenues to Paris being closely guarded.

In this extremity I applied to W---, formerly under-secretary to a Viceroy of Ireland, a man of whose honour and integrity I had repeated proofs. He not only offered me his assistance, but proposed to accompany me, if I should succeed in getting off. In consequence of which, the next day we set out together on foot for Rincy, where, as I have already observed, the Duke of Orleans had a country-house.

While we waited for a favourable opportunity of procuring a carriage we strolled into the Park, and had proceeded but a few paces when we saw the execrable proprietor himself walking towards us with a hook in his hand.

Having had the misfortune of being introduced to him before the Revolution, he recollected me. But my friend and he had been upon intimate terms. He seemed much surprised at meeting us, and asked a number of questions as to the cause of our being there.

When we had fully satisfied him he invited us to dinner, and promised us a passport to Brussels that should secure us from either insult or interruption on the way. As we walked towards the house he took notice of Mr W---'s being in mourning, and without ceremony demanded the occasion. Mr W--- told him he wore it in honour of the good King who had been recently murdered.

I shuddered at the boldness of his expression, but Orleans, with well-dissembled candour and an affectation of a deep sense of public justice, observed that as it was an act the sole object of which was the good of the people, it was not only justifiable in itself but such as every true Frenchman should glory in. 'However that may be' replied W---, 'every man is at liberty to judge for himself, and our opinions, I believe, can never coincide upon that subject'.

I wished to give a turn to the conversation and for the present succeeded, but at dinner it was impossible to exclude politics, and this infamous modern Nero, equally detestable as a father, a husband or a subject, and even a traitor to the cause he espoused, manifested throughout the whole of his political discussion that evening a degree of depravity which till then I thought human nature incapable of.

I felt so uneasy in his company that I could have gladly quitted it even without the passport which, however, we at last obtained, with a letter to the mulatto St George, then commandant at Lisle.

I shall always regret the necessity I was under of being obliged to such a monster; but our very critical situation at that time rendered it unavoidable, and necessity often silences every other consideration.

It was seven in the evening when we reached Lisle. The Gates were shut, and we could not get admittance until I produced my letter for the Commandant, who came himself to receive it. This officer gave us a very friendly and polite reception, and during our stay treated us with the utmost respect and civility. What he may have done since I know not, but certain it is that though a creature of the Duke's he seemed composed of very different materials, and consequently possessed very different sentiments from those of his detestable Superior. Not only he, but all the officers who were with him spoke with detestation and horror of the act perpetrated by Orleans and his gang of assassins.

St George had the precaution to send with me a friend of his as far as Brussels, where, without his assistance, I should certainly have been assassinated for my opposition to sans-culottism.

I was one night at the theatre where a new Republican piece was performed, composed for the express purpose of insulting the memory of the late unfortunate King. It afforded high entertainment to the audience but only served to fill my mind alternately with indignation and melancholy ideas, till at length I felt my situation so disagreeable that I was on the point of leaving the house when a Jacobin, who stood near me, asked why I did not seem to participate in the general satisfaction. To which I answered that every man may be supposed master of his actions, but could not always command or suppress his feelings, and that what produced joy in some minds, may have quite the contrary effect on others. 'You are then an aristocrat', said he, to which I imprudently answered in the affirmative. I had scarcely pronounced the word, when he vociferated 'Here is a rascally aristocrat got among us.'

In an instant the whole house was in confusion – every eye sought me with evident malignancy, and I should certainly have paid very dearly for my temerity had not the officer who accompanied me, by threatening to call in the National Guard, rescued me from their clutches and conveyed me home in safety

The next day I met Prince Louis de A--- who by his revolutionary principles had acquired popularity, and even some ascendancy over the Jacobins.

He found no difficulty in persuading them that what I said was merely in jest, and without any intention of giving offence, so that for the time I remained among them, which was near a month, I met with neither insult nor molestation.

From Brussels I proceeded to Dunkirk, where I obtained a passport to Calais, as I entertained the pleasing hope of meeting my companion there and taking her with me into Switzerland. In this I was disappointed but I had the pleasure of meeting with many of my countrymen here, who were waiting with impatience for an opportunity of returning to England.

In the hotel where I lodged was a French duke, who endeavoured with unremitting assiduity to draw me into an intimacy with him, but as his conversation shewed him to be of the most violent democratic principles, I shrunk from his advances as much as I could consistently do with propriety and good manners. One night as I was preparing to go to bed he begged leave to accompany me to my chamber, having, as he said, something of importance to communicate, to which I assented.

When we were in the room he observed little Tom in bed, and asked if he understood French; I told him he did, but that he might speak freely as the boy was fast asleep. He then spoke thus to me: 'My dear sir, from what I have heard of you, and the disinclination you have manifested to enter into any degree of familiarity with me, I feel myself warranted in giving you my entire confidence, and disclosing to you my real sentiments particularly on the subject of modern politics, which are the very reverse of what you may be induced to imagine from the tenor of my conversation on that favourite subject. But it is of the utmost consequence to me and some others, whom I highly esteem, that we should thus assume a character and outwardly profess sentiments which we despise and inwardly disavow. Grant me your confidence and esteem, and you shall never find me unworthy of either. There are many others whom you have it in your power to serve, and who, you may rest assured, will always preserve a grateful sense of their obligations to you. Is it in your power to set out directly for Paris and repair to a hotel I shall point out to you? There you will meet a man whom you will readily distinguish by the description I shall give you. He will give into your hands 1,000 louis d'ors, and to him you are to consign this letter'.

I asked him what the purport of the letter might be; to which he answered that he was not at liberty to discover, but solemnly declared, upon his honour, that it was such as could not in any wise tend to involve me in either difficulty or danger, even should the contents be made publicly known. I told him I felt highly honoured by the confidence he was pleased to repose in me, but that the offer of the money was totally unnecessary, as I should without any such inducement readily undertake what he proposed, were it not that I was waiting for the arrival of a lady from England who would be much embarrassed and distressed should she not find me there, but if he could postpone the business till then, I should with alacrity enter upon and execute it to the utmost of my power and abilities. He expressed his thanks, but said that the delay of a few hours would render the whole scheme abortive. Since that time I have heard no more of the French duke and the letter.

While I thus remained in expectation of some intelligence from England, I became acquainted with an American lady who was then at Calais with her two daughters, waiting for the arrival of her husband from Vienna, where he had been sent in a diplomatic capacity from the United States. These ladies took a great liking to my little boy; asked me his name and age, and after some conversation I discovered that the old lady was acquainted with my mother. When she understood my situation she kindly offered me every assistance in her power, and very soon had an opportunity of shewing the sincerity of her professions.

At length a signal was given of a Packet from England being in sight; upon which I went down to the Quay, and by the help of my glass discovered my dear companion among several other females on board. I had very little time to rejoice at the prospect of my troubles and anxiety being nearly at an end, when I was informed that the Municipality of Calais had refused to admit the Packet-boat into the harbour. I immediately wrote a letter and endeavoured to get it conveyed on board, offering a reward of 20 louis d'ors to any person who would engage to convey it safe. But no one would undertake the office without permission from the Municipality. I applied to them myself and shewed them the letter, which contained nothing more than to inform my friend of my being there, and to desire she would return to London, and wait there till I could find an opportunity of joining her. I requested they would permit me to send this letter by the boat that was to convey their determination to the Packet, but this they refused, and I had the mortification of seeing the vessel leave the coast, without being able to give my dear companion the least information concerning myself or any measures I may have had in contemplation for our mutual accommodation.

Vexed to the soul at seeing all my hopes thus frustrated, and having no prospect of an end to my misfortunes, I applied to the American lady for advice. As she had determined on going to Ostend she proposed that I should accompany her, and accordingly we dispatched a courier to Paris for permission to quit France. He soon returned with a direct refusal to our request, the only reason alleged for which was, that in the present critical state of affairs no person whatsoever could be allowed to leave the country.

Notwithstanding this prohibition, we did not give up our determination or hopes of visiting Ostend, and to this end we availed ourselves of an old passport which the lady had for herself, her two daughters and her son, who was then absent and whom, on this occasion, I was to personate.

Having procured four stout horses, and harnessed them to my carriage, we proceeded as far as Farnese without interruption, as we travelled for the most part through by-roads, but here we were stopped, and after receiving many insults from the soldiers on guard, we were carried before the Commissary, though he was then in bed. Fortunately for us, this gentleman was of a mild and humane disposition, and after having examined our passports, and understanding that we were subjects of the United States, he not only imprisoned the soldiers who had insulted us, but gave us a fresh passport, and sent an escort to conduct us safe out of the town.

We now resumed our journey with less apprehensions on our minds than when we first set out, and travelled without stopping till we arrived at a small town within six leagues of our journey's end, where we found it necessary to halt in order to refresh our horses. While this was doing I took a walk to a small eminence to enjoy the prospect, leaving the ladies in the carriage. On my return I found the inn beset by ten or twelve hundred Republicans, a part of whom surrounded me as I approached the carriage and strictly interrogated me as to my name and country, backing each impertinent question with a bayonet pointed at my breast.

Notwithstanding I repeatedly assured them that I was an American, yet I should have hardly escaped with life, if the officers, who were more rational beings, had not interposed and rescued me from the hands of these drunken scoundrels.

It was with the utmost difficulty I could approach the carriage, where I found another set of those miscreants, and the ladies half dead with apprehension. They had, however, presence of mind to make signs to me, not by any means to shew the least appearance of resentment. By dint of entreaties and fair words, I was at length suffered to step into the carriage but we had scarcely recovered from our agitation and apprehensions when we were assailed by another set and again relieved by the officers, though not without being obliged to cry out repeatedly 'Vive la Republique!' to which, with true politeness, they answered 'Vivent les Americains!' We were then permitted to prosecute our journey; but every half league we met with parties of the National Guards, who all took care to lay us under some contribution.

In this pleasant way of travelling we arrived under the walls of Ostend, and after waiting a short time, were admitted into the town, having announced ourselves as English, the garrison being at that time in anxious expectation of a fleet with troops from England.

In ten days after my arrival I had the satisfaction of seeing the British flag flying in the harbour, and among the officers recognized some of my old acquaintance, who supplied me with money sufficient to pursue my route with the American ladies, and we accordingly embarked in the first Packet for Dover, where we soon arrived.

After having procured proper accommodations for the ladies, the first thing I did was to inquire after my companion. For this purpose I repaired to the York Hotel, where I was well known from an act of folly I had committed there some years before.

I had laid a wager with a young man as giddy and inconsiderate as myself that I would leap out of the window on the second floor, over the roof of the mail-coach that was then standing near the door. By laying mattresses in the street to break the fall, I performed the feat and had the honour of winning the wager which was 2,000 guineas, besides the good fortune to escape with whole bones.

To return, however, from this digression, I was informed in the hotel that my friend had gone to Deal, in hopes of procuring a passage to France. I instantly set out for Deal where I learned that she had proceeded directly from thence to London without taking any refreshment. Now I had not a guinea in my pocket, and to complete my embarrassment I had sufficient reason to apprehend that, on my arrival in the capital, I should be arrested by the creditors of two young men for whom I was security.

While I was revolving in my mind the extent of my present distress, I discovered that my friend Admiral M--- was then at Deal, under orders for Ostend. To him I gave a succinct detail of all my distresses, of the fatigue I had undergone, not having been in bed for the last five days, and of the extreme desire I had of getting to London, whatever might be the consequence.

Like a true friend he removed all my difficulties, and I immediately set out for London, accompanied by an officer charged with dispatches for the Admiralty.

We arrived at six in the morning and my first visit was to my old lodging, where I indulged myself with the pleasing hope of finding my companion or, at least, of gaining such intelligence of her as would remove those apprehensions which our separation had occasioned. But by a strange fatality she had, a short time before, returned to Deal with an intention of embarking for Ostend.

These repeated disappointments did not cool my ardour or abate my activity. I therefore returned directly to Deal, where I had the additional mortification of finding that, only three hours before, she had embarked in the Packet that sailed for Ostend. By the powerful bait of 20 guineas, I prevailed on the master of a boat immediately to take me on board, and exert all his nautical skill and powers to overtake the Packet. 'Tis true I had not in my possession the means of fulfilling my engagement, but I knew that could I overtake my friend, she had money sufficient to answer every exigency.

After five hours' rowing we came alongside of the Packet, not above three leagues from land, where she had come to an anchor owing to contrary winds. Here I found my Eurydice, who was then in bed, worn out with fatigue and anxiety. After we had recounted our adventures to each other and described the dangers we had passed, through flood and field, she desired me to observe a petticoat she then wore, and which, she said, had not been off for three weeks. I begged to know what charm it possessed that could thus peculiarly attach her; upon which she shewed me £2,000 sewed in the binding. But alas! This sum, considerable as it was, did not prove of much advantage to us, as will shortly appear.

We had now no motive or inducement to proceed any farther on our way to Ostend, and therefore we returned to Deal and from thence to London, where I was no sooner arrived than I encountered one of my creditors, to whom I was under the necessity of giving £1,700 to stop his mouth and prevent his giving intelligence to the rest. But still this could give me no hope of perfect security; and as my debts amounted to upwards of £10,000, I knew it would be impossible for me to remain in the heart of London without being every moment under the painful apprehensions of a discovery.

I therefore took a lodging in the suburbs, in the neighbourhood of Moorfields, where I lived as retired and private as possible, never stirring out but on Sunday evenings, and associating with no person except-ing my brother. I had only one servant, and of his fidelity I could not, without doing him the highest injustice, entertain the smallest doubt.

One day, as he was out for beer, a man followed him unperceived, and the instant my servant opened the door, he forced himself in and was followed by six more who ranged themselves in the passage, while the first entered the room where I was sitting. 'Good morning to you Mr W---' said he with a sneer. 'I am very glad to see you again in London'. As I then passed under another name, for the same reason which induced me to live in that part of the town, I told him he was mistaken, that my name was not W---. 'No, no', replied he, 'I am not mistaken, and your memory must be very bad indeed, if you do not know me to be the waiter at Brook's, to whom you are indebted £400. I have here a writ against you for that sum, which you must either pay or go to prison'.

While this was passing, the landlord and my servant entered the room and prepared to defend me. I seized a sword and pistol and retired through a door leading to a room the windows of which fronted the street. While I was meditating an escape by this means, the people called to me not to risk my neck by such an attempt, which must prove fruitless, as the house was surrounded by at least twenty constables. I then returned to the room I had quitted and, assisted by my two friends, endeavoured to keep at bay the whole gang, who were just entering.

But my companion, who was at that time very ill, entreated me not to hazard my life in opposing so many, who could not fail to overpower me in the end. Her entreaties, and a conviction in my own mind that resistance would be in vain, induced me at length to surrender, upon which I was instantly conveyed to the Bridewell, a prison solely designed for thieves and murderers.

My female friend intended to accompany me, but was refused admittance, and I was thrust into a common room, amidst wretched criminals of all descriptions. I represented to the Jailor that I was not committed on a charge of any crime and that I was a gentleman. 'That may be', said the Jailor, 'but here we make no distinction but according to the money a man can afford to spend. I have excellent champagne and claret and if you choose to call for either, I can accommodate you with one of my own apartments.' I acceded to the proposal and was shewn into a room which, immediately upon my entrance, suggested an idea of my being able to effect my escape.

With this view, I desired my servant to wait in the street within a few yards of the prison, and invited the Jailor to take a glass of wine with me, an offer which I had no occasion to repeat, and accordingly I plied him so closely with his own home-brewed champagne that he was soon in a fit condition for my purpose, which was that of descending from the window into the street, and this I could have easily effected but for a circumstance I was not aware of.

I had scarce made the attempt when the Jailor's daughter, a stout athletic wench, assisted by two of the understrappers, seized me and immediately conveyed me to the common room, where I should have been very roughly handled were it not for the interposition of 10 guineas, which I fortunately had then in my pocket, and with which I appeased the infernal crew there assembled and prepared to load me with blows and insults.

The Jailor, on recovering from the state in which I had left him, shewed a grateful remembrance of my generous hospitality without once adverting to the motive, and not only liberated me from the purgatory, but even gave me up his own bed.

In the meantime my faithful friend had gone to my brother and related to him the whole of my misfortune. He bade her be of good cheer, as he had just learned that my brother-in-law, the Chancellor was then in London, to whom he would immediately communicate my situation.

He accordingly went to his lodging, but as he had dined abroad that day it was impossible to do anything effectual till the next day. In the morning, however, they were both at the prison door by six o'clock. My brother-in-law readily undertook to discharge the action but before I could obtain my liberty it was necessary to search the office, which luckily happened to be in the county of Surrey. Had it been in Middlesex, there would in all probability have been detainers to the amount of all my debts. As it was he had only £400 to pay with the costs.

I was now determined not to stay another hour in London and immediately set out for Dublin.

The first thing I did after my arrival was to dispose of all my estates for the discharge of my personal debts, and with the remainder, amounting to about £5,000, I resolved to try my fortune at play and either retrieve myself or complete my ruin.

The latter was my fate, as may easily be supposed; for in one winter I lost £10,000, which obliged me to sell all my own jewels, and those I had given to my companion in my better days, so that in the course of a few years I dissipated a fortune of near £400,000, and contracted debts to the amount of £30,000 more, without ever purchasing or acquiring contentment or one hour's true happiness.

Deprived now of all means by which I could support my rank in a society the only cement of which is gold, I had leisure to look a little into myself and for the first time saw my conduct in its true light. I am at present, as I have already related, retired from the world, and my principal occupation, since the above mentioned period, has been the compiling of this narrative, which I hope from its candour will, in the estimation of my friends, make some atonement for the folly and extravagance of the author.

# Conclusion

As I committed many of the preceding events to paper, I frequently paused to compare my present mode of thinking with the notions of life and happiness I had formerly entertained, and as I occasionally sighed, I have often doubted whether I really was the principal actor in the scenes I have here related.

When the effervescence of youth and the violence of passion are past, when the imagination has lost its power and novelty no longer invites because life has nothing new, the mind, viewing things with the clear and unimpassioned eyes of reason, retraces the follies of our juvenile years with pity and astonishment.

The vanity of human happiness has ever been an inexhaustible theme for the moralist and the philosopher. These by the incontrovertible evidence of experience and the sound arguments of reason, to which they have not infrequently added the lesson of instruction, have endeavoured to prove the fallacy of our fondest pursuits, and laboured to give to youth the judgement and solidity of age. But the inefficiency of their labours teaches us that our knowledge, in order to be productive of the advantages they boast of, must proceed from the same source, and that the precepts of the sage avail but little till they have been enforced by the sanction of experience.

A sigh involuntarily rises when we reflect that the most enviable period of our existence must be thus sacrificed, and we cannot help lamenting that we are ignorant in what true happiness consists whilst we are best fitted for the enjoyment, and are not able to make a true estimate of it till the finest feelings of the heart have been destroyed by disappointment and dissipation.

The attainment of happiness has ever been the principal incentive to the pursuits of man, and according to the propensity of his disposition, he has sought it in the daring paths of ambition, in the possession of riches, the voice of fame, or in the more rational enjoyment of intellectual acquisitions.

Ambition, fortune and fame, even where they have bestowed their united favours, have only served to convince him of their inability to content the heart. The attainment of knowledge and the cultivation of literature have, amidst their boasted utility, failed to satisfy the curious and active nature of man. He has found that on conjecture many of his inquiries must rest, and over what he would have wished the light of truth and certainty to shine, the dark and impenetrable veil of ignorance has been drawn. Hence, in what he was unable to investigate, doubts have arisen and here it is that Scepticism has reared her dauntless head, and from this source has drawn her too powerful arguments to silence her believing opponents.

But if man has been disappointed in his promised happiness, it is not because our life has no enjoyment to bestow, but because he expected to derive happiness from a false source, has sought her in paths which she frequented not, and has used to excess those pleasures which induce pain when they exceed the bounds of prudence, moderation and virtue.

Ambition, when directed to proper objects, becomes a virtue, and the voice of praise will be ever grateful to the ear, when it is attended with the consciousness of being merited. It is the application of riches that stamps their value, and if the gifts of fortune add not to our happiness the fault arises from ourselves.

If in the intellectual pursuits we could be content to confine our researches within the limits that are enlightened by the eyes of reason, if we knew how to stop at the point where it has been ordained that our knowledge should terminate, and could persuade ourselves that we knew sufficient for our happiness, we should not be prompted to bewilder ourselves in those paths of doubt which lead to infidelity.

My own example will give the sanction of truth to most of the preceding observations. I was born with strong passions, a lively imagination and a spirit that could brook no restraint. I possessed a restlessness and activity of mind that directed me to the most extravagant pursuits, and the ardour of my disposition never abated till satiety had weakened the power of enjoyment; till my health was impaired and my fortune destroyed. In the warmth of my imagination I formed schemes of the wildest and most eccentric kind, and in the execution of them no danger could intimidate, no difficulty deter me.

The remonstrances of my friends, the tender solicitude and affection-ate entreaties of my mother, though I always listened with emotion and gratitude to the voice of love and reason, could not recall me from my eccentricities, nor stop me in the career of folly and dissipation which led me from precipice to precipice into an abyss of misfortunes.

But if to my natural disposition many of my follies are to be attributed, no small share may be laid to a neglected education.

The very causes from which many of my extravagancies sprung, would, if properly directed, have been a spur to actions which might have rendered me of use and an ornament to the age I live in. But either the good nature or indolence of my tutor forbore to control the impetuosity of my disposition, till he found himself unequal to the task, and neglected to enforce the utility of instruction till my mind had contracted a habit of indolence that rendered the idea of study and application painful and disgusting.

If the ardour and activity of my mind had been directed to intellectual attainments, I should not have experienced the vanity of thought which made me delight in change and any expedient that could beguile the time and retrieve me from the most insupportable of maladies, ennui.

The calm shades of domestic life, the pleasures of social converse and the tranquil enjoyment of friendship, experience has taught me, have the most extensive power of conferring happiness, but for the enjoyment of these it requires a mind enriched with information and refined by a cultivated taste, it requires that station where poverty excites not discontent, nor riches tempt to improper pursuits, and which affords a sufficiency for the necessities and a little for the elegancies of life.

Removed from the noise and bustle of the world, I have lost all relish for the tumultuous pleasures of life, and little remains of all that is past but the melancholy reflection of having applied to an improper use the gifts with which nature and fortune had richly endowed me.

Blessed with the reciprocal friendship of a tender and beloved companion, and the society of a few rational friends; dividing my time between their company and literary pursuits, my days might now roll on in serenity and repose, if retrospection did not sometimes damp the pleasure of enjoyment. But in proportion as the recollection of the past is painful, the mind directs its views to the future, and I feel no trifling satisfaction from the prospect that this simple narrative may persuade the young and inexperienced, if the language of truth has the power of persuasion, that a life of dissipation can produce no enjoyment, and that tumultuous pleasures afford no real happiness.

# Appendix

*Extracts from Capt. Moore's MS Journal*

The following sheets, written on board ship, are not to be consider'd as a Composition deliberately put together, or as a work sufficiently digested to be submitted to the inspection of the Public – the undertaking I meant merely as a *passé-temps* at sea, to dissipate the many heavy hours of ennui which I must, without an employment of this kind, have been subject to – intended merely as a future gratification to myself, by enabling me to recollect the occurrences of a long tour, I have not an idea of its ever appearing more publicly than within the small circle of my most particular Friends…

Page 1

Gibraltar, 6 November, 1788.

Having determined to accept an invitation I received from Mr Whaley (who with a Mr Wilson made a stay of ten days at Gibraltar on their way to Smyrna) to accompany him on a tour to the Levant, Constantinople, and the coast of Syria, and to penetrate as far as Jerusalem in consequence of a bet he had taken on in Ireland that he would go there, we embarked on 6 November, 1788. We travelled on board the *London* of London, a ship bound to Smyrna, of which Mr Whaley had hired the cabin. We sailed out of Gibraltar Bay that evening with a fair wind…

Page 32

19 December

We all return'd to Constantinople. Soon after our arrival at the Palace, Sir Robert's painter, a Signior Mayer, permitted us to examine a set of views he had just finish'd for the Ambassador to present to the King; they represented the most beautiful views of Constantinople, Ephesus, Athens, the Bosporus, etc., etc…

Page 60

27 December

We started from Belgrade, near the Black Sea, early this morning, expecting an excellent day's sport, as the country, we were inform'd, abounded with game of every kind. We, however, found the snow so very deep that . . . we return'd home at one o'clock, and order'd an early dinner, as we determin'd to set off immediately after for Constantinople by land, the Ambassador having kindly sent his horses for us. We arrived in town soon after it was dark, and as soon as we had paid our respects to Sir Robert we retired early to bed. About eleven o'clock my friend Whaley, who lay in a bed near mine, awoke me. He found himself extremely indisposed, and on going to him, I was not a little alarm'd to find him in a very violent fever, which, as he afterwards acknowledged, he had brought on by eating a quantity of snow, the morning before, to quench his thirst, while he was in a great perspiration. Mr Franklin, surgeon's mate of the *Pearl*, was fortunately in the Palace. I immediately sent for him, and as in the course of an hour he found the fever augment rapidly, attended with a strong delirium, he administer'd large quantities of James's Powders, . . and to our great joy the delirium was soon remov'd.

Page 62
…Until 18 January, 1789 he was not thought at all in a situation to embark for Smyrna…

Page 63
Through the whole of that distressing period the attention and politeness of our worthy Ambassador were such as never to he forgotten by either of us.

Page 113
On 1 Jan, 1789, my friend found himself much better… and was unfortunately prevail'd on by Mons. le Comte de Choiseul French Minister at Constantinople, to dine with a party at his Palace… In the evening there was a ball. The temptations to dance were too strong for my friend to resist… At nine o'clock he was obliged to go home… and the following morning… his fever was attended with the most alarming symptoms, of a putrid nature. On the 3, 4, and 5 the malady had increased to so alarming a height that it fell to my lot to perform the most distressing and truly painful office of friendship, which was to assist in the final arrangement of his worldly affairs.

Page 115
On 18 Jan. my friend found himself so much better that he determin'd to embark for Smyrna, though contrary to the advice of his physician.

Page 129

2 February

This evening being fix'd on for our departure, we return'd the visits of all
the gentlemen who had come to see us, and prepared other matters for
our embarkation in the course of the morning. We were prevail'd on to
postpone our going on board till after supper… We went after the Play to
the Casino, where we were presented to the Prince Victoire Giminé, of
the Rohan family, with several of whom Whaley had been intimate when
in France. He commanded a very fine frigate, the *Badine*. He is an active
spirited young man, passionately fond of his profession, imitates as nearly
as possible the customs of the British Navy, and spares no pains to acquire
a knowledge of their regulations. When we met him he was just return'd
from Athens, where he had been in search of antiquities, and where he had
procured some beautiful pieces of Grecian sculpture, etc..

Page 298

The Procurer then accompanied us to the Apartments of the Superior of
the Convent, whom we had not before seen, as he was indisposed when
we arrived… he appear'd to be a good deal oppress'd by a feverish cold.
He raised himself and received us politely. He was a man far advanced in
years, yet he possessed a natural vivacity in his countenance, which a life
of retirement had not entirely deprived him of, and which a long beard,
with the cowl and dismal Cordelier habit, could not altogether disguise.
We conversed for some time on the late transactions in Europe, and he
question'd us particularly concerning the motives of our journey, which
we told him we had undertaken both through religion and curiosity. . . .
We took our leave, and return'd with the Procurer to his apartments. The
Superior here sent us a Certificate of our having visited Jerusalem, which
we were inform'd it was customary to give to every pilgrim who visits the
convents, and which we were glad to obtain, as a voucher of our having
perform'd the journey required by the articles of my friend's bet. I here
annex the original Certificate for the gratification of any person who may
read this.

MS No.2, Vol. II, pp. 114-118

## *Episode of Theresina.*

I shall ever [sic] forget my tender, faithful and lovely Theresina, when I
had bought her from her parents. When I first saw her, she was sitting

before the door. The beauty of her complexion, the regularity of her features, and above all, the innocent, modest and tender simplicity of her countenance, made me gaze on her with wonder, delight and admiration. The parents soon observed the lively impression their lovely child made on me, and they immediately determined to turn it to their advantage. Within a quarter of an hour the bargain was struck, I paid about £130 and Theresina was mine. Strange as it may appear, I was the only person that was astonished at so extraordinary a transaction. Theresina shed a few tears on quitting her parents, but they were soon dried up when I had provided her with all the most costly dresses that Eastern magnificence could produce.

She [sic] pleased and happy in her new situation. She was but thirteen, her mind perfectly corresponded with the wonderful simetry [sic] of her person; courteous and affable to everybody, without regretting the past, or caring for the future, her only study was to promote the happiness of a person whom she considered as a master and benefactor.

It was both my duty and inclination to provide for so charming a girl, as I was convinced that she could not be insensible to the personal accomplishment of my dear Paoulo, who was returning to his own country, I proposed a match between them, which both accepted with eagerness and gratitude. Theresina was happy with the idea of returning to her own country and of having her freedom, while Paoulo thought it a great honour and found it his interest to marry the pretty slave of his master. They had saved some money, I doubled it and paid their passage; now they are comfortably settled at Smyrna, where Paoulo carries on some trade, and they live in a simple and happy mediocrity.

Happy simplicity! I leave it to our modern philosophers and modern beaux to comment upon it. As for my part, I do not blush to acknowledge, that however customs and manners may differ among nations, I cannot help admiring the passive submission and un [sic] philosophy of my dear Theresina, while I am at a loss to find expression sufficiently strong to reprobate the selfish and interested character of her parents.


Page 295, ante.

During the period of my residence at Neufchatel (1792-1794), it was also visited by Mr Beckford, the well-known author of *Vathek*, who made his journey in a style that would astonish the princes of the present degenerate days. His travelling ménage consisted of about thirty horses, with four carriages, and a corresponding train of servants. Immediately upon his arrival Mr Beckford set up a fine yacht upon the lake, and by his munificent hospitality, soon ingratiated himself with the young Englishmen of rank whose names I have mentioned. The friendship, however, was not of long endurance: in the course of a few weeks, letters came from England to Captain Arbuthnot, as the result of which our visits to Mr Beckford ceased.'

(*Personal Recollections of Valentine Lord Cloncurry*, page 11)

Page 394, ante
William Beckford, in his Portuguese Letters, refers to his stay at Evian at an earlier date. Writing from Falmouth, where he was detained by contrary winds on 11 March, 1787, he says: 'What a fool I was to leave my beloved retirement at Evian! Instead of viewing innumerable transparent rills falling over the amber-coloured rocks of Melierie [sic], I am chained down to contemplate an oosy beach… Instead of the cheerful crackling of a wood fire in the old baron's great hall I hear the bellowing of winds in narrow chimneys. You must allow the aromatic fragrance of fir-cones, such heaps of which I used to burn in Savoy, is greatly preferable'.
(Letter V)

Among other expensive luxuries in which Beckford indulged about the period when Buck Whaley met him was the purchase of Edward Gibbon's library at Lausanne.

*Haliday Pamphlets (Royal Irish Academy)*
Vol. 550, page 140. Mis. Verse, 1789

> I travers'd Judah's barren sand,
> At beauty's altar to adore-
> But there the Turk had spoil'd the land,
> And Sion's daughters were no more.
> In Greece the bold imperious mien,
> The wanton look, the leering eye,
> Bade Love's devotion not he seen,
> Where constancy is never nigh.
> From thence to Italy's fair shore
> I urged my never-ceasing way,
> And to Loretto's temple bore
> A mind devoted still to pray.
> And there, too, superstition's hand
> Had sketch'd every feature o'er,

And made me soon regain the land,
Where beauty fills the Western shore.
Where Hymen with celestial power
Connubial transports doth adorn;
Where purest virtue sports the hour
That ushers in each happy morn.
Ye daughters of old Albion's isle,
Where'er I go, where'er I stray,
O! Charity's sweet children, smile
To cheer a pilgrim on his way.

Ibid. Vol. 358, page 52

Now Wh-l-y comes adorn'd with Beauty's flowers,
But comes resplendent with superior powers,-
What tho' that cheek exceeds the Peach's bloom,
That fragrant breath Arabia's rich perfume;
Faint in the eye of sense those charms are seen,
To that intelligence which rules within:
That polish'd mind, by every truth imprest,
And the meek virtues which adorn her breast

This and the two pieces following refer to Buck Whaley's sister Anne, who married the Rt. Hon. John Fitzgibbon in 1786. At a later period, when Lady Clare, she was distinguished for her wit and cleverness in the gay society which the Prince of Wales collected about him in the Pavilion at Brighton.

Mr W.H. Wilkins, in his *Mrs Fitzherbert and George IV*, London, 1905, Vol. 1, 157, speaking of Canton House in the year 1786, and the entertainments there over which Mrs Fitzherbert presided as hostess, states that Lady Clare was among the 'beautiful and brilliant women' who were frequently present. She was still, however, Mrs Fitzgibbon at that time, her husband not being Lord Clare until 1795. Later in the same volume (p. 268), referring to the rollicking parties continuously given by H.R.H. at Brighton in 1790, he mentions a number of favoured Irish guests whose 'merry recklessness of temperament had a great attraction for the Prince of Wales, and indeed bore a peculiar affinity to his own character', and adds – 'among whom was the witty and fascinating Lady Clare, an Irish lady who was a friend of Mrs Fitzherbert'.

Ibid. Vol. 572, page 3
From *The Mirror*

> See smiling Fitzgibbon in negligence bright,
> With a person of elegance, eye of delight;
> Behold how she swims through the mazes of fashion,
> No stranger, tho' gay, to the joys of compassion;
> Her charms are confess'd, yet more bright they appear
> When refresh'd by the dew of benignity's tear.

Ibid. Vol. 538, page 22, 'The Promenade, or Theatre of Beauty.'
    Mrs F-tz-bon.

> With loveliest form F-tz-bon next is seen,
> Grace rules her step, and elegance her mien;
> The sweet impression which our hearts pursue,
> In her resplendent meets th' admiring view;
> Strikes the quick sense, in majesty array'd,
> And casts each meaner Beauty into shade.
> Not with more swiftness darts the rapid course
> Of fires electric shot with fiercest force.

(Extract from *Memoir of Joseph Holt, General of the Irish Rebels* in 1798.
Ed. by T. Crofton Croker. Lond., 1838.)

Vol 1, page 160 (Holt, speaking of his enemies)
'They had as many setters about me as Buck Whaley when he got the Duke
of Y---, Miss---, into his keeping.'

On which Croker has the following note: 'I am not able to illus-
trate the scandalous anecdote here alluded to by Holt. Those curious in
the chronicles of slander may, no doubt, readily have their curiosity gratified by referring to the pages of the *Court Magazine*, or the *Town and
Country Magazine*, if such worse than useless publications have been preserved. Buck Whaley, however, was a notorious character, from his pilgrimage to Jerusalem and other achievements, famous in the annals of
sporting. The *Annual Register* for 1788 has the following notice of the
first of these affairs. 'A young Irish gentleman, for a very considerable
wager, set out on Monday, 22 instant September, to walk to Constantinople
and back in one year. It is said that the young gentleman has £20,000
depending on the performance of his exploit.' ... Whaley's extraordi-

nary achievement, as it was then considered, gave rise, in Dublin, to a popular song, known by the name of its burden, 'Round the world for sport'.

Mr Whaley's sister, Isabella [sic], married the first Lord Clare, and to Mr Whaley belonged the seat more than once mentioned [in Holt's Memoirs] as Whaley's Abbey. It is situated on the side of the mountain west of the first Meeting of the Waters in the Vale of Avoca

'Mr Whaley is said to have been the possessor of some of the best-bred horses in Ireland. His town residence was in St Stephen's Green, Dublin, from the drawing-room window of which, for a considerable wager, he is commonly believed to have leaped, on a favourite little Arabian horse, over a mail coach. This fete [sic] was accomplished by taking out the window-frame, and having a quantity of straw laid on the pavement below to receive the gallant horse and its determined rider. I do not vouch for the accuracy of this sporting anecdote; I merely 'tell the tale as told to me'.' Croker in the same note mentions that 'General' Holt at one period of the Rebellion rode a blood mare which had belonged to Whaley.